Heresy literally means 'choice' or 'choosing.' The very nature of people actively choosing for themselves what to believe and practice was considered a crime against the Roman Catholic Church, whose priests developed 'The Inquisition' to discourage further stray from the church's established dogma of suppression of basic human rights and needs.
   Very little has changed today.
—William Garner

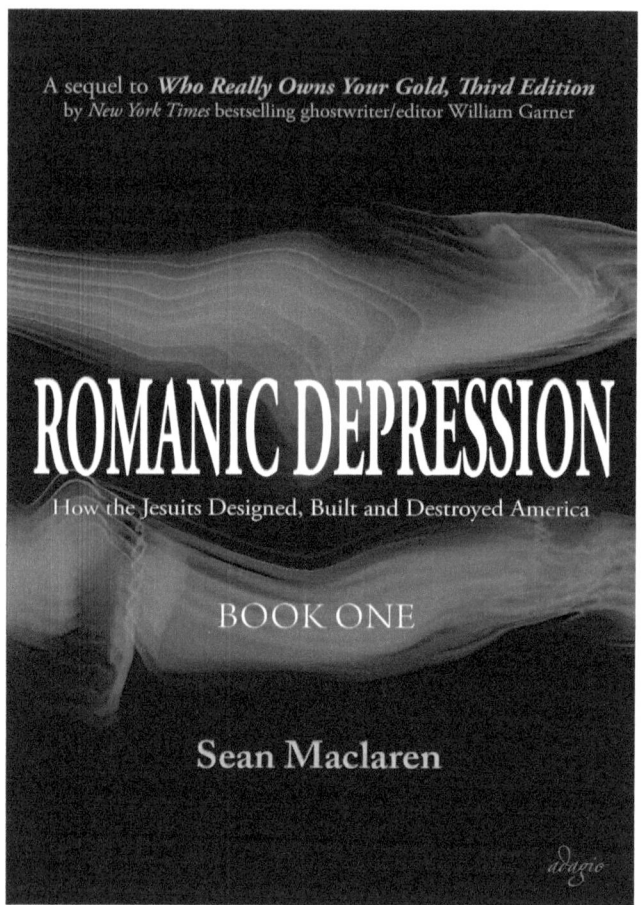

Romanic Depression
Available from Amazon.com and other bookstores

eBook available from Amazon.com, AdagioPress.com and WilliamDeanAGarner.com

The first book in a four-part series that reveals how the Jesuits have designed, built and destroyed every sector of American society, from Law and Government to Politics to Healthcare to Education. Also with more than 200 excellent references.

Edited by William Dean A. Garner
New York Times bestselling ghostwriter/editor

Burke McCarty

The Suppressed Truth About The Assassination of Abraham Lincoln

The Suppressed Truth
About the Assassination of Abraham Lincoln
Available from Amazon.com and other bookstores

eBook available from Amazon.com, AdagioPress.com and WilliamDeanAGarner.com

Burke McCarty was a courageous ex-Catholic who conducted diligent research on the details surrounding the murder of President Abraham Lincoln by the Jesuits.

Edited by William Dean A. Garner
New York Times bestselling ghostwriter/editor

Machiavelli's *The Prince*
Available from Amazon.com and other bookstores

eBook available from Amazon.com, AdagioPress.com and WilliamDeanAGarner.com

The Prince is a raw and bloody field manual for upper- and mid-level managers on predatorial ethics and power: what it is, how to obtain it, and what to do with it once you have found, stumbled across, or been granted it.

Edited by William Dean A. Garner
New York Times bestselling ghostwriter/editor

Sun Tzu *The Art of War*
Available from Amazon.com and other bookstores

eBook available from Amazon.com, AdagioPress.com and WilliamDeanAGarner.com

This contemporary edition of Sun Tzu's timeless masterpiece is just as, if not more, relevant today as it was 2,500 years ago, and is wholly effective on the battlefield, and in the boardroom and bedroom. The wisdom of *The Art of War* teaches us that war is unnecessary. Peace is always the goal.

Edited by William Dean A. Garner
New York Times bestselling ghostwriter/editor

The Escape and Suicide of
John Wilkes Booth
The Jesuit Assassin of Abraham Lincoln
Available from Amazon.com and other bookstores

eBook available from Amazon.com, AdagioPress.com and WilliamDeanAGarner.com

Researcher, author and attorney Finis L. Bates did exhaustive work to uncover the accurate history about Jesuit assassin John Wilkes Booth after he murdered President Abraham Lincoln.

Edited by William Dean A. Garner
New York Times bestselling ghostwriter/editor

Fifty Years in the Church of Rome
Available from Amazon.com and other bookstores

eBook available from Amazon.com, AdagioPress.com and
WilliamDeanAGarner.com

Rev. Charles Chiniquy chronicles his 50 years as a servant of the Church of Rome, while also revealing the evil machinations of the Jesuits and their Roman Catholic minions. He includes information about the assassination of President Abraham Lincoln by the Jesuits, and their controlling the United States and other countries.

Edited by William Dean A. Garner
New York Times bestselling ghostwriter/editor

ARCANUM

A critical analysis of the original 36 sermons of Jmmanuel, the man known to the world as Jesus Christ

Available from Amazon.com and other bookstores

eBook available from Amazon.com, AdagioPress.com and WilliamDeanAGarner.com

In Part 1, Maclaren psychoanalyzes Jmmanuel's sermons, which are featured in Part 2. In Part 3, Maclaren reveals The Laws of Creation that Jmmanuel discussed but never actually revealed in depth.

Edited by William Dean A. Garner
New York Times bestselling ghostwriter/editor

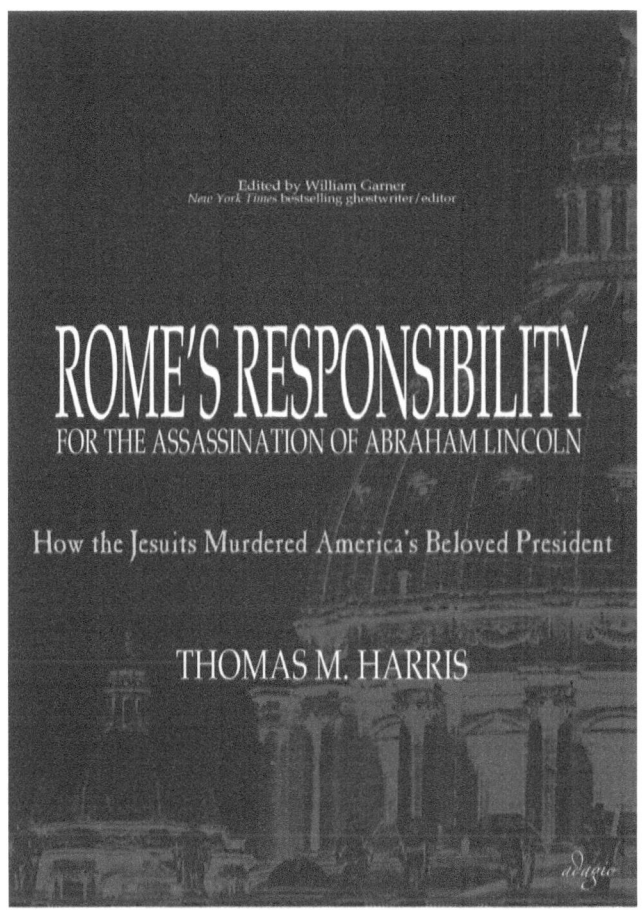

Rome's Responsibility
for the Assassination of Abraham Lincoln
How the Jesuits Murdered America's Beloved President
Available from Amazon.com and other bookstores

eBook available from Amazon.com, AdagioPress.com and
WilliamDeanAGarner.com

General Thomas M. Harris, a member of the Lincoln Assassination Military Commission, possessed first-hand information about how the Jesuits plotted over many months in different cities in Rome, Italy, Canada and the United States to murder America's President Abraham Lincoln and take further control of the American government and her people.

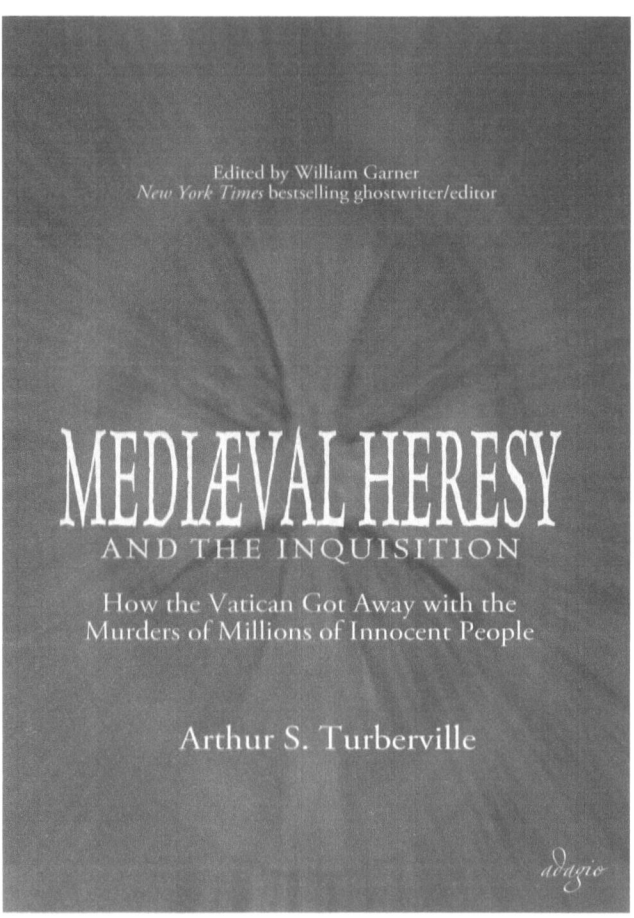

Mediæval Heresy & The Inquisition
How the Vatican Got Away with the Murders of Innocent People
Available from Amazon.com and other bookstores

eBook available from Amazon.com, AdagioPress.com and
WilliamDeanAGarner.com

Arthur S. Turberville published a fairly detailed account of the infamous Roman Inquisition, a medieval method of torture that was designed to punish and discourage all who opposed the Roman Catholic Church's established dogma. Orginally published in 1920, this important work reveals information about the doctrine of the Inquisition, rather than adding background on the overall history.

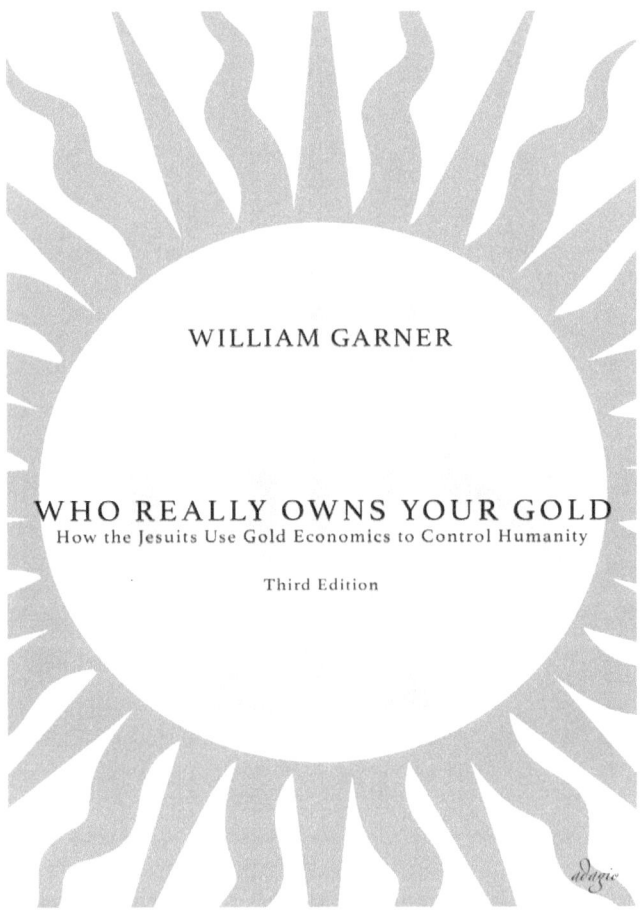

Who Really Owns Your Gold, 3rd Edition
How the Jesuits Use Gold Economics to Control Humanity
Available from Amazon.com and other bookstores

eBook available from Amazon.com, AdagioPress.com and WilliamDeanAGarner.com

Who Really Owns Your Gold, Third Edition, is about much more than just gold economics. It's about the manipulation of every sector of life across the globe by a dynastic group of men in Rome, the Jesuits, who are successfully building a world that is counter to every good belief we hold dear and true.

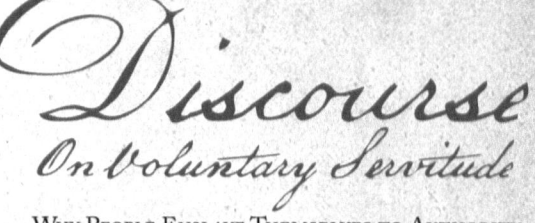

Discourse on Voluntary Servitude
Why People Enslave Themselves to Authority
Available from Amazon.com and other bookstores

eBook available from Amazon.com, AdagioPress.com and WilliamDeanAGarner.com

Étienne de La Boétie's masterpiece is still highly relevant today. While short in words, it speaks volumes to all those who value liberty on all levels, but who are currently trapped in the yoke of oppression by the many tyrants in every government and institution. This book may be considered the flip-side to Machiavelli's *The Prince*, which teaches would-be dictators how to acquire and maintain power over people and institutions.

VA Disability Claim, 3rd Edition
How to Prepare, File and Maintain a VA Disability Claim and Appeal
Available from Amazon.com and other bookstores

eBook available from Amazon.com, AdagioPress.com and
VADisabilityClaimBook.com

VA Disability Claim, Third Edition, has been revamped to reflect the hundreds of suggestions from discerning and caring veterans who commented on the first two editions.

The current book omits the considerably damning intel on VA malpractice and malfeasance, and strictly focuses on how to prepare, file and maintain a VA disability claim and appeal.

How To
~~1. Sex it like a porn star~~
2. Write your first book
~~3. Earn a million bucks~~

A Simple & Practical Method For Anyone Who Can Tell A Story

New York Times bestselling ghostwriter & editor

WILLIAM GARNER

adagio

How To Write Your First Book
A Simple and Practical Method for Anyone Who Can Tell a Story
Available from Amazon.com and other bookstores

eBook available from Amazon.com, AdagioPress.com and WilliamDeanAGarner.com

This gem is much more than just a book about writing. It reveals metaphysically how our subconscious functions during the creative process to produce the finished product, and how we grow spiritually as this process evolves before us to create our first book.

Garner employs a simple, step-by-step method we have used all our lives, and includes easy-to-follow examples and exercises, plus anecdotes from his work as a ghostwriter/editor.

Edited by William Garner
New York Times bestselling Ghostwriter/Editor

MEDIÆVAL HERESY
AND THE INQUISITION

How the Vatican Got Away with the
Murders of Millions of Innocent People

Arthur S. Turberville

AN INDEPENDENT PUBLISHING CRUISE
est. January 1, 2001

Katharine L. Petersen
Publisher / Senior Editor
William Dean A. Garner
Editor

Copyright © 2016 Adagio Press
All rights reserved

Published in America by Adagio Press

Adagio and colophon are Trademarks of Adagio Press

Library of Congress Control Number: 2016962349

ISBN: 978-1-9448-5507-9

Adagio website: AdagioPress.com

Cover design and interior: Dean Garner

B20161216
First Print Edition

for You, dear Reader

Contents

Preface xxiii
PART 1: HERESY
Chapters
   I: Origins of Mediæval Heresy 2
   II: Waldenses and Cathari. 14
   III: 'The Everlasting Gospel'. 33
   IV: Averrhoïst Influences 54
   V: Reform Movements of the Fourteenth Century and the
Council of Constance 75
   VI: The Magic Arts. 102

PART 2: THE INQUISITION
Chapters
   I: Attitude of the Church towards Heresy prior to the
Institution of the Inquisition. 121
   II: The Beginnings of the Inquisition 137
   III: The Spread of the Inquisition through Europe. 156
   IV: The Composition and Procedure of the Tribunal 174
   V: Inquisitorial Penalties. 201
   VI: Conclusion 223

Note on Authorities 238

Preface

The aim of this book is to provide, within a short space, and primarily for the general reader, an account of the heresies of the Middle Ages and of the attitude of the Church towards them.

The book is, therefore, a brief essay in the history not only of dogma, but, inasmuch as it is concerned with the repression of heresy by means of the Inquisition, of judicature also.

The ground covered is the *terrain* of H. C. Lea's immense work, *A History of the Inquisition of the Middle Ages*, but that was published more than thirty years ago, and since then much has been written, though not indeed much in English, on the mediæval Inquisition and cognate subjects.

As the present work has been undertaken in the light of some of these more recent investigations, it is hoped that it may be of utility to rather closer students, as well as to the general reader, as a review of the subject suggested by the writings of Lea's successors, both partizans and critics.

At the same time this book does not profess to be a history, even the briefest, of the mediæval Inquisition. Its main concern is with doctrine, and for that reason chapters on Averrhoïsm and on Wyclifitism and Husitism have been included, though they have little bearing on the Inquisition.

The entire subject, on both its sides, is complex and highly controversial. Probably no conceivable treatment of it could commend itself to all tastes, be accepted as impartial by the adherents of all types of religious belief. It can, however, at least be claimed that this work was begun with no other object in view than honest enquiry, with no desire whatever to demonstrate a preconceived thesis or draw attention to a particular aspect of truth.

The conclusion arrived at in these pages is, that the traditional ultra-Protestant conception of ecclesiastical intolerance forcing a policy of persecution on an unwilling or indifferent laity in the Middle Ages is unhistorical, while, on the other hand, some recent Catholic apologists, in seeking to exculpate the Church, have tended to underestimate the power and influence of the Church, and to read into the Middle Ages a humanitarianism which did not actually then exist.

Heresy was persecuted because it was regarded as dangerous to society, and intolerance was therefore the reflection, not only of the ecclesiastical authority, but of public opinion. On the other hand, clerical instruction had a large formative influence in the creation of public opinion.

This book inevitably suffered a prolonged interruption owing to the War. That there was not a complete cessation at once I owe to my Father, who most ungrudgingly devoted valuable time to making transcriptions from needed authorities in the British Museum, at a time when other duties debarred me from access to books.

My friend and former colleague, Mr. W. Gannon Jones, Dean of the Faculty of Arts of the University of Liverpool, gave me the benefit of his ripe scholarship and fine judgment in reading through the greater part of the work in manuscript, though I need hardly say that any errors in statement or opinion are to be attributed to me alone. I have to thank the Rev. T. Shankland of this College for generously undertaking the thankless task of reading the proofs, and my Wife for the compilation of the Index and for other help besides.

A. S. TURBERVILLE
BANGOR, April, 1920

Part 1: Heresy

I

Origins of Mediæval Heresy

Ages of Faith—the term has often enough been applied to the long era that separates the days of the Carolingian empire from those of the Italian Renaissance.

Like most of the other generalizations that it is customary to make of the Middle Ages the statement is true only with important qualifications.

It is with the qualifications that this book is concerned. But to appreciate the exceptions, it is first necessary to realize the full significance of the rule—the very pregnant reality concerning Church and State upon which the general statement is based. That reality, the understanding of which is essential to a grasp, not only of the ecclesiastical, but of any aspect of mediæval history, is the magnificent conception of the *Civitas Dei*.

The Kingdom of God on earth was conceived, not as a vision of the future, but as a living and present reality—the Visible Church, Christendom. Church and Christendom were one, for the Church was catholic. The distinction which we of the modern world, as the Renaissance and Reformation have made it, are wont to make between Church and State, spiritual and temporal, was wholly foreign to mediæval thought.

I: ORIGINS OF MEDIÆVAL HERESY

There was but one society, not two parallel societies. Society had indeed two aspects—one which looked to things mundane and transient, the other which looked to things heavenly and eternal.

To safeguard its earthly interests the world had its secular rulers and administrators; to aid its spiritual life it had as guides and mediators the sacred hierarchy. But the secular rulers, on the one hand, and the priesthood, on the other, were officers in the same polity.

The secular authority of the Empire was in the days of Frederick Barbarossa acknowledged to be derived from the Pope by consecration; later, as in Dante, it was conceived as collateral with that of the Pope. But always the two authorities were regarded as essentially related.

It is true that the reality never corresponded with the august theory, that the *Respublica Christiana* never was universal, that there were always those who disputed the authority of Emperor or Pontiff or both; worse still, that Christendom was distracted by bitter strife between Emperor and Pontiff. But always such warfare was regarded as domestic, not one between two different states, but between two officers in one state.

It is important to bear in mind that the conception of the universal church and empire was not regarded simply as an idea which the philosopher and the publicist wrote and disputed about, but as manifest in facts, which every eye could see and every mind realize.

There actually existed an empire, an imperial crown and coronation; there actually existed a Holy See and a ministering priesthood. And the authority of the rulers of the universal state was not simply vague and theoretical; it was discernible in crusades, in pilgrimages, in the 'Truce of God.' Men realized themselves no doubt in an ever increasing degree through the Middle Ages, national characteristics becoming more and more pronounced, as Englishmen, Frenchmen or Spaniards; but they also thought of themselves quite naturally as members together of the common society of Christendom. [1]

If we comprehend the *oneness* of human society in the Middle Ages, as actively believed in by the average thinking man and unquestioningly accepted as a patent fact by the average uneducated man, we can realize what is meant by the phrase 'ages of faith' and at the same time avoid some of the pitfalls that lie in the path of any one seeking to study the exceptions to the rule, namely, the heresies of these ages of faith.

What were the conditions that generated heresy? First, there were psychological conditions. In contrast to the bustling and multiform activity of the modern world the Middle Ages may at a first glance give an impression of inactivity and sameness.

Such an impression, if it is encouraged by the intellectual dormancy of the ninth and tenth and, in some degree, of the eleventh centuries, is completely at variance with the facts of the twelfth and thirteenth centuries, in which the mind of Western Christendom was very much awake indeed.

The impression also ignores what is one of the most marked characteristics of mediæval history as a whole —the clash and conflict and the dissonances of it. While the idea of the universal empire still held sway, secular princes, pursuing purely separatist ambitions, made war one upon another and the nations of Europe were in the throes of parturition.

Typical of the incongruities of mediæval life was the glaring contrast between the glorious minster and the mean and filthy hovels round it to be seen in every city; but that there was incongruity in spending immense wealth, time and labour on building a house for God to dwell in, while housing themselves in dwellings rude and insanitary was not apparent to the occupants.

There was another incongruity inside the churches themselves. Together with images that were sacred and beautiful there were hideous gargoyles, grotesque figures, whose inspiration was not Christian but pagan. Congregated together were saints and satyrs, and Pan is found in company with Christ.

Art was made the handmaiden of religion: that did not mean that she was wholly consecrated. St. Bernard complained that the eyes of monks as they walked round their cloisters were too often assailed by pictures which could only awaken thoughts unsanctified.

If the first of these two discords is eloquent of the faith which set the worship of God far before the common needs of men, the second is indicative of that alien spirit, untamed and powerful, which fights against the higher nature and the devoted life. From rebellious nature sprang all manner of unholy lusts and ambitions, productive of wars and enmities and other kinds of evil, which rendered the reality of human existence so divergent from the Christian ideal.

But Christianity accepted these inevitable consequences of original sin, providing through repentance and penance reconciliation and the possibility of amendment. In the elemental passions, however, the Church found itself faced by a problem which presents one of the most interesting features of the ecclesiastical history of the Middle Ages.

It is ever a hard task to expel nature, and often, where she has been renounced and thwarted, she has her revenge by returning, clothed in her grossest forms. The literature of the Thebaid and of mediæval hagiology is eloquent testimony to the fact that extreme asceticism and extreme profligacy are often found in close proximity.

The fugitive from the insurgent passions of his own being, seeking to overcome the temptations of the flesh by severe macerations and scourgings, has only too often found his voluntary existence of self-discipline intolerable without the relief of an occasional wild debauch or has found that in his savage attempt to subdue the senses he has come to take a sensual delight in self-torture and that he is falling into the lowest depths of bestiality.

The very fervour of religious zeal in the Middle Ages is a token of the fierceness of the passionate fires that tortured men's hearts.

It was always doubtful what outlet these fires would find. Would they glorify God in the martyrdom of the lower nature or would they rage untamed, flames solely of desire, destroying the soul?

Was it a pure religious passion or a depraved sensual passion that, when the Albigensian Crusade was being preached in Germany, drove women who could not take the cross to run naked through the streets in ecstasy?

Which was it that was really evidenced by the practices of the Flagellants, who at one time obtained considerable influence in different parts of Europe?

They were simply doing in public what the monk did in seclusion and in the perfect odour of sanctity.

The idea of bringing the soul nearer to God by the wounding of the sinful flesh had the Church's fullest sanction. Yet the Flagellants were eventually declared heretics. Why? Because it became plain after a time that the motive of some of those who joined the sect was unholy—not a desire to seek salvation, but only a perverted lust. Secondly, because alike the genuine and the false devotee were moved in the excess of their strange enthusiasm to build upon it a theory of the efficacy of flagellation which made it the only means to salvation, a sacrament, indeed the essential sacrament.

In yet another way the unregenerate part of man's nature might breed heresy. The lust not perhaps of the flesh so much as of the eye and the pride of life led men to take a delight in pleasure, in the sensuous pagan world, that was not a wholly hallowed delight. Such superabundant joy in life was apt to produce over-confidence in the individual's powers unaided by religion, leading to presumption and disobedience.

The phenomenon of such rebelliousness in the later Middle Ages is sometimes forgotten. Yet the legends of the blossoming pastoral staff and of the Holy Grail pictured also the Venusberg and the garden of Kundry's flower-maidens.

In remembering the figures of the anchorite and the knight-errant one must not lose sight of the troubadour and the courtesan. Eloquent of the movement of revolt is the famous passage in 'Aucassin et Nicolette' in which Aucassin, threatened with the pains of hell if he persists in his love for the mysterious southern maid, exclaims that in that case to hell he will go.

> For none go to Paradise but I'll tell you who. Your old priests and your old cripples, and the halt and maimed, who are down on their knees day and night, before altars and in old crypts; these also that wear mangy old cloaks, or go in rags and tatters, shivering and shoeless and showing their sores, and who die of hunger and want and misery.
>
> Such are they who go to Paradise; and what have I to do with them? Hell is the place for me. For to Hell go the fine churchmen, and the fine knights, killed in the tourney or in some

grand war, the brave soldiers and the gallant gentlemen. With them will I go.

There go also the fair gracious ladies who have lovers two or three beside their lord. There go the gold and silver, the sables and the ermines. There go the harpers and the minstrels and the kings of the earth. With them will I go, so I have Nicolette my most sweet friend with me. [2]

Comparable with the fearless scepticism of this romance is the outspoken unorthodoxy produced by the intellectual ferment of the twelfth century. That epoch which saw the new movement of monastic reform which gave birth to the order of Grammont, of the Carthusians and the Cistercians, is most notable in the history of the universities—of Paris, Oxford, Bologna.

From one to another, from the feet of one learned doctor and teacher to another, flocked wandering scholars athirst for pure knowledge which, if it had a theological bias and a religious garb, nevertheless inevitably tended to produce a spirit of rationalism, to substitute freedom for discipline, the individual consciousness for authority. The philosophy of the day—the Scholastic Philosophy—sprang from the concentration of the thought of theologians trained in logic on the question of the relation between the individual unit and the universal, the $εἶδος$: for if the Middle Ages knew little of Plato they were conversant with his doctrine of ideas.

The scholastic philosophers are remarkable for their great erudition within the limitation of contemporary knowledge: but still more for the extreme acuteness and subtlety which came from their dialectical training. Such subtlety might at times be no better than verbal juggling; but it always indicated alertness of mind. Such intellectual nimbleness was generally at the service of the Church, to elucidate doctrine, uphold and defend the Catholic faith.

On the other hand, the curious mind, even when starting with the most innocent, most orthodox intent, was sometimes beguiled into surmises and speculations of a dangerous nature.

Logic, if untrammelled, has a way of leading to untraditional conclusions. When this happened it was possible to escape from an awkward dilemma by submitting that philosophy was one thing, theology another, and that there could be two truths, in the two different planes, subsisting together though mutually contradictory.

But this convenient compromise was obviously only a pious subterfuge and grotesquely illogical. Unfortunately both of the two principal schools of thought were prone to lead to error. Realism, which found reality in the universal substance, subordinating the individual to humanity and humanity to the Godhead, logically led to Pantheism; while Nominalism, finding reality solely in each disjointed unit, if applied to theology, left no choice except between Unitarianism and Tritheism.

In the year 1092 a nominalist philosopher Roscellinus was condemned at Soissons for teaching Tritheism and denying the Trinity. Another nominalist, Berengar of Tours, skilfully dissected the doctrine of Transubstantiation, which had grown up in its grossest form during the Dark Ages and was first really developed in an answer to Berengar by Anselm of Bec.

There was a greater than either Roscellinus or Berengar, who was neither a nominalist nor a realist, but a conceptualist, the greatest of all the wandering scholars of his time, gifted with extraordinary vividness of personality and brilliance of intellect.

Abelard's love story in the world of actual fact is as wonderful as that of Aucassin in the world of romance. His teaching has the same note of freedom and fearlessness as that which sounds so clear in the old French story.

There was nothing very alarming in his doctrines; his conclusions were generally orthodox enough. It was the methods by which he arrived at those conclusions that aroused the fear and the wrath of his adversaries. For he put Christian dogma to the touchstone of reason, accepting it because it was reasonable, not following reason just as far as it was Christian.

To St. Bernard, Abelard appeared as a virulent plague-spot, a second Arius. But there were coming other heresies of a more disturbing nature, for the source of whose influence if not inspiration we must seek among facts of a different character.

Though their extent is certainly a matter of dispute, there is no doubt about the fact of serious clerical abuses in the twelfth and thirteenth centuries.

I: ORIGINS OF MEDIÆVAL HERESY

There is no need here to trench upon contentious ground; and it should be said that when a catalogue of offences is produced as a picture of the mediæval church without giving the other side of the picture, only a most erroneous impression can be created.

There was extraordinary greatness in a church that could produce a St. Bernard, a St. Francis, an Anselm, a Grosseteste. Yet even if we leave out of account the invectives of professed enemies altogether and only rely upon the unimpeachable authority of the Church's leaders themselves, we are left with rather a dark picture.

We must remember that would-be reformers are prone to indulge in highly coloured language with reference to the evils they seek to eradicate. Yet, simony must have been a crying abuse, or it would not have received so much attention from zealous pontiffs. We know too of many bishops who neglected their spiritual duties and were nothing more than feudal barons, sometimes fattening upon riches amassed by extortion.

It cannot be denied that there were numerous instances of absenteeism and pluralities; while for the sexual immorality to be found among both regular and secular clergy we have the excellent authority of great men who were scandalized by it and sought to produce amendment, such as Honorius III, St. Bernard and Bishop Grosseteste. Monastic reforms had been tried, the Cluniac being followed by the Cistercian and others of a like severity.

A fine attempt had been made to assist the endeavour of the parish priest to strive after personal holiness by the institution of the orders of the Praemonstratensians and the Austin Friars. And much good was unquestionably accomplished; yet order after order eventually fell away from its pristine purity and the seed of corruption remained uneradicated.

At the very least, we can say that most men must have had from personal experience knowledge of some glaring contrast between clerical profession and accomplishment. That some such contrast should at all times in greater or less degree exist is only the inevitable result of the weaknesses of human nature. It has invariably been the case, however, that when the ministers of a religion have failed to proclaim their gospel in their lives as well as in their preaching, they have sowed doubt and distrust and lost adherents.

Bishop Grosseteste told Pope Innocent IV that the corruption of the priesthood was the source of the heresies which troubled the Church.[3] We may feel sure that it was one source at all events when we note in the twelfth century a most marked revival of the Donatist doctrine that the sacrament is polluted in sinful hands.

By similar reasoning the score of a great composer might be regarded as tainted for our hearing because the members of the orchestra performing it were not all high-minded men. That would be similar reasoning: but it would not be the same.

Skill in his art is what we expect from the musician; without it he cannot mediate between the composer and his audience, he cannot interpret the music, he can only jar and lacerate the feelings of his hearers. There is the skill also of the priest. He has to interpret spiritual things and needs therefore to be spiritually-minded. God may not be dependent upon the worthiness of His interpreters; none the less their unworthiness may jar upon and lacerate the feelings of worshippers, conscious of the scandal of such unworthiness.

When, for example, priests are found abusing the confessional by actually soliciting their female penitents to sin, a moral revulsion against such a practice is inevitable. Such a revulsion may in some cases generate an attack upon the whole system of confession—and that is heresy.[4]

An intense dissatisfaction with the moral condition of the world, more especially as revealed in the Church, is one of the dominant features of the neo-Manichæan heresy, known as Catharism or Paulicinianism, of Waldensianism, of Joachitism. The last actually postulated that Christianity had failed and that mankind stood in need of a new revelation and a new Saviour, Corruption in the Church was, then, one of the contributory causes of mediæval heresy, and anti-sacerdotalism was one of its features.

It must not be assumed, however, that because heretical sects protested against scandals in the Church, they necessarily exhibited a higher standard of morality themselves. The reverse is in some cases the truth. Among the heresiarchs and their

I: ORIGINS OF MEDIÆVAL HERESY

followers are found men who were mere half-crazed fanatics, others whose passion was more of lust than for righteousness.

We have to bear in mind that our knowledge of the heretics is almost entirely derived from their adversaries unbiased contemporary testimony there is none. Yet, even remembering this, we can appreciate the repugnance which many heretical sects inspired in their own day.

In the second place, the Church was itself alive to the need of reform. The best minds always were; and to all the outbreak of heresies in the twelfth and thirteenth centuries, though it was so ruthlessly and thoroughly suppressed, was a significant warning. Unhappily the abuses actually tended to increase in the fourteenth century, and the papacy in particular lost heavily in moral and spiritual authority when it allowed itself to become the mere catspaw of the French monarchy at Avignon, when it became rent asunder by the even greater disaster of the Schism.

But the task of the Church in reforming itself was one of very great difficulty. It was essential in purifying conduct to take the utmost precautions against adulterating the purity of the faith, in reforming the papacy to maintain the fundamental continuity of the Church, of its orders, its sacraments, its traditions. Individual would-be reformers were carried away by their perfervid zeal, led into proposing the most unheard-of innovations. Wycliffe actually demanded the sweeping away of the higher orders of the priesthood and the monastic orders as a condition of the suppression of corruption.

Such theories were clearly heretical, and it was no solvent of the spiritual troubles of the Church to weaken it still further by making concessions to revolutionaries, by invalidating sound doctrine. Such was the point of view of moderate reformers like Gerson, D'Ailly, Niem—men perhaps just as earnest as Wycliffe and Hus in their desire for purity, but anxious, as these were not, for the preservation of the Catholic faith untouched.

And it is easy to understand the position they adopted. The general conditions of their time, political and social as well as religious, made a strong appeal to the conservative instinct.

England and France were both suffering from the havoc of the Hundred Years War. There was schism in the empire as well as in the papacy. The terrible scourge of the Black Death laid all countries low. Social unrest was widespread and alarming. Vagrant, masterless men devoured with avidity any doctrines of a communist saviour, and to such the Wycliffite thesis of dominion founded on grace had an obvious and dangerous attractiveness.

Just as in the twelfth and thirteenth centuries, so now in the case of Wycliffitism and Husitism, heresy was regarded not as a purely religious matter, but also as a social danger.

Another phenomenon which conservatives naturally viewed with misgiving was early translations of the Scriptures into the vernacular. Parallel to the peril of revolution from social ideas among the servile classes of the community was that of the 'open' Bible among the ignorant, uninstructed laity.

For many reasons, then, the conservatives were prompted to be cautious. Their heroic attempt to secure reform from within—made in the great Conciliar movement—definitely failed. It failed in the main because it was not sufficiently drastic, and because, while it healed the Schism, it did not secure the moral elevation of the papacy. The Council of Basel proposed the most elaborate measures for reform; but they were never confirmed by the papacy.

The loftiest aspirations were represented within the Church. They had always been. The Canon law had been clear and unequivocal enough on the subject of clerical conduct. The difficulty lay in making these aspirations, reflected alike in the Canon law and in the proposals of the Councils, thoroughly effective.

The history of mediæval heresy takes us as far as the Conciliar movement. There we stand on the threshold of the modern world, the scene changes, with new actors and a new atmosphere. The Protestant Reformation is much more familiar than the earlier movements. Yet the subject of these is one of great and manifold interest.

For the heresies of the Middle Ages were of various types and arose from a variety of causes. Broadly speaking, we may say that any circumstances which tended to break up the unity of the *Civitas Dei*, whether in the sphere of action or of theory, might be productive of heresy.

I: ORIGINS OF MEDIÆVAL HERESY

That is obviously a very rough generalization indeed; but only broad generalization can include such diverse sources of heresy as the obsessions of fanatics like Eon de l'Etoile and Dolcino, the dialectical disputations of theologians like Roscellinus and philosophers like Siger, the anti-sacerdotalism of Waldenses and Cathari, the profounder searchings of heart and mind that inspired the revolts of Wycliffe and Hus.

Nor must we forget the influence of the political factor, the contention between papacy and secular princes regarding rights and jurisdiction, which was a potent encouragement to controversy.

Such strife, where in theory there should have been complete harmony, was in itself productive of doubt and unsettlement. The very heinousness of heresy to the mediæval mind lay largely in its challenge to the essential social, ecclesiastical, doctrinal unity of Christendom. Whether the springs of its being were an emotional afflatus, a moral revulsion, or an intellectual ferment, heresy was in any case a challenge to the existing order. Its adherents were always a comparatively small and unpopular minority. Society as a whole regarded it as dangerous and was convinced of the necessity of its repression.

By far the most important, as it is the most notorious, instrument devised for the repression of heresy in the Middle Ages was the tribunal of the Inquisition. [5]

---

[1] See O. Gierke, *Political Theories of the Middle Ages* (trans., with introd. by. F. W. Maitland, 1900), p. 10.

[2] F. W. Bourdillon's translation.

[3] See *Compendium of Ecclesiastical History*, by G. C. E. Gieseler (English ed., Edinburgh, 1853), vol. iii, p. 388.

[4] See H.C. Lea, *History of Auricular Confession* (1896), vol. i, pp. 380 *et seq.*; *History of Sacerdotal Celibacy* (3rd ed., 1907), vol. ii, chapter on 'Solicitation,' pp. 251-96.

[5] On the subject-matter of this chapter see H. O. Taylor, *The Mediæval Mind* (2 vols., 1911), especially on the influence of the Latin Fathers and the transmission into the Middle Ages of patristic thought, vol. i, pp. 61-109; on the effects of Christianity on the character of mediæval emotion, pp. 330-52; and on the scholastic philosophy, vol. ii, pp. 283 *et seq.*]

II

Waldenses and Cathari

In the year 1108 there appeared in Antwerp a certain eloquent zealot named Tanchelm. Apparently there existed in Antwerp only one priest, and he was living in concubinage. In these circumstances the enthusiast easily obtained a remarkable influence in the city, as he had already done in the surrounding Flanders country.

His preaching was anti-sacerdotal, and he maintained the Donatist doctrine concerning the Sacrament. He declared indeed that owing to the degeneracy of the clergy the sacraments had become useless, even harmful, the authority of the Church had vanished.

He is also credited with having given himself out to be of divine nature, the equal of Christ, with having celebrated his nuptials with the Virgin Mary, with having been guilty of vile promiscuous excesses, with having made such claims as that the ground on which he trod was holy and that if sick persons drank of water in which he had bathed they would be cured.

We need not necessarily take these stories seriously. Our knowledge of Tanchelm and his followers is derived mainly from St. Norbert, Archbishop of Magdeburg and founder of the

II: WALDENSES AND CATHARI

Praemonstratensian order, who after the leader's death undertook the task of winning back his followers to the true faith. The evidence comes, as usual in these cases, entirely from hostile sources, and may easily be based on credulous gossip.

Certain it does, however, appear to be that the man succeeded in obtaining a remarkable influence, surrounding himself with a bodyguard of 300 men and making himself a power and even a terror throughout the neighbourhood. That he cannot have regarded himself as an apostate is clear from his having paid a visit to Rome in 1112 on the question of the division of the bishopric of Utrecht.

On the way back he was, together with his followers, seized by the Archbishop of Cologne. Three of the disciples were burned at Bonn; he himself escaped, to be killed three years later by a clout on the head administered by an avenging priest. [1]

Somewhat similar to Tanchelm, but indubitably a madman, was Eudo or Eon de l'Etoile, who created trouble a little later on in Brittany, declaring himself to be the son of God. The madman had convinced himself of his divine origin from reading a special reference to himself in the words: 'Per *eum* qui venturus est judicare vivos et mortuos.'

Eon, in virtue of this high claim, plundered churches and monasteries, giving their property to the poor, nominated angels and apostles and ordained bishops.

It is not easy to be certain as to the extent of his influence; for it is not possible to tell whether there was any direct connection between him and a sect who were spread abroad in Brittany about the same time, 1145-1148, but were connected with others calling themselves Apostolic Brethren who, having their headquarters within the diocese of Châlons, were found in most of the northern provinces of France, their main tenets being that baptism before the age of thirty, at which Christ Himself was baptized, was useless, that there was no resurrection of the body, that property, meat and wine were to be adjured. [2]

Of much more serious consequence than either of these two fanatics was Arnold of Brescia, who, a pupil of the errant Abelard and accused of sharing his master's heterodoxies, was proclaiming a much more inconvenient heresy when he invoked the ancient republican ideals of the city of Rome, maintaining that the papal authority within the city was an usurpation; and indeed that the whole temporal power of the papacy and all the temporal concerns of the Church as a whole were an usurpation — so that his crusade in Rome involved a larger crusade against the alleged secularism, wealth and worldliness of the clergy. [3]

After his death, there remained a certain obscure sect of Arnoldists, calling themselves 'Poor Men,' a devoted unworldliness their gospel, who no doubt provided a receptive organism in which the later culture of Waldensianism might thrive.

But it was neither in the Low Countries and northern France nor in Italy that heresy was first recognized as a formidable menace. The danger came from southern France, particularly from Provence, from the country of the *langue d'oc*.

In the fertile and beautiful territories of the Counts of Toulouse, between the Rhone and the Pyrenees, a land altogether distinct from the rest of France, where there was a vernacular language and literature much earlier than elsewhere in Europe, there existed a civilization unique, vivid and luxuriant.

It was distinctive in that it was not in inspiration and essential character Catholic, for it owed much to intercourse with the Moors from across the Pyrenees, whose trade, whose special knowledge and skill, in particular medical skill, were welcomed there. The population was itself of mixed origin, having in it even Saracenic elements.

This Provencal country, peculiar in Christendom, was pre-eminently the land of chivalry, of the troubadour, of romance and poetry and the adventures of love, of all the grace and mirth and joyousness that were in the Middle Ages. Clearly the atmosphere was not religious, the Church had little influence and the priesthood were disliked and despised. It was an atmosphere in which any anti-sacerdotal heresy might flourish.

In this country there was preaching early in the twelfth century a certain Pierre de Bruys, denouncing infant baptism, image-worship, the Real Presence in the Sacrament, the veneration of the Cross. He declared indeed that the Cross—simply the piece of wood on which the Saviour was tortured—should be regarded as an object rather of execration than of veneration. As nothing save the individual's own faith could help him, vain and useless were churches and prayers and masses for the dead. No symbol had efficacy; only personal righteousness.

Pierre de Bruys was burnt, but a small sect of Petrobrusians survived him for several years, their heresies being dissected by Peter the Venerable of Cluny. [4]

Much more numerous and more troublesome than the Petrobrusians were the followers of Henry, a monk of Lausanne, of whose original doctrines little is known save that he rejected the invocation of saints and preached an ascetic doctrine, with which was inevitably associated a denunciation of worldliness among the clergy.

Later on he became more venturesome, rejecting the Sacrament and avowing many of the tenets of Pierre de Bruys. So successful was his teaching in the south of France that St. Bernard was wellnigh in despair. Christianity seemed almost banished out of Languedoc.

With fiery zeal Bernard threw himself into the work of reclamation, and apparently met with much success, the refusal of Henry of Lausanne to meet him in a disputation going a long way to discredit his influence.

His sect survived his death, the nature of which is uncertain. It is possible that the Apostolic Brethren found in Brittany and elsewhere in France, if they were not connected with Eon de l'Etoile, were really Henricians. [5]

The chief interest of the heresies so far mentioned is the indication they afford of the potential popularity of any anti-sacerdotal propaganda. Apart from the crusade of Arnold of Brescia, which had a special significance of its own belonging less to the history of dogma than of politics, none of the movements had within them the power of inspiration and sincerity to make them of permanent influence and importance.

It was otherwise with the movement set on foot by Peter Waldo, a wealthy merchant of Lyons, uncultured and unlearned, but filled with an intense zeal for the Scriptures and for the rule of genuine godliness. From diligent study of the New Testament and the Fathers he came to the conclusion that the laws of Christ were nowhere strictly obeyed.

Resolved to live a Christ-like life himself, he gave part of his property to his wife and distributed the proceeds of the remainder among the poor. He then started to preach the gospel in the streets, and soon attracted admirers and adherents, who joined him in preaching in private houses, public places and churches. As priests had been very neglectful of that part of their duty, the preaching apparently had something of the charm of novelty.

The small band, adopting the garb as well as the reality of poverty, came to be known as the Poor Men of Lyons. At first their ministrations were approved, and even when the Archbishop of Lyons prohibited their preaching and excommunicated them, the Pope, Alexander III, appealed to by Waldo, gave his benediction to his vow of poverty and expressly sanctioned the preaching of himself and his followers, provided they had the permission of the priests.

This proviso, however, in time came to be disregarded, and the Poor Men, becoming more and more embittered in their denunciation of clerical abuses, began to mingle erroneous doctrines with their anti-sacerdotalism. The clergy, who naturally resented the onslaught upon their alleged shortcomings, resented also the usurpation of the function of preaching.

It was not difficult to maintain that such usurpation was itself indicative of heresy. Richard, monk of Cluny, writing against the Waldenses near the close of the century, while admitting the merit of the rich man in voluntarily embracing poverty, on the other hand found that Waldo read the Scriptures with little understanding, that he was:

> "...proud in his own conceit, and possessing a little learning assumed to himself and usurped the office of the Apostles, preaching the Gospel in the streets and squares. He caused many men and women to become his accomplices in a like presumption, whom he sent to preach as his disciples. They being simple and illiterate people, traversing the village and entering into the houses spread, everywhere many errors." [6]

That they were a heretical sect and no part of the true Church is demonstrated by Moneta, the chief authority on Waldensianism, from the question of orders. Who gave the Poor Men of Lyons their orders, without which there can be no Christian Church? No one but Waldo himself! From whom did Waldo obtain them? No one. Waldo 'glorified himself to be a bishop; in consequence he was an antichrist, against Christ and His Church.' [7]

From preaching it was an easy transition to hearing confessions, absolving sins, enjoining penances. The Poor Men came eventually to undertake all these offices.

By the time of the Council of Verona of 1184, when the attitude that the Church ought to adopt towards the new organization was first seriously discussed as a matter of urgent moment, the points of importance were—that the Waldenses refused obedience to the clergy, held that laymen and even women had the right to preach, that masses for the dead were useless, and that God was to be obeyed rather than man. [8]

The last article is clearly a butting against sacerdotal authority. In fact, anti-sacerdotalism is still the real sum and substance of the teaching. There was no explicit doctrinal, intellectual error of the first magnitude.

Implicitly, however, there was; for underlying the whole Waldensian propaganda lay a heretical principle that which bestows authority to exercise priestly functions is not ordination at all, but merit and the individual's consciousness of vocation. [9]

The Church felt Waldensianism to be a serious menace because it speedily became popular and spread rapidly. The Poor Men later came to believe themselves the true Church, from which Catholicism had in its corruption fallen away. And in support of this they were wont to point to their own personal purity.

To secure godliness was ever their main concern. A simple adherent of the Waldensian creed, interrogated as to the precepts his instructors had inculcated, explained that they had taught him 'that he should neither speak nor do evil, that he should do nothing to others that he would not have done to himself, and that he should not lie or swear.' [10]

It would be difficult to find an apter summary of the ideals of Christian conduct!

On certain points of behaviour the Waldenses laid particular stress—perhaps most of all upon the necessity of scrupulous truthfulness; and like many people who have a keen sense of the compelling beauty of truth for its own sake, they strongly disapproved of the taking of oaths.

Simple goodness and high-mindedness have rarely at any time of history failed to make their appeal to men's hearts; and it is clear that in the Middle Ages especially a strict rule of life, particularly if it had something austere and ascetic in it, held a remarkable attraction and influence.

A writer, inveighing against the Waldenses towards the end of the fourteenth century, admits the efficacy of their purity in promoting their teaching. "Because their followers saw and daily see them endowed with exterior godliness, and a good many priests of the Church (O shame!) entangled with vice, chiefly of lust, they believed that they are better absolved from sins through them than through the priests of the Church." [11]

An inquisitor bears testimony—and no testimony could be less biased in their favour—to the moral excellence of the sect.

"Heretics," he goes so far as to say, "are recognized by their customs and speech, for they are modest and well-regulated. They take no pride in their garments, which are neither costly nor vile. They do not engage in trade, to avoid lies and oaths and frauds, but live by their labours as mechanics —their teachers are cobblers.

"They do not accumulate wealth, but are content with necessaries. They are chaste and temperate in meat and drink. They do not frequent taverns or dances or other vanities. They restrain themselves from anger. They are always at work; they teach and learn and consequently pray but little. They are to be known by their modesty and precision of speech, avoiding scurrility and detraction, light words and lies and oaths." [12]

That the Waldenses should sometimes have been accused of hypocrisy and have met with ridicule from sophisticated enemies is not surprising; but generally there is striking evidence as to their simple piety. There were some stories told at times of sexual immorality among them. These we need not take very seriously.

Similar stories were told against all heretical sects; and they can be accounted for easily in this case by a confusion found frequently between the Waldenses and the Cathari. The preponderating evidence in favour of the moral excellence of the former is strong. It is not perhaps too much to say that the distinctive dangerousness of the former lay in the fact of such excellence, such fruits of the spirit being brought forth among a sect which arrogated to itself apostolic functions without lawful authority.

The other great contemporary heresy—Catharism—has some striking points of resemblance with Waldensianism, but more important points of contrast.

The new Manichaeism emanated from the East, being found in the Balkans in the tenth century tolerated and flourishing under John Zimiskes, especially in Thrace and Bulgaria, after a period of attempted extirpation under Leo the Isaurian and Theodora.

The Manichæan belief appeared in Italy about 1030, and speedily made its way into France, first entering Aquitaine, then spreading over the whole country south of the Loire. Early in the twelfth century it penetrated further north—into Champagne, Picardy, Flanders; and at the same time in one form or another it was found in Hungary, Bohemia, Germany. It was so far-spread indeed that its existence presented a very serious problem for the Church. [13]

There were several varieties of Manichæan doctrine, corresponding with the different sects of Bogomiles, as they were called in Bulgaria and other Slavic lands, Paulicians among the Greeks, Cathari in Western Europe; but the different varieties were united in their fundamental dualism.

The Manichæan idea started in an attempt to find a solution for the problem of good and evil presented by the assumption that God the Creator is all-good and all-wise. [14]

Could such a Creator be the author of all the evil abroad in the world? Yet evil could not be fortuitous; the material universe presented too much evidence of purpose and design. A creator of the evil there must have been; but an evil person or principle. To this creator—call him Satan or Lucifer, what you will—must be due sin and such disasters as famines, wars and tempests. [15]

For such a dualism—two creators, one beneficent, the other malign—the Catharan discovered abundant evidence in the Scriptures. In the Temptation Satan offers Christ all the glories of the earth, which must mean that they, constituting the material world, belong to Satan. [16]

There were numerous passages descriptive of the discrepancy between the earthly and the heavenly. Christ said, 'My Kingdom is not of this world.' One Catharan tenet was that Jehovah, the God of the Old Testament, was the malign creator. For he was a sanguinary deity, dealing in curses and violence, wars and massacres. What single point in common, urged the Catharan, was there between this deity and that of the New Testament, who desired mercy and forgiveness?

The Catharan dubbed Jehovah a deceiver, a thief, a vulgar juggler. He strongly condemned the Mosaic law, declaring it radically evil. Had it not been entirely abrogated by the law of Christ, according to Christ's own statement? [17]

There were differences among the Manichæans as to whether the evil deity was equal to the other or not. The Bogomiles believed that God had two sons, the younger Jesus, the elder Satan, who was entrusted with the administration of the celestial kingdom and the creative power. Satan revolted, was turned out of heaven, and thereupon created a new world and, with Adam and Eve, a new race of beings.

Another Manichæan system saw in Lucifer, not a son of God, but an angel, expelled from heaven. Two other angels—Adam and Eve—agreed to share his exile. In order to secure their permanent allegiance to himself Satan created Paradise to drive the idea of heaven from their minds.

Not satisfied with this device he hit upon another—the union of the sexes. He accordingly entered into the serpent and tempted Eve, awakening the carnal appetite, which is original sin, and has ever since been the main source of the continuance of the Devil's power. [18]

The Manichæans of all sections regarded Jesus as having been sent by the good God to destroy the power of the evil one by bringing back the seed of Adam to heaven. In their view Jesus was inferior to God, not God Himself, but rather the highest of the angels. [19]

Denying His divinity, they also denied His humanity. For holding Satan to be essentially the lord of the material world and the originator of the propagation of the human race, they could not allow that Christ's body was of the same substance as of the ordinary man.

According to them, the transfiguration was Christ's revelation of His celestial body to the disciples. [20] The Passion and Crucifixion had no significance for the Cathari. Indeed Christ's death was a delusion. The Devil tried to kill Jesus, under the impression that His body was vulnerable; whereas in reality it was as invulnerable as His spirit. There was, therefore, no death, and of course no resurrection. [21]

The dogma of the expiatory character of Christ's life the Cathari necessarily rejected. He came, according to them, solely to teach the duty of penitence and to show the way to salvation, which lay only through membership of the Catharan church.

The Virgin Mary possessed the same form of celestial body as Christ; though apparently a woman, she was actually sexless. Some Cathari held that the Virgin was only symbolical—of the Catharan church. [22]

Some, too, held that John the Baptist was one of the demons of the evil god, who acted as an obstacle to the beneficent God, by preaching the material baptism of water instead of the true baptism which is purely spiritual. [23]

Such were some of the main doctrinal features of Catharism. Its ethical teaching was intimately connected with its theology. Refusing to credit that the good God could predestine any to perdition, they held that salvation ultimately awaited all.

What gain, in these circumstances, had the Catharan over his unconverted neighbours? Only a gain in point of time. Life on earth, the Devil's domain, was thought of as a dwelling in and with corruption, a penance, a probation. The aim was to have done with such life, such probation, as soon as might be. The unbeliever, though he eventually reached heaven, did not do so immediately after death, but had to continue his penance in another material form. One of the essential ideas of Catharism, then, was the transmigration of souls. [24]

But for the Catharan, death meant the instant discarding of the filthy garment of the decadent flesh, the entrance at once into glory.

It was in the ability to cast aside the bondage of the material world that there consisted the Catharan's supreme advantage over other people. The feeling that this was an advantage clearly depended on one's attitude towards human life.

To the Catharan the essential sin was worldliness. The Catharan made no distinction between mortal and venial sins for this reason. All concern and pleasure in the affairs of the world was mortal sin. Money-making was of course depraved but so also was devotion to parents, children, friends. Had not Christ said as much? [25] The Catharan must give up everything he held dear in life for the sake of the truth, which was the Catharan faith. [26]

While the Bogomiles sanctioned prevarication in order to escape persecution, the stricter adherents of the creed combined together with a Waldensian devotion to strict truthfulness without oaths, a conviction that to deny the smallest article of their faith was a heinous offence. [27]

His belief in metempsychosis meant that the Catharan was a vegetarian. He abjured cheese, milk and eggs as well as meat; but flesh was worst of all, because all flesh is of the Devil. [28]

But the human spirit was regarded with the greatest sanctity. The effusion of blood was always wrong, the circumstances made no difference — it was always murder. The parricide was no wickeder than the soldier in battle or the judge condemning the criminal to death. [29]

No human being was ever justified in preventing his fellow men from following out their own course to salvation. It may seem at first sight curious that the Catharan, so strongly condemning the taking of another's fife, should in certain cases condone and even encourage suicide.

The explanation is, however, simple enough. Once granted the conception of the radically evil nature of the world and, secondly, of entrance into the Catharan fold as ensuring immediate entrance into glory without further probation after death, it was legitimate for a believer, conscious of his having accomplished the object of his earthly penance and made his salvation secure, to hasten the time of his departure into heaven.

Hence the initiated would sometimes escape the sufferings of illness, or the recent convert flee from the temptation of the desire for the temporal things he had renounced, by suicide. Such Catharan suicide was known as the Endura. Yet more remarkable than the sanction of suicide was another consequence of the Manichæan creed—the condemnation of matrimony. [30]

The connection of thought was logical and the conclusion perhaps logically inevitable. If it be accepted that the carnal body is the invention of the Devil and the propagation of the species his device for prolonging his power, the love of the sexes original sin, then it is clear that marriage is service of Satan. So the Cathari enjoined the severest possible chastity. [31]

As usual they found evidence of their belief in the Bible. But for them there was no difference between one form of sexual intercourse and another. Adultery, even incest, was not one whit more iniquitous than marriage. On the whole they were rather less evil. For adultery was only temporary and produced a feeling of shame whereas marriage was permanent, a lasting living in sin, contemplated without shame. The bearing of children was regarded with horror. Every birth was a new triumph for the evil one; a pregnant woman was possessed of the Devil, and if she died pregnant, could not at once be saved. [32]

Catharan beliefs inevitably involved the denunciation of Catholicism. [33] It was the Catholic that was the heretic; the wearer of the pontifical tiara could not possibly be even a disciple of Him who wore a crown of thorns, was indeed antichrist. The clergy from the highest to the lowest were pharisees; the sacraments —infant baptism, the sacrificial mass—were declared to have no warrant in Scripture, to be mere figments of the imagination. [34]

The Cathari, it has to be remembered, were a church. They had an organization, held services with a certain very simple ritual, for example substituting for the mass a simple blessing of bread at table, the Catharan meal bearing a close resemblance to the early Christian ἀγάπη. Confessions were made to elders of the church once a month.

But the most distinctive ceremony of the sect was the Consolamentum, an imposition of hands whereby the ordinary believer was admitted into the select ranks of the Perfected. The number of the latter was always small, and consisted principally of the avowed ministers of the faith. The Consolamentum, which meant re-entrance into communion with the spiritual world, was the desire of all true Cathari, but was apt to be postponed until late in life, often until the death-bed.

The actual ritual of the Consolamentum—or hæretication, as Catholics termed it—was very brief. The candidate, after a series of genuflections and blessings, asked the minister to pray God that he might be made a good Christian. [35]

Such prayer having been offered, the candidate was then asked if he was willing to abjure prohibited foods and unchastity, and to endure persecution if necessary. When the Consolamentum was given to a man on his death-bed, it was frequently followed by the Endura, which commonly took the form of suffocation or self-starvation.

The Perfected consisted of four orders—bishop, filius major, filius minor, deacon—their duties being to preside at services and missionary work, in which the Cathari were zealous.

Outside their ranks were the simple adherents, the Believers or, as they were sometimes called, Christians. These bound themselves eventually to receive the Consolamentum; but, generally speaking, they were under no obligations save to venerate the Perfected who, in the strictest sense, composed the true Catharan Church, and to live the pure life their faith enjoined. But they were under no coercive authority, and were even permitted to marry.

Wherein lay the attraction of the Catharan doctrine and system? For evidently they were attractive, as their great and rapid spread over Europe shows.

It is at first difficult to discern anything attractive in teaching so austere; and if the Catharan promised a reward in heaven, so also did the Catholic. In his case purgatory had first to be faced, but then the ordeal on earth was less exacting. There would appear to be two explanations, the one high-minded, the other the reverse.

In its early days the gospel of Catharism probably made to some a lofty appeal. It denounced palpable clerical abuses, repugnant to the moral consciousness. The austerity of its ethical principles seemed to point to a higher standard of living in days

II: WALDENSES AND CATHARI

when any outstanding examples of asceticism, whether in the Church or outside it, evoked admiration.

In its hatred for the evil spirit of materialism, in its detestation particularly of that worst of human passions, cruelty, there was an element of nobility which finds a response in the instinct which we to-day call humanitarian. [36]

In so far as its appeal was of this nature, it was sincere and fine. Unhappily, however, Catharism unquestionably developed another appeal of a wholly different character, which resulted almost inevitably from the complete impracticableness of its ideal. A creed that approved of suicide and denounced marriage stands self-condemned. It was at war with the very principles of life itself.

The ascetic rule it enjoined was one 'more honoured in the breach than the observance.' There was taint of unhealthiness and corruption in a rule so hopelessly at variance with nature; while a creed which, if it meant anything, held as its highest hope the speediest possible destruction of all human life, was devoid of the balance and sanity which is essential in any doctrine that is to be of any practical service in the world.

Such a religion as Catharism could not harmonize with the most elementary facts of life and human nature. The consequence was—and herein lies the greatest condemnation of the sect—that it went on proclaiming an impracticable ideal while admitting that it was impracticable, sanctioning a compromise, itself antithetical to its essential dogma, whereby alone the heresy was able to continue at all.

The compromise is seen in two practices—the distinction made between the Perfected and the Believers and the postponement of the Consolamentum, or complete initiation, until the end of life. The Believers—the great bulk of the adherents of the creed—might do pretty well as they liked, in fact ignore all the Catharan precepts of conduct, might marry, have riches, make war, eat what they chose, provided only they were prepared to receive the Consolamentum before they died.

Such an arrangement is merely the apotheosis of the system of the death-bed repentance, it is an encouragement to insincerity and hypocrisy.

This does not mean that most, or necessarily even many, Cathari were hypocrites. Most of them, probably, were originally simple-minded labourers and artisans, attracted by a novel gospel, which discerned the evils of the times, gave hopes of heaven and was marked by the ascetic and missionary enthusiasms which were then regarded as the hall-mark of a spiritual origin and divine inspiration.

Nevertheless, the temptation to insincerity was clearly present. 'Believe in the Catharan creed, venerate the Perfected, receive the Consolamentum before death,' made a simple and an attractive faith for one who wished to enjoy the pleasures of life to the full, yet to whom the tortures of a material hell were painfully vivid.

'We are the only true Christians, the Catholic church is but an usurpation, utterly corrupt,' made a convenient excuse for the feudal lord, by whom only the excuse was wanted, to harry the clergy and make inroads on their property.

Nor need we wonder that these holders of a doctrine of ultra-asceticism, of a complete celibacy, were credited with even the foulest of sexual orgies. The distinction between Perfected and Believers was an antinomian arrangement. Intense asceticism among the very select number of the former was made compatible with excesses among the latter.

Was not the very rigour of existence among the completely initiated an invitation positively to extreme indulgence prior to such initiation?

It would be highly uncritical to place a great deal of credence in the many stories told of immoral practices among Cathari. Such stories were bound to be told. We find them in connection with practically every mediæval heresy; it was such an obvious device for the discrediting of unholy beliefs to demonstrate that they involved unholy lives.

But it would also be uncritical to reject the stories altogether. There is an inherent probability that a certain percentage—it may be only a small percentage—of those told of the Cathari were true.

The critic's objection, 'what abomination may one not expect of those who hold incest no worse a crime than marriage?' is pertinent and sound. [37]

II: WALDENSES AND CATHARI

What results are likely, once given the impossibility of complete continence, from such a perverted teaching?

Indeed, notwithstanding its better qualities, its still better possibilities, Catharism was essentially perverted: and the antagonism it aroused and the efforts made to suppress it are in no way surprising. It has been termed 'a hodge-podge of pagan dualism and gospel teaching, given to the world as a sort of reformed Christianity.' [38]

A hodge-podge it undoubtedly was, an amalgam of ancient Manichaeism and elements of eastern origin, which were not Christian at all but Mazdeist, together with certain features of pure Christianity. It is no wonder that the Catholic Church viewed with alarm the challenge made by a faith so compounded when it claimed to be the only true Christianity.

Catharism was not an antagonist to be despised. Its missionary enterprise, its anti-social tendencies and the evident popularity of its anti-sacerdotal features made it undeniably dangerous. Moreover, it did not stand alone. Taken together, the different anti-sacerdotal heresies, of which Waldensianism and Catharism were the chief, which were abroad in Europe before the end of the twelfth century, presented a serious problem and indeed a menace. Was not the widespread phenomenon of organized heresy a challenge to the whole conception of the Civitas Dei alike on its spiritual and its secular side?

If only in self-defence must not the Church—society on its spiritual side—take special measures to counteract the influence of rebels, who had deliberately made war upon it by declaring themselves alone to be the true repositories of the sacred truths upon which God's Kingdom here upon earth was founded?

There were three possible methods of answering the challenge of heresy. The first was reform, the weeding out of those abuses which gave anti-sacerdotalism its case and its opportunity, reform whereby all might be enabled to recognize incontestably that Christ was plainly revealed in the life of His Church.

The second was missionary propaganda, the utilization of the same weapon which the enemy so trenchantly wielded—that of persuasion.

The third possible method was constraint.

[1] For Tanchelm see the following: P Frédéricq, *Corpus documentorum Inquisitionis haereticae pravitatis Neerlandicae* (Ghent, 1889-96), vol. i, pp. 22-9, nos. 14-29; J. J. Döllinger, *Beiträge zur Sektensgeschichte* (Munich, 1890), vol. i, pp. 105-9; H. C. Lea, *A History of the Inquisition of the Middle Ages* (New York, 1887), vol. i, pp. 64-5.

[2] For Eon de l'Etoile see Döllinger, *op. cit.*, vol. i, pp. 98-103; C. Schmidt, *Histoire et Doctrine de la secte des Cathares ou Albigeois* (Paris, 1848), vol. i, pp. 48-9.

[3] See T. de Cauzons, *Histoire de l'Inquisition en France* (Paris, 1909, 1913), vol. i, p. 259. 'On voit donc la lutte fortement engagée entre l'Église et l'esprit révolutionnaire.'

[4] See Gieseler, vol. iii, pp. 390-1, n.; Döllinger, vol. ii, p. 29. 'Quod Deus passus est ibi mortem et nunquam dedecus, et ponebant exemplum, si aliquis homo suspendebatur in aliquo arbore, semper illa arbor amicis suspensi et parentibus esset odiosa et eam vituperarent, et nunquam illam arborem videre vellent, a simili locum in quo Deus, quem diligere debemus, suspensus fuit, odio habere debeamus et nunquam deberemus ejus presenciam afiectare.'

[5] See Lea, vol. i, p. 72.

[6] Pius Melia, *The Origin, Persecutions and Doctrines of the Waldenses, from Documents* (London, 1870), p. 1. Other origins of the term Waldenses have been suggested: (1) Vaux or valleys of Piedmont, where the sect came to flourish most, (2) Peter of Vaux, a predecessor of Waldo.

[7] Melia, quoting *Venerabilis Patris Monetae Cremonensis Ordinis Praedicatorum adversus Catharos et Waldenses, Libri quinque* (1244), p. 6.

[8] See Döllinger, vol. ii, pp. 306-11, for list of eighty-nine errors alleged against the Waldenses.

[9] Bernard Gui, *Practica Inquisitionis haereticae pravitatis* (ed. C. Douais, Paris, 1886), p. 134. 'Item, circa sacramentum vere penitentie et clavis ecclesie perniciosius aberrantes, tenent et docent se habere potestatem a Deo, sicut sancti apostoli habuerunt, audiendi confessiones peccatorum sibi volentium confiteri, et absolvendi, et penitentias injungendi; confessiones talium audiant et injungant sibi confitentibus penitentias pro peccatis, quamvis non sunt clerici, nec sacerdotales per aliquem episcopum Romane ecclesie ordinati, nec sunt layci simpliciter; talemque potestatem nec confitentur se habere a Romana ecclesia, sed pocius diffitentur, et revera nec a Deo nec ab ejns ecclesia ipsam habent, cum sint extra ecclesiam et ab ipsa ecclesia jam precisi, extra quam non est vera penitentia neque salus.' Cf. *ibid.*, pp. 244 *et seq.*

[10] Quoted in Lea, vol. i, p. 85.

[11] Peter de Pilichdorff, quoted in Melia, p. 25.

[12] Quoted in Lea, vol. i, p. 85.

[13] See Schmidt, vol. i, pp. 7-24.

II: WALDENSES AND CATHARI

[14] The Paulicians had originally, in the seventh century, in Armenia, been anti-Manichæan. They became definitely Manichæan in the ninth. The French *bougre*-heretic means Bulgar. For Catharan doctrines and manners of life generally, see Bernard Gui, *Practica*, pp. 235 *et seq*.; for its theology see Döllinger, vol. i, pp. 34-50; vol. ii (*Documents*), pp. 282-96. The errors of the Cathari are summarised in Nicolas Eymeric, *Directorium Inquisitorum* (Rome, 1585), part ii, question xiii, pp. 290-2.

[15] See Schmidt, vol. ii, pp. 9, 11, 16.

[16] *Ibid.*, pp. 21-2; also C. Douais, *Documents pour servir à l'histoire de l'Inquisition dans le Languedoc* (Paris, 1900), vol. ii, pp. 95-6. Examination of a Catharan, Pierre Garcia. Garcia said, 'quod erat unus Deus benignus qui creavit incorruptibilia et permansura, et alius Deus erat malignus qui creavit corruptibilia et transitoria.'

[17] *Ibid.*, p. 91. 'Lex Moysi non erat nisi umbra et vanitas.' *Cf.* Döllinger, vol. i, p. 40.

[18] Schmidt, vol. ii, pp. 37-68.

[19] *Ibid.*, p. 73.

[20] *Ibid.*, p. 36.

[21] Schmidt, vol. ii, pp. 38-9.

[22] *Ibid.*, p. 40, and Douais, *Documents*, vol. ii, p. 40; Döllinger, vol. ii, p. 155.

[23] Schmidt, vol. ii, pp. 39-40; Döllinger, vol. ii, p. 34.

[24] Schmidt, *ibid.*, pp. 44-8

[25] S. Matt., x. 37.

[26] See Schmidt, vol. ii, p. 82.

[27] Döllinger, vol. ii, pp. 3, 83-4

[28] *Ibid.*, p. 4; Schmidt, vol. ii, p. 84.

[29] Schmidt, *ibid*.

[30] Döllinger, vol. ii, pp. 30-4, 56. This was a survival of the Marcionite heresy. The continuity of the same fundamental types of heresy which had vexed the early Church into the Middle Ages is remarkable.

[31] Döllinger, vol. ii, pp. 30 *et seq.*, 56; mainly from *Acita inquisitionis Carcassonensis contra Albigenses*, 1308-9.

[32] *Ibid.*, vol. ii, p. 33. See also E. Vacandard, *The Inquisition, a Critical and Historical Study of the Coercive Powers of the Church* (trans. by B. L. Conway, 1908), pp. 90-4.

[33] Döllinger, vol. ii, pp. 25, 44. Catholic churches were the dwellings of evil spirits. Satan's first home on earth had been the temple of Jerusalem, *ibid.*, p. 45. Whenever one of their children by some chance was baptized in a Catholic church, they washed off the taint with dirty water.

[34] See Vacandard, pp. 73-6. Also Douais, *Documents*, vol. ii, p. 94. 'Audivit

dictum Petrum Garcia (m) dicentem quod non erat missa celebrata in ecclesia usque ad tempus beati Sylvestri; nec ecclesia habuerat possessiones usque ad illud tempus; et quod ecclesia deficiet citra xx annos; et quod missa nostra nihil valet; et quod omnes praedicatores crucis sunt homicide; et quod crux quam illi praedicatores dant nihil aliud est nisi parum de pella super humerum; idem cordula cum qua ligantur capilli.'

[35] Douais, *Documents*, vol. ii, pp. 250-1, 263, 291, where the ceremony is described in confessions before inquisitors.

[36] Douais, *Documents,* vol. ii, p. 100. 'Dixit etiam idem Petrus quod si teneret ilium Deum qui de mille hominibus ab eo factis unum salvaret et omnes alios damnaret, ipsum dirumperet et dilaceraret unguibus et dentibus tanquam perfidum et reputaret ipsum esse falsum et perfidum, et spueret in faciem ejus, addens "de gutta cadet ipse."' Such language, which is typical of many Catharan utterances, is simply that of a *saeva indignatio*, aroused by the ascription to the Deity of the cruelty and injustice which conscience reprobates in human beings.

[37] Eymeric, *Directorium*, part ii, question xiv, p. 196. 'Quod melius est satisfieri libidini, quocunque actu turpi, quam carnis stimulis fatigari: sed est (ut dicunt, & ipsi faciunt) in tenebris licitum, quemlibet cum qualibet indistincte carnaliter commisceri, quandocunque & quotiescunque carnalibus desideriis stimulentur.' Cf. Schmidt, p. 151 n., on the Cathari of Orleans in 1012.

[38] Vacandard, p. 80.

III

'The Everlasting Gospel'

In 1196 Pope Celestine III gave his sanction to a new order, of which the mother-house was in Fiore. From this place its founder derived his name, and he is generally known as Joachim of Flora.

Born of a noble family and intended for a courtier, he had joined the Cistercians in the desire for a life of austere discipline, but finding its severities insufficient to satisfy his zeal had retired into a hermitage, where however would-be disciples sought him out, so that he had to put himself at their head.

Joachim, who has been described as 'the founder of modern mysticism,'[1] regarded himself as inspired, and in his own lifetime obtained the reputation of a prophet. As a prophet he is recognized in Dante.[2]

There is no question that Joachim was much under Greek influences. Calabria itself, the scene of most of his labours, was half-Greek; he paid more than one visit to Greece, came in contact with the Greek Church and also almost certainly with the Cathari, for Greece was a hotbed of their doctrines.

There is some common ground between Catharism and the peculiar teachings with which the name of Abbot Joachim is associated. Except for a few unimportant pamphlets against the Jews and other adversaries of the Christian faith there are only three works of which he was the undoubted author—a concordance, a psalter and a commentary on the book of the Revelation.

The authenticity of two epistles ascribed to him is probable, but many other works put down to his authorship after his death are certainly spurious. [3]

The contemporary reputation of Joachim would appear to have been derived as much from his spoken utterances as from his writings: but Adam Marsh prized the smallest fragments of his works, sending them whenever he could obtain them from Italy to Bishop Grosseteste.

On the other hand, however interesting and indeed startling they may have been, they were not during their author's lifetime regarded as in any way injurious. His reputation as a seer was wholly orthodox and unexceptionable. In 1200 he submitted his books to the Holy See for its approval, and the verdict was that they were undoubtedly of divine inspiration.

Thirteen years later, indeed, certain speculations concerning the Trinity in one of his minor tracts were condemned by the Council of the Lateran. But the author was not personally condemned, and his order was definitely approved; while in 1220 Honorius III issued a bull declaring Joachim to have been a good catholic. [4]

It is doubtful if the name of Joachim of Flora would ever have been of any more than very transitory importance had it not been for the appearance in 1254 of a work entitled 'The Eternal Gospel,' of which he was stated to be the author.

No book of that title figures among the authentic works of Joachim, nor did he give that name to any collection of them. It seems that the book which appeared in Paris in 1254 consisted of Joachim's three principal works—which had none of them been hitherto deemed heretical—with explanatory notes and a lengthy and all-important introduction (*Introductorius in Evangelium Aeternum*).

It must have been rather in the notes and introduction than in the text that the heresy lay, in the interpretations put upon Joachim's apocalyptic effusions rather than in the effusions themselves.

III: THE EVERLASTING GOSPEL

The true author, therefore, of the heresies associated with 'The Everlasting Gospel' would appear to be the commentator, not the originator. The authorship of the introduction and the glosses was early ascribed to one of two persons—to a certain Gherardo da Borgo San Donnino by the contemporary chronicler Salimbene, to John of Parma by the inquisitor Eymeric in his 'Directorium Inquisitorum,' written more than a century later.

In any case the author was a Franciscan. [5]

And between the conceptions contained in 'The Everlasting Gospel' and the Franciscan Order, it will be seen, there was a very close and a very significant connection.

We may take it that the compiler of the work which startled the world in 1254—whether it was Gherardo or John of Parma—is to be regarded less as an expounder of the teaching of Joachim of Flora than as an original thinker, either honestly finding a preceptor and a kindred soul in the prophet and simply elaborating his thesis, or else utilizing the apocalyptic utterances of a man who had died in the full odour of sanctity in order to build up a thesis essentially his own on esoteric writings easily susceptible of a new construction.

It is sufficient that 'The Everlasting Gospel' has direct reference to that section of the Franciscans which was at the time led by John of Parma, and that in the new religion which the work predicts the Friars are to play the leading part as inaugurators. The work is indeed astoundingly revolutionary. In much the same way that Mazzini in his 'From the Council to God' proclaimed the emergence of a new religion of Humanity superseding Christianity did 'The Everlasting Gospel' proclaim a new religion, that of the Holy Ghost.

But whereas condemnation of the Catholic Church was commonplace in the nineteenth century and humanitarian ideas familiar; in the thirteenth century it is rather astonishing to find an admission that Christianity has failed and that a new dispensation is necessary for the salvation of mankind.

The text of 'The Everlasting Gospel' is the words in the book of the Revelation, 'And I saw another angel fly in the midst of heaven, having the everlasting gospel to preach unto them that dwell on the earth, and to every nation, and kindred, and tongue, and people, saying with a loud voice, Fear God, and give glory to him, for the hour of his judgment is come.' [6]

Joachim had foretold in his 'Concordia' that the world would go through three cycles, those of the Father or the circumcision or the law; of the Son, crucifixion, grace; of the Holy Ghost, peace and love.

The first had been the era of Judaism, of the Old Testament. It had led on to that of the New Testament and the Christian Church. The second period was very shortly to reach its accomplishment, and the third and last era, that of 'The Everlasting Gospel,' to be inaugurated by a new religious order. By mystic computations the date of the commencement of the final era was found to be 1260.

Fundamental to such a mystic conception of human history is the assumption that Christianity is not the whole and the sole truth, that it is not complete in itself, but only a partial revelation of God to man, destined to be superseded by a fuller, ampler revelation in the same way in which it had superseded Judaism.

Such an assumption could only rest upon a pessimistic view of contemporary life and society, a feeling that it urgently needed a new saviour. Joachim strongly denounced the evils of his day, especially those evinced by the Church, which was given up to carnal appetites and neglected its duties, to the advantage of proselytizing heresies, for which it was thus itself indirectly responsible.

The author or authors of 'The Everlasting Gospel' illustrated this very conception by elaborating a thesis really more destructive of the Catholic faith than Catharism itself.

The ending of the second era was to be accompanied by great tribulations, but these grievous troubles would usher in the millennium, days of perfect justice, peace and happiness, in which God would be worshipped everywhere and in which the Eucharist and indeed all other sacraments would be needless, mankind being liberated from such burdens, so complete would be the knowledge of God in the heart of the individual man.

The conversion of the world to this new dispensation, in which each man would live the devoted life of a monk, was to be brought about by the new mendicant order, in which would be

III: THE EVERLASTING GOSPEL

manifested all the highest powers of man. What order could this be but the Franciscan?

The personality and career of St. Francis of Assisi are of profound significance in the history of mediæval Christianity. Their sanctity and spiritual power gave other men, such as Peter Damiani, Bruno, Stephen Harding, Norbert, Bernard, Dominic, a great reputation and authority even in their own lifetime.

But Francis stood apart from and above all of them, even Bernard. His intense sincerity, his absolute, unconditional renunciation of all worldly things, the charm and beauty of his character made the man, upon whose body the στίγματα of Christ were said to have been seen, appear to his own day as one different from all other men—indeed so miraculously near to the spirit of his Master as to be hailed by some even as a second Christ.

Simple, unlearned, not interested in intellectual matters, making religion an inward matter of spiritual experience, intense conviction of sin and of repentance together with unreserved devotion of life and soul to God in personal service, St. Francis was no organizer, and when the nucleus of an order gathered round him viewed the future with the utmost disquietude, fearing in the very fact of organization a falling away from those ideas of strictest poverty and personal holiness which marked out the Minorites from all other religious associations.

Yet if the influence of St. Francis was to survive his death, organization, whatever its drawbacks, was an imperative necessity. This work was carried out by a man of rare energy and constructive powers, Elias of Cortona, with the active support of Gregory IX. Elias did for the Franciscans what St. Paul did for primitive Christianity. But between the spirit of Elias and that of Francis there was a difference equivalent to that between the zeal of a prophet and the skill of a statesman.

The Franciscan Order as it came to be, if it gained something by its organization, lost also, as the founder had foreseen. With organization there came indeed recruitment from the ranks of scholarship, and the followers of the unlearned saint of Assisi included in Alexander of Hales, Bonaventura and Roger Bacon men who could take stand with Albertus Magnus and Thomas

Aquinas himself among the followers of the learned Dominic de Guzman.

But there came also with organization temporal influence and worldly wealth, entirely out of harmony with the mind and ideals of Francis, and proving indeed a snare and a temptation to those very clerical abuses against which the whole life of Francis had been a protest.

Accordingly, there came about a very serious and indeed irreconcilable cleavage among the Grey Friars. There were on the one side the followers of Elias who came to be known as the Conventuals, arguing that a strict compliance with the principles of Francis was impracticable, indeed fanatical, that compromise involving the abandonment of the mendicant ideal and the acceptance of property was not only justifiable but unavoidable for the continued existence of their society.

On the other side were the Spirituals, arguing that the policy of compromise meant nothing less than the repudiation of the distinctive characteristics of the order which had led to its creation and justified its continuation, and urging to the full the strictest conformity with all their uncompromising sincerity.

The dispute between the two parties had been some years in progress when 'The Everlasting Gospel' was published, the John of Parma to whom the authorship of the work was by some attributed being at that time General of the order and a most perfervid Spiritual.

St. Francis himself had indeed been orthodox enough, for the most part accepting the articles of faith in a spirit of unquestioning obedience, though the bent of his mind and his marriage to the Lady Poverty caused him to attach more importance to some dogmas than to others, and in particular to shorten and to simplify all forms and ritual.

But in the beautiful fancifulness of Francis there was a strong element of mysticism, and this element was a marked characteristic of those who sought to retain his ideal of asceticism in the order. To such the mystical outpourings of the Abbot Joachim made a powerful appeal. For they perceived in his predictions a clear reference to themselves, found in Francis the forerunner and in themselves, his true followers, the destined preachers of the new era of the Holy Ghost in which the carnal-mindedness of a decadent Church and the corruption and indeed the worldliness of the whole human race were to be known no more.

To some extremists Francis figured not as a great saint and servant of Christ seeking to reclaim the world to His truth, but as an equal with Christ—not as the restorer of an existent religion, but as the creator of a new religion. So completely heterodox a construction was it possible to place upon the mission of St. Francis, in the light of Joachite prophecy. [7]

It can easily be understood that the taint of Joachitism among the Spirituals gave a splendid opportunity to their adversaries, which the latter were not slow to take.

The Pope, Alexander IV, was appealed to; John of Parma was forced to resign, and his successor, Bonaventura, who belonged to neither party, was made, however unwillingly, to take action against John himself and his most outstanding adherents.

Already evidence was accumulating of heretical dangers which might accrue from the wedding together of Franciscan ideas of poverty with Joachitic myticism, and Spirituals began to be looked upon askance. Already Languedoc, abundant source of all manner of onslaughts upon the faith, was beginning to welcome the ideas of Joachim, and it was possible for the Conventuals to argue that their opponents were no better than a heretical sect, another form of Cathari.

Later on there came successors to the author of 'The Everlasting Gospel,' in the Franciscan Pierre Jean Olivi in France, in Italy Arnaldo da Villanova, who pronounced the vices of the clergy to be eloquent signs of the presence of Antichrist.

To begin with the Spirituals were in the ascendant. Bonaventura, in controversy with William of Saint Amour, a virulent enemy of the whole Franciscan order, maintained that poverty was an essential feature of Christianity and that neither Christ Himself nor His disciples owned property of any kind.

Pope Nicholas III by the bull *Exiit qui seminat* gave the sanction of the Holy See to the view that St. Francis had been inspired in his creation of the Rule by the Holy Ghost; that Christ had completely renounced the ownership of property and that such renunciation was most laudable and Christian.

At the same time he drew a distinction—no new one, because it had already been put into practice by Innocent IV and Alexander IV—between ownership and use, and laid down as a rule always to be followed that the ownership of Franciscan property was vested in the Holy See, the Franciscans themselves simply having the usufruct. This bull did not, as might have been anticipated, settle the dispute between the two Franciscan factions. Laxity increased among the Conventuals, and Joachite tendencies still subsisted among their opponents. The pontificate of Boniface VIII, which began in 1294, brought upon the scene a man most eminently practical, essentially worldly.

To the Pope, who had designs on the temporal power and eventually announced categorically, 'I am Caesar, I am Emperor,' the ascetic ideal of the Spirituals was a ridiculous fanaticism, which was also a positive nuisance.

The mendicant orders had been especially the servants of the papacy the Spirituals were apt to refer to it as Antichrist. Moreover, the existence of wandering friars, actually beggars, under no proper discipline and supervision—as some of the Spirituals had become—outraged his sense of order and decency. Boniface decided that these lawless bands must be hunted down, and utilized the Inquisition for this purpose.

Under Clement V the lot of the Spirituals considerably improved, and inveighing against the abuses of their false brethren they very nearly succeeded in securing a permanent separation into an order of their own. Instead of this Clement, while declaring in favour of the ascetic party and favouring them generally during his pontificate, endeavoured to induce the rival factions to drop their quarrels and live together in amity.

His efforts at settlement were defeated by the action of Spirituals in Italy, who at the very time when a Council at Vienne, sitting in 1311-12, was declaring in favour of the Spirituals and prohibiting their enemies from referring to them as heretics, proclaimed themselves a separate community and brought down the Pope's wrath upon them as rebels and schismatics and indeed founders of a pestilential sect.

The controversy came to a head under Clement's successor, the resolute and aggressive John XXII, to whom the pauper ideal was particularly obnoxious. He was extremely avaricious and full of worldly ambitions which involved him in frequent wars in Italy. This pontiff—possessing in his nature not one single feature in common with St. Francis—determined on restoring order within the Franciscan fold and bringing the Spirituals to obedience. [8]

The first attack on the ascetic party was made in Languedoc. One of the minor distinctive features of the Spirituals was their wearing smaller gowns and hoods than the Conventuals. The Spirituals in the province of Aquitaine, in Beziers, Narbonne and Carcassonne, were forbidden to wear this distinctive garb.

Twenty-five, to whom the wearing of their habit was symbolical of the whole principle for which they stood, refused to submit and were delivered to the Inquisition at Marseilles. Already the Pope had declared that all the wandering Spirituals in Languedoc who styled themselves *Fratres de paupere vita* or *Fraticelli* were heretics, and had stated very significantly in the bull *Quorundam* that however praiseworthy poverty might be, more praiseworthy was obedience.

Four of the twenty-five remained obdurate to the last, were handed over to the secular arm, and burnt. This proved to be but the beginning of a persecution carried out most rigorously by means of the Holy Office, particularly in the south of France, but also in Spain and Italy.

The rebel Franciscans were persecuted because they were heretical, and it is important to note in what their heresy consisted. It was not because of Joachite tendencies—these might or might not exist, they were not a criterion—it was because of disobedience pure and simple.

To disobey the constitution *Quorundam*, to dispute its ruling as to the wearing of a habit and the question of ownership of property—that was heresy.

It is true that the motive which induced the recalcitrant to refuse obedience to the bull was a repudiation of papal authority to lay down such a regulation regarding the Franciscan Rule, and that such repudiation was connected with Joachite views as to the degeneracy of the Church and the unique reforming rôle of the Franciscan order. None the less the fact remained that in running directly counter to the ruling of the bull *Exiit qui seminat* and the decisions of the Council of Vienne John XXII had actually created a new heresy, had asserted that what had seemed most Christian and laudable to Nicholas III and Clement V was an error in the faith.

The persecution had the result of actually encouraging Joachitism. 'As well to be hanged for a sheep as a lamb' is a proverb of very general validity.

If it was heresy to disobey a papal bull—granted that that had to be disobeyed—why not go to the full length of rejecting the papacy and declaring it superseded by the era of St. Francis and the Holy Ghost?

The papal pronouncement made the fanatical Spirituals more and more convinced that the Roman Church was indeed 'the whore of Babylon,' the Pope veritable Antichrist. And certainly we may regard the extremists latterly, under the goad of persecution, as having developed into a sect, definitely believing itself to be the true Church—that of St. Francis and the Holy Ghost.

But such fanatical Spirituals were exceedingly small in numbers, their influence very restricted, and their extinction was brought about without very much difficulty.

But it was not only the extremists that were made victims.

On November 12, 1323, John XXII, to whom the Spirituals' conception of the place of poverty in the Christian Church was definitely anathema, so irreconcilable was it with his papal policy, issued the bull, *Cum inter nonnullos*, in which it was authoritatively denied that Christ and His Apostles possessed no property. To assert that they held none was error and heresy. [9]

This question of dogma became involved with secular politics, when Lewis of Bavaria, being claimant to the imperial crown and at enmity with Pope John, found it convenient to adopt the cause of the Franciscans and to denounce the Pope himself as a heretic for not believing in the absolute poverty of Christ, as he did in a formal indictment of John known as the Protest of Sachsenhausen.

A controversy between Empire and Papacy was thus started which is of great interest because it evoked the 'Defensor Pacis' of Marsiglio of Padua and the numerous polemical works of William of Ockham on the imperial side. This controversy is

III: THE EVERLASTING GOSPEL

of much greater interest and significance than the story of the persecutions of the *Fratres de paupere vita*, or *Fraticelli*, which continued as the result of John XXII's action, more especially in Italy, into the later decades of the fourteenth century.

The significance of the persecutions lies in the virtual creation of a heresy by a papal bull. That it should be possible for any individual wearer of the papal tiara to declare heretical what his predecessors had held to be praiseworthy and to stigmatize as heretics his opponents in secular politics revealed a great danger. To hold fast to an immutable faith is easy, but what if the immutable faith does as a matter of fact change!

The bull *Cum inter nonnullos* made it possible that a man might be condemned as a heretic because he held a certain view as to Christ's poverty, although perfectly able and willing to subscribe to every article in the Christian creed as defined in the great councils of the early Church.

Catharism may have been a real peril to the Church but to maintain that men who had no other wish but to preserve the strict Rule of St. Francis in the order constituted such a peril is impossible. And men might well be bewildered by the fact that whereas the revolutionary teachings of Joachitism were not at first proscribed, the wearing of a particular type of hood became heretical not many years later.

The importance of 'The Everlasting Gospel' lies principally in its influence on the Franciscan order, but it had several other developments which are of distinct interest as remarkable illustrations of the strange fanaticisms and superstitious credulities possible in the thirteenth century.

The Joachite idea of a new era and new religion led to the astonishing discovery of incarnations of the divine. One was found in a certain woman, a native of Milan, called Guglielma, who seemed to have been in no way remarkable save for her piety.[10]

Yet the little band of followers who gathered round her came to venerate her as a saint and a miracle worker. The biographies of mediæval worthies are full of tales of the miraculous, and there was nothing strange in this.

But the extraordinary absurdity followed of finding her to be the Holy Ghost in female form. The woman herself never countenanced such fantastic ideas and expressly repudiated any supernatural powers. But after her death a small circle of fanatic devotees established her worship in Milan with a certain Maifreda at their head, performing high sacerdotal functions and destined in the eyes of her associates to succeed to the papal throne when the corrupt Roman Church should have passed away.

The Guglielmites were a very insignificant sect, easily extinguished. Potentially more dangerous were the followers of one Gherardo Segarelli, a very ignorant and very demented enthusiast of Parma, who, being rejected on his seeking admission into the Franciscan order, determined to outdo St. Francis in the exact reproduction of the life of Christ. [11]

His method of accomplishing this purpose was to have himself circumcised, wrapped in swaddling clothes and suckled by a woman—after which preliminaries he stalked into the streets of his native town, a wild, uncouth figure, calling all men to repentance.

In time the madman succeeded in attracting devotees from among herdsmen as ignorant and almost as foolish as himself. The movement began to be formidable when it spread beyond Parma, even beyond Italy, being found in 1287 in Germany; and it appeared that Segarelli aimed at proselytizing the world. The papacy was roused, the Inquisition put into action, Segarelli himself in 1300 burnt in Parma, his disciples, known as Apostolic Brethren, energetically persecuted.

They were not, however, entirely eradicated. Some remained—men of more intellect than the lunatic heresiarch and his half-witted herdsmen—and among them a certain Fra Dolcino, who saw in the appearance of Segarelli in the all-fateful year 1260 a fulfilment of the prophecies in 'The Everlasting Gospel.' [12]

He chose to regard himself as a heaven-appointed messenger of the new dispensation. As fanatical as Segarelli himself, he was more dangerous because apparently gifted with the capacity of leadership and of inspiring even enthusiastic loyalty. Beginning in Milan, Bergamo, Brescia, Vercelli, he had by 1304 created a distinct religious community among the Italian Alps.

It appears that, in order to maintain their supplies of provisions they were wont to resort to robbery, and must have become a

III: THE EVERLASTING GOSPEL

public nuisance. But they were also dangerous heretics; it is a remarkable tribute to the mark made by Dolcino's personality that Dante makes Mohammed send a warning message to Dolcino, as to a kindred false prophet, lest he fall into the same ill-case as himself. [13]

In June, 1305, Clement V resolved upon drastic measures to wipe out this 'son of Belial who had been polluting Lombardy.' [14] A crusade was organized against the Dolcinists in their mountain fastnesses, and after a desperate defence against no fewer than four different expeditions, in which there was much bloodshed and ferocity and in which the heretics were so reduced as to have recourse to cannibalism, they were forced to surrender. [15]

The punishment of Dolcino—for the nature of which, it should be remembered, the state and in no way the Inquisition was responsible—was terrible in the extreme. He was gradually torn to pieces by red-hot pincers—an appalling torment which he bore with an almost incredible fortitude.

Indirectly connected with the ascetic and mendicant enthusiasm of the Spiritual Franciscans were certain heretical movements in Germany—those of the Beghards or Beguines.

The names are used somewhat indiscriminately to denote Fraticelli, who were simply wandering Spirituals asserting the supreme virtues of poverty, and other sectaries, much more extravagant, whose only likeness to the Spirituals lay in their mendicancy.

The indiscriminacy of nomenclature undoubtedly denotes a very comprehensible failure at times to distinguish between vagrants outwardly alike and all of them at least under the suspicion of heretical tendencies. [16]

Among the extravagants to whom this title was given were followers of two teachers of a crude mysticism and pantheism— one Amaury de Bène [17], whose doctrine had a very marked antinomian tinge, for he maintained that no one filled with the Holy Ghost and the spirit of love could commit sin; the other, Ortlieb of Strassburg, whose pantheism caused him to include Satan in the divine essence, so that his followers, generally known as Brethren of the Free Spirit, were also sometimes known as Luciferans and credited with devil-worship and the perpetration of the most disgusting obscenities at the initiation of novices into the faith.

The Brethren of the Free Spirit were never numerous, but in spite of constant persecution they appear to have existed right up to the days of Lutheranism. Their doctrines were not without significance, because together with an exalted claim to impeccability which prescribed the severest tests of sexual purity they combined a mystic belief, which under the term Illuminism, a name they themselves adopted, had a considerable influence on the theological thought of Germany.

The most remarkable of these was the distinguished Dominican, Master Eckhart, who appears to have maintained that man shared the divinity of God and that in the eyes of God virtue and sin were alike. [18]

The existence of such venturesome pantheistic speculations as these broad-cast in Germany reacted very unfavourably on all unrecognized, and particularly on migratory, religious associations, which became involved in the persecutions set on foot in consequence of the undoubted heresies of the pantheists.

Such associations tended to increase in the thirteenth century. They were not necessarily connected with the Spiritual Franciscans or Fraticelli; but they certainly owed their origin to the popularity of the mendicant idea as practised by the friars, in particular the Minorites.

They are found in France, Germany, Italy and the Low Countries; and to such voluntary fellowships there could be no legitimate objection in themselves; they might be the most laudable instruments for the exploitation of religious zeal.

Only they called for thorough supervision. Beguinages, therefore—large permanent houses—were established in such towns as Cologne, Ghent, and Paris, such establishments being under careful management, the special protection of the popes and secular princes, and enjoying often the highest reputation for sanctity.

But with wanderers it was different. They could not be supervised, and to distinguish between the orthodox and the schismatic mendicant was difficult. Undisciplined vagrancy was in itself an invitation to temptation.

III: THE EVERLASTING GOSPEL

The Inquisition in Germany represented to Boniface IX in 1396 that for a hundred years all manner of heresies had lurked under the outward fair-seeming of the Beghards and that their suppression was impeded by certain papal constitutions urged in their protection. [19]

It is true that at times, owing to the extent to which the innocent were wont to suffer with the guilty, the papacy had ere that come to the rescue of the former, as for example Benedict XIV in 1336 and Gregory XI in 1374. It had in particular been necessary to protect women, large numbers of whom joined themselves not only to the permanent mendicant communities, but to the wandering mendicants.

In times that were hard and wild and disordered, when there was no system of poor-relief save through the Church, the lot of widows and of women and girls who had no male protectors was exceedingly hard, and for such the mendicant associations had a clear attraction as a means of asylum and refuge.

The war upon the Beghards in many cases led to many respectable women being led into a life of misery and want and sometimes prostitution, until Benedict XIV intervened on their behalf. [20]

At the Council of Constance certain rules were drawn up for the regulation of beguinages, but beguines did not thereby escape persecution. In 1431 we find Eugenius IV intervening for their protection.

Ever in danger of persecution, wanderers over the face of the land, these mendicant communities, whether remaining within the Church's fold or not, were a source of religious unrest, of dissatisfaction with the hierarchy, of aspiration for new doctrines which would attune with the intense individualism of a mystic illuminism. By such men and women Lutheranism might well be welcomed and its progress materially assisted. [21]

One of the strangest of the fanatical outbursts of the Middle Ages, especially in Germany, is indirectly connected with the Brethren of the Free Spirit, some of whom joined themselves with the Flagellants. The latter first made their appearance in Europe in 1259 in Italy, whence the movement spread to Bohemia and Germany.

A more important outbreak occurred in the middle of the next century, when the appalling ravages of the Black Death had no doubt brought home to many thousands of the survivors the awful fragility and insecurity of human life and the need for repentance and godliness.

It was the consciousness of the impotence of man probably that gave popularity to the abasement and self-torture of the scourge. There was a positive luxury of misery in the suggestion of so drastic a means of grace for a polluted people, smitten by the heavy hand of an angry God.

Through Hungary, Germany, Flanders, Holland marched these penitents, proclaiming complete regeneration for all who should persevere in flagellation for thirty-three days and a half, chanting weird prayers in which this creed was enshrined. For example,

               'En commencant no pénitence
               Soit la Vierge et la Trinité,
               Et, tout en parfaicte puissance,
               Des cieulx, le hault divin secret,
? cessiez. Sire Dieu, croissiez vo venjeance,
               Les fruits des ventres respitez.
               Car esté a en grant balance,
               Longtemps toute crestienté.

               'Or, avant, entre nous tait frère,
               Batons nos charoinges bien fort,
               En remembrant la grant misère
               Du Dieu et sa piteuse mort,
               Qui fut prins de la gent amère
               Et vendus et trahis à tort,
               Et battu sa char vierge et clère;
               En nom de ce, batons plus fort.' [22]

Theirs was a new gospel—the all-sufficient efficacy of the voluntary effusion of blood. [23]

It is no wonder that the authorities became alarmed. Legitimate exception was taken to the enthusiasts' indecency—

III: THE EVERLASTING GOSPEL

men went virtually naked, women insufficiently clad, all were under a temptation to sexual excesses. [24]

Worse was the doctrinal error involved—the attack upon sacraments and priesthood contained in the preaching of the strange means of grace by these new priests of Baal. [25]

In 1349 Clement VI, condemning the movement on the ground of the contempt of the Church implied in the formation of such an unlicensed fellowship, ordered the suppression of the Flagellants, who thereafter came under the purview of the Inquisition.

The heretical doctrine inherent in the Flagellant mania was enunciated in its most extravagant form by a native of Thuringia, named Conrad Schmidt, who in 1414 was maintaining that all spiritual authority had passed from the Catholic Church to the Flagellants, that not only were the sacraments useless, but they had been proscribed by God and it was mortal sin to partake of them, so that, for example, the ceremony of marriage polluted the union.

The fundamentally anti-sacerdotal character of the Flagellant movement was shared by another contemporary mania in Flanders and the Rhinelands—a dancing mania, under whose impulse fanatics would leap and convulse themselves in the most violent contortions in fierce ecstasies of religious frenzy. [26]

It is a most curious and remarkable story that is made by these interconnected heresies, more especially of the thirteenth century, and by others like them.

In the midst of the Ages of Faith individual emotional outpourings or intellectual speculations would lead to strange results of fanaticism or dogma. There were indeed some that were mainly sensual in origin, but others betokened an earnest desire for a new heaven and a new earth and demanded a moral progression in human affairs not visible in existing human society.

Such an aspiration is implicit in all the strange theories connected with 'The Everlasting Gospel' and in all the ideas of the Spiritual Franciscans, their offshoots and their companion sects.

How much of such aspiration, such opinions could the mediæval Church absorb within herself? It was ever doubtful. It would have been impossible to predict beforehand upon which side would eventually be found many of the remarkable men referred to in this chapter—Francis, John of Parma, Bonaventura, Marsiglio of Padua, William of Ockham, Roger Bacon, Amaury, Master Eckhart.

The pope who condemned the Spiritual Franciscans might easily have regarded Francis himself as a heretic. Fortunately for herself the Church, while repudiating doctrines which were obviously unchristian, those that were the mere frenzies of the ignorant and the demented, succeeded in absorbing a large measure of the enthusiasm and the thought of the age, incorporated the mendicant orders, produced the scholastic philosophy.

Nevertheless there were abroad in the mediæval world moral and intellectual ferments, yearnings for regeneration and guesses at truth which found within her fold no satisfaction.

NOTE:—In O. Holder-Egger's (complete) edition of Salimbene (*Monumenta Germaniae Historica*, vol. xxxii, Hanover and Leipzig, 1905-13) the most important references to Joachitism are on pp. 231-41, 292-4, 455-8.

---

[1] Lea, vol. iii, p. 10.

[2] Paradiso, xii, 139-41.

[3] On Joachim's writings, the problem of *The Everlasting Gospel and Joachitism* generally, see J. J. Döllinger, *Prophecy and the Prophetic Spirit in the Christian Era* (tr. A. Plummer, 1873), ch. vii; E. Renan, *Nouvelles Études d'histoire religieuse* (Paris, 1884; English ed. 1886); the Essay on Joachim in *Franciscan Essays* (1912), by E. G. Gardner, pp. 50-70; also E. Gebhart, *L'Italie mystique; la renaissance religieuse au moyen âge* (1908), esp. pp. 49-84, 183-253. The whole story of the Spiritual Franciscans, so far as it affected Italy, is told in this admirable work.

[4] J. à Royas, *De Haereticis, eorum que impia intentione et credulitate, cum quinquaginta analyticis assertionibus, quibus universae fidei causae facile definiri valeant*, in F. Ziletus, *Tractatus Universi Juris* (Venice, 1633), vol. xi, pt. ii, p. 211. The fact of the submission of his works in 1200 is disputed, *Franciscan Essays*, p. 56.

III: THE EVERLASTING GOSPEL

[5] See Renan, *op. cit.*, p. 248; Lea, vol. iii, pp. 22-3 and notes; F. H. Reusch, *Index der verbotenen Bücher* (Bonn, 1883). *Bücherverbote im Mittelalter*, pp. 18-21; Chronicle of Salimbene in *Monumenta Historica ad provincias Parmensem et Placentiam pertinentia* (Parma, 1857), pp. 235-6. See *Directorium*, part ii, question ix, pp. 269-72, on the heresies of John of Parma. 'It is… the substitution of the idea of the Everlasting Gospel as a written book to supersede the Gospel of Christ, for the original one of the Everlasting Gospel as an unwritten spiritual interpretation based upon that Gospel—that separates Gherardo of Borgo San Donnino and the Joachists from the authentic creed of Joachim himself.'—*Franciscan Essays*, p. 63. The prophecies of Joachim himself were esteemed by the Church; it was the subsequent gloss upon them that was suspect. See Döllinger *Prophecy and the Prophetic Spirit* (London, 1873), pp. 121 *et seq.*

[6] Rev. xiv, 6.

[7] See Lea, vol. iii, pp. 18-19. 'Unless the universe were a failure, and the promises of God were lies, there must be a term to human wickedness; and as the Gospel of Christ and the Rule of Francis had not accomplished the salvation of mankind, a new gospel was indispensable. Besides, Joachim had predicted that there would arise a new religious Order which would rule the world and the Church in the halcyon age of the Holy Ghost. They could not doubt that this referred to the Franciscans as represented by the Spiritual group, which was striving to uphold in all its strictness the Rule of the venerated founder.' Salimbene was not a very spiritually-minded Franciscan. That most entertaining chronicler took a not entirely holy delight in the bright and frivolous things of life, and even the gross. But he was very much impressed by the prophecies of the Abbot Joachim. All prophecies appealed to his curious and inquisitive mind, those of Merlin as well as Joachim; but he was genuinely interested in their spiritual significance also, and for a time a professed Joachite. See his Chronicle, especially relating to the testimony of one, Brother Hugo of Montpellier, concerning Joachim, *op. cit.*, pp. 97 *et seq.* There is a summary in Taylor, *op. cit.*, vol. i, pp. 494-517. The place of poverty in the Franciscan Rule is discussed in *St. Francis and Poverty—Franciscan Essays*, pp. 18-30.

[8] For the persecution of the Spirituals generally see Lea, vol. iii, pp. 23-89, 129-80; also Döllinger, *Beiträge*, vol. ii, pp. 417-526, a *Chronicle of the Persecution of the Brothers Minor*, also p. 606. See also *Directorium*, on Arnaldo da Villanova, p. 282, Fraticelli, pp. 313-22.

[9] The formula of abjuration from the heresy defined by John XXII's bulls was: 'I swear that I believe in my heart and profess that our Lord Jesus Christ and His Apostles while in the mortal life held in common the things which Scripture declares them to have had, and that they had the right of giving,

selling and alienating them.'—Eymeric, *Directorium*, p. 486.

[10] For Guglielma see Lea, vol. iii, pp. 90-100.

[11] See Bernard Gui, *Practica*, pp. 340 *et seq.*; also Salimbene, *op. cit.*, pp. 112 *et seq.*; *Directorium*, pp. 286-8.

[12] For Dolcino see *ibid.* and *Practica*, pp. 340-55.

[13] *Inferno*, Canto xxviii.

[14] *Practica*, p. 340.

[15] Inquisitors found difficulty in proceeding against Dolcinists, *ibid.*, p. 343. 'Est autem valde difficile ipsos examinare et veritatem contra eos invenire pro eo maxime quod, quantuscumque juraverint in juditio se veritatem dicturos, nolunt tamen manifeste suam detegere falsitatem, nec suos errores publice confiteri, nec directe respondere ad interrogata, set palliate et per astucias et tergiversationes multas deviant et mendaciis se juvant, et se ipsos contegunt, et ideo multum est ars necessaria contra ipsos et industria inquirentis.'

[16] See Lea, vol. ii, pp. 351-2, 355.

[17] Lea, vol. ii, p. 320. E. Renan, *Averroës et l'Averroïsme* (Paris, 1861, 2nd ed.), p. 222.

[18] See Lea, vol. i, p. 360; vol. ii, p. 359. For views ascribed to Beghards see Döllinger, *Beiträge*, vol. ii, pp. 378-401 (*passim*). '…se esse vel aliquos ex istis perfectos et sic unitos Deo, quod sint realiter et veraciter ipse Deus, quia dicunt se esse illud idem et unum esse quod est ipse Deus absque distinctione.' See also *Directorium*, pt. ii, question xv, pp. 299-308.

[19] For proceedings against Beguines, modes of interrogation and sentences, etc., see Bernard Gui, *Practica*, pp. 141-4, 277 *et seq.*

[20] Frédéricq, *op. cit.*, vol. ii, p. 93. 'Verum quia in multis mundi partibus sunt plurime mulieres similiter Beghine vulge vocate, quarum alique in propriis, alique in conductis, alique in communibus sibi domibus habitantes vitam ducunt honestam' …proceeds to rule that these must on no account be molested.

[21] Lea, vol. ii, pp. 413-14.

[22] See Frédéricq, *Corpus*, vol. iii, No. 25, pp. 23-4.

[23] *Ibid.*, vol. ii, p. 101. See also No. 61.

[24] *Ibid.*, vol. ii, pp. 100-1.

[25] *Ibid.*, vol. iii, p. 35. See also p. 31: '…yperbolice loquendo, qua locutione solet frequenter uti scriptura ad exprimendum eius magnam quantitatem seu multitudinem, congrue dici possit per omnes christianitatis provincias jam esse diffusa.' From a sermon preached before Clement VI, descanting upon the seriousness and extent of the attraction of the Flagellant mania for the ignorant crowd.

[26] These acrobatic performances were of course of a convulsive nature and were by contemporaries ascribed to demoniac possession. But the idea

III: THE EVERLASTING GOSPEL

of dancing and leaping as a form of religious devotion suggests the very charming story, *Our Lady's Tumbler*, which has been rewritten by Anatole France and is included in *Aucassin et Nicolette and other Mediæval Romances in Everyman's Library*.

IV

Averrhoïst Influences

The great intellectual achievement of the Middle Ages was the recovery of the learning of the world that had vanished before the onset of the Hun, the Vandal and the Lombard.[1]

That learning was in part classical, in part patristic. But as the process of absorption was the achievement of the Church, the emphasis was on theology, and the works of the Fathers bulked very much more largely than the profane literatures of Greece and Rome. There was much in the teaching of Augustine that was Neoplatonic, that was akin to the speculations of Plato himself. But the whole point of view, method and cast of mind of the mediæval thinker were radically different from those of the pagan philosopher.

The latter set out upon the search for abstract truth without any preconceptions; the former started from the postulate of a divine revelation. His primary object was not to investigate, but to justify the ways of God to man. For him all knowledge must be a theodicæa.

He was not, therefore, an original thinker; for the foundations of his scholarship being revealed truth, his most marked characteristic was a sincere deference to authority.

IV: AVERRHOÏST INFLUENCES

He was, moreover, ever conscious that the salvation of the soul was a matter of greater cogency than even the exposition of God's dealings with the world. At the same time mediæval philosophy was of a peculiarly formal pattern; and to the modern world it is apt to appear pedantic indeed, 'cabined, cribbed, confined.' It rested upon the tripod of grammar, rhetoric, logic. It was a matter very largely of dialectic, and it may seem to us of mere verbal juggling.

The *Trivium* was an introduction to metaphysics, but the metaphysics were strongly theological in bias and nakedly logical in form. Their clue to the processes of thought being logic, not psychology, mediæval thinkers did not clearly distinguish between problems of the human mind and problems of reality, assuming an exact correspondence between mental conceptions and the ultimate facts of the universe.

Yet whatever the defects of the scholastic philosophy, it holds a great and significant place in the history of the intellectual development of western Europe, since it was the means whereby the learning of the ancient world was recovered and preserved and an intellectual continuity rendered possible. Such is one out of many of the great contributions made by the mediæval Church to the cause of civilization.

Secular knowledge was not proscribed, but on the contrary adopted and utilized, by the Church; enquiry and research not looked askance upon, but encouraged. The universities of the Middle Ages were ecclesiastical in origin; their teachers and scholars were clerks. The great University of Paris, the very centre of the intellectual life of Christendom in the thirteenth and fourteenth centuries, was an object of very special solicitude to the Holy See.

The two great mendicant orders, the Prædicants and the Minorites, taking the lead in the schools and universities only a few years after their own inception, speedily produced some of the most erudite and the most brilliant minds of the Middle Ages.

In the twelfth century the leading scholastics were Augustinians; in the middle of the thirteenth the dominant philosophy was still of a Neoplatonic character. The great Franciscans Alexander of

Hales, Bonaventura, Peckham belonged to that school of thought. In many of them, notably in Bonaventura, there was a marked strain of mysticism. The mystic note in Plato, his insistence on moral and spiritual values had made his doctrine harmonize easily with Christian dogma.

The appropriation of pagan thought and secular science had not so far produced any discord with the truths of the Christian faith, or any serious tendency to question them.

It is indeed significant that the pupils of Anselm of Bec should have asked him for a *rational* justification of Christian dogma; but that had not betokened any doubt as to the possibility of reconciling faith with reason, but only an appreciation of the desirability of being able to demonstrate that, however superfluous, such justification was perfectly possible.

Again, in the vast compendious treatises of such encyclopædic scholars as Vincent of Beauvais, Hugo of St. Victor and Peter Lombard, there was the explicit recognition that, while secular learning is a thing to be desired for its own sake, yet its stages of *cogitatio* and *meditatio* are only the threshold before the portal of the shrine, wherein the divine nature may be contemplated. Reason cannot unaided explain the ineffable; the visible world is but the simulacrum of the unseen. [2]

Once or twice indeed there had been hints of danger. Right back in the ninth century a certain very self-confident Irishman, by name John Scotus Eriugena, had declared the supremacy of reason over authority; for while authority sometimes proceeded from reason, reason never proceeded from authority.

In the eleventh century there had been the aberrations of Berengar of Tours and Roscellinus.

In the next century a new and more brilliant Eriugena arose in the person of Abelard, a man even more self-opinionated and self-confident, one who treated the seeming contradictions of the Fathers as opportunity merely for mental calisthenics, whose whole method of thought appeared to enthrone reason at the expense of authority.

But the potential danger was never realized. The trained dialectician trembled before the unlearned spiritual dictator of Christendom; the man who exalted himself in his own eyes

IV: AVERRHOÏST INFLUENCES

dared not face Bernard, to whom God was all in all and man as nothing: and at the last Abelard, a monk of Cluny, died humbled, in the odour of sanctity.

Up to the end of the twelfth century, then, the free play of enquiry and discussion in the schools had not threatened defilement of the purity of the Christian faith. Heresy had indeed been a serious danger; but not among the learned, not in the precincts of the university, had it been bred.

The succeeding century, however, did bring with it an anxious problem. There came a large influx of new learning out of the pagan past—the encyclopædic knowledge of Aristotle. Aristotle had been introduced into the world of Latin Christianity long ere this through the medium of Boëthius in the days of Theodoric. [3]

The Dark Ages had intervened since then. Now came a second and a much more significant advent of Aristotle. This time he came through a non-Christian medium, through the interpretations of the 'great commentator,' the Moslem Ibn-Roschd, Averrhoës.

Could the Stagirite be won for Christ; could his teachings be enlisted for the Christian theodicæa? The Church could not but be alive to the risks involved in any converse with Aristotelianism.

There were radical contrasts between the Platonic and Aristotelian methods. The latter was inductive, non-committal, denoted an impartial examination of natural phenomena, the range of which was infinitely more comprehensive than anything which any other human mind had ever attempted.

Aristotle seemed intent rather upon coldly collecting evidence from the operations of a soulless Nature than extolling the wonders of God in a beatific vision.

The extent of secular knowledge opened up in the writings of Aristotle was, then, vast and their attraction to the alert and curious mind correspondingly vivid; but the attractiveness had to be viewed with caution.

The Church perceived that there were in the Peripatetic philosophy elements which must be repugnant to truly devout minds. This would have been true even had the pure unadulterated text of Aristotle been in question; it was the more cogently true seeing that Aristotle was presented to the Christian world through the voice of Averrhoës and the commentary was more familiar than the original.

During the tenth and eleventh centuries when Christendom was for the most part wrapped in a barbarous ignorance, Saracen culture, in the caliphates of Bagdad and Cordova, had kept alive the sciences—mathematics, astronomy, medicine—and speculative thinkers had preserved, not indeed uncorrupted, yet always as a vital influence, the ancient philosophy of Greece, when to the Christian world it was lost in oblivion.

Side by side with an orthodox philosophy in consonance with the teachings of the Koran, Islam had produced a heretic philosophy, which though written in a Semitic language and modified by an oriental environment, was essentially Greek, essentially Aristotelian. [4]

To the Arabian thinkers the Stagirite represented the utmost limit of the human intelligence; they could not conceive that there could ever be improvement upon knowledge so catholic, synthesis so complete. The first of the great Arabian philosophers, Alfarabi, had been Neoplatonist in thought, Aristotelian in method. [5] His great successor, Avicenna, was Aristotelian both in the content and the logical scheme of his work. [6]

The distinctive teachings of Avicenna were, first, the nominalist doctrine that universality exists not in reality, but in thought only; secondly, that matter is uncreated and eternal; thirdly, that the first and only direct emanation from God or the First Cause is Intelligence, $νους$, but that this communication of intelligence to lesser beings is not a single act in time, but a constant process or an everlasting act.

While in the eastern caliphate these bold speculations were strongly denounced by the later philosopher of Bagdad, Ghazali, and were repudiated in a powerful orthodox reaction [7]; in Spain at the beginning of the twelfth century Avempace and Abubacer were teaching that the life of the soul is a progress from a purely instinctive existence shared with the lower animals to a spiritual absorption in the divine essence and intellect; while the latter philosopher added the contention that religious creeds were but types of, or approximations to, absolute truth, which the philosopher, but never the mere theologian, may attain.

IV: AVERRHOÏST INFLUENCES

The greatest of all the Arabian thinkers, Averrhoës, whose life extended over the greater part of the twelfth century was, in even greater degree than Avicenna, a worshipper of Aristotle.[8] While Avicenna occasionally questioned his great original, Averrhoës never did. He laid no claim to originality. To him the substance of human wisdom could never alter, being enshrined for ever in Aristotle's pages. If Averrhoïsm differs from Aristotelianism, it does not differ consciously. Averrhoïsm is simply and solely the undiluted gospel of Aristotle, as Averrhoës conceived it.

Its principal theses—the Averrhoïst version of Aristotle—are the eternity of matter and the unity of the intellect.[9] Matter is uncreated. God did not create; He is Himself the primordial element in things, the latent force or impulse in the universe, which gives it both its being and continuance.

Emanating from the First Cause is the active intellect. For Averrhoës makes an important distinction between νους ποιητικός and νους παθητικός, the latter being the human intellect. Averrhoës explains the difference by the analogy of the sun and the human vision. Just as by the light which it sheds the sun produces the capacity to see, so the active intellect produces the capacity to understand.

But the human intellect has no individual immortality, being at death absorbed in the universal mind. Man, indeed, possesses no personal immortality. Only in man's power of reproducing his species can there be said to be any human immortality. The human race is permanent. In the fullest sense, however, only the active intellect is eternal.

The attitude of Averrhoës to Islam, and indeed to all religion, is important. It may be summed up by saying that he was the friend of religion, the enemy of theology, for which he could see no excuse. There could be no compromise between faith and philosophy.

The theologian was at the outset hopelessly hampered in the search for truth, because he had to premise all the articles of his creed. His system, thus conditioned, became a mere hodgepodge of sophistic quibblings, groundless distinctions, fanciful allegories, which did but serve to obscure and distort the religion which it pretended to expound. The sincere and exact thinker could accept no such postulates, start with no preconceptions. Philosophy and religion must be kept completely apart; the attempt to suffuse them—made in theology—did but corrupt both. They were not, however, mutually subversive.

Religion was no branch of knowledge, no matter of arid formularies; it was an inward power, an inspiration. It was indispensable, because it was the basis of morality for the multitude who could not aspire to philosophy.

But while Averrhoës thus discountenanced any attempt to instil religious doubts into the popular mind, his attitude towards religion was exclusively utilitarian, and he obviously regarded it as the inferior of philosophy. The special religion of philosophers, he declared, was to study what exists, for the noblest worship of God was in the contemplation of his works. Philosophy, in short, the pursuit of wisdom, was the highest form of religion, higher than that which is based upon prophecy. [10]

Averrhoïsm speedily penetrated into Christendom. Aragon and Castile naturally received it early. In Languedoc, at the schools of Montpellier, Narbonne, Perpignan, Arabian medicine and philosophy both flourished. Scholars from central and western Europe, visiting the medical schools of the Moors, no doubt brought back with them the current views of the Saracen philosopher as well as the Saracen physician. The first Latin version of Averrhoës' commentaries is attributed to Michael Scot, who came fresh from Toledo to the court of Frederick II; while there is a tradition that the son of Averrhoës lived for a time in the palace of that most eclectic potentate. [11]

From Saracen Toledo itself, from Christians and Jews in Spain and Provence, came translations of Averrhoës. It was probably with extraordinary rapidity that the ideas of the Arabian philosopher became the common property of the Christian schoolmen. [12] Quite certainly Latin Averrhoïsm was a force to be reckoned with by the middle of the thirteenth century. [13]

The Averrhoïst was not the only Latin version of Aristotle current in western Christendom in the twelfth century. The capture of Constantinople by the crusaders in 1204 had brought Catholic Europe directly into contact with Greek philosophy, and translations direct from the Greek into Latin had been

IV: AVERRHOÏST INFLUENCES

attempted, one of the earliest being made by Bishop Grosseteste. Various translations of Aristotle were, then, available.

Were they to be regarded as open without restriction to the curious eye of scholarship? The Church decided against such freedom.

In 1210 a council of the ecclesiastical province of Sens, held at Paris, having publicly condemned the heresies of Amaury de Bène, went on to protect the unwary from another source of possible contamination by commanding that neither the works of Aristotle nor the commentaries upon him should be read in Paris under pain of excommunication. [14] The commentaries referred to must be either those of Averrhoës or similar Arabian treatises.

In 1215 this prohibition was renewed by the papal legate, under whose supervision the schools of Paris came. Gregory IX, in a regulation addressed to the masters and students of Paris on April 13, 1231, made the prohibition provisional, until such time as the books of Aristotle could be examined and expurgated. At the same time he entrusted this important task to William of Auxerre and two others.

The project is very much to the credit of the Pope, a genuine supporter of learning who, however, had probably not realized how great an undertaking it was. At all events it came to nothing; and the prohibition, although renewed by Urban IV, in January 1263, would appear to have remained a dead-letter.

In 1255 the 'Physics' and 'Metaphysics' of Aristotle were prescribed for the course in the Arts' faculty in the University. In fact the Aristotelian impulse in the vivid and vigorous atmosphere of the youthful Parisian schools was too strong. Neither Aristotle nor Averrhoës could be got rid of by papal inhibition. The keenest interest had been aroused in them. It were better, as it was simpler, to utilize such keenness rather than to attempt to combat it.

Of all the great services rendered to the Church by the Dominican order none was greater than its capture of profane learning for orthodox Christianity. The great Franciscans were expounding the current theology of the day with its tinge of Platonism; the Dominicans now came forward to adapt Aristotle for the service of Christianity.

In 1256 Alexander IV commissioned Albertus Magnus to write his 'De unitate intellectus contra Averroëm': a fact that is proof positive of the headway that had already been made not only by Aristotelianism but by the tenets of the 'great commentator.' The tractate is indeed written against Averrhoës himself, not Averrhoïsts, but the fact that the Pope entrusted Albert of Cologne with the task of answering the former is evidence of the activity of the latter. [15]

Fifteen years later Thomas Aquinas produced another work on the same subject: but this one definitely 'contra Averroïstas.' Between the years 1261 and 1269 Aquinas was, together with William of Moerbeke, at the court of Rome engaged upon the great task, now at length undertaken under the auspices of the Holy See, of making a translation and commentary on Aristotle.

In the latter year he appeared at Paris on the occasion of the assembly there of a chapter-general of the Dominican order. It has been maintained that the real reason of his presence was to clear the Prædicants of the suspicion of Averrhoïsm. [16]

The middle and the latter half of the thirteenth century were years of violent controversy in the University of Paris. Fundamentally the source of this was the jealousy of the secular clergy against the Mendicant orders, which had succeeded in establishing themselves in the University earlier in the century, the Dominicans securing their first chair in 1217, the Franciscans theirs in 1219.

Apprehensive lest the Friars should achieve a complete predominance, the seculars under the leadership of Gerard of Abbeville and the acrimonious William of Saint-Amour led a heated attack upon them, first only on the practical question of university privileges. But it was not long before matters of doctrine were involved, and regulars and seculars were soon denouncing each other as heretics and antichrist. [17]

It is not easy to discover what was the doctrinal position of the seculars, but they seem to have reproached the Dominicans at all events with overfondness for philosophy as distinct from theology. [18] Together with the contest between seculars and regulars in the University there went also one between the two great Mendicant orders.

IV: AVERRHOÏST INFLUENCES

The same charge seems to have been preferred against the Prædicants by their rivals. They cared too much for knowledge that was not wholly sacred; they were too scientific, too intellectualist. [19]

Such is the gist of the diatribes launched against the Dominicans, especially Thomas Aquinas, by Archbishop Peckham. [20] There is no doubt that he deliberately tried to involve Aquinas in the suspicion of Averrhoïsm.

A certain Gilles de Lessines, sending to Albertus Magnus a list of fifteen errors current in Paris, includes in the number thirteen definitely Averrhoïst doctrines together with two theories of Aquinas, not Averrhoïst, to which, however, the Augustinians took exception. [21] Clearly the Franciscans were endeavouring to discredit not only the Averrhoïsts, but the Aristotelians.

In the year 1270 there appeared two important treatises: the one by a certain Siger of Brabant, entitled 'De anima intellectiva,' the other by Aquinas, 'De unitate intellectus contra Averroïstas.' The latter is defending himself vigorously against the charge of Averrhoïsm by himself vigorously attacking the Averrhoïsts.

In a sermon preached before the University of Paris St. Thomas vehemently denounced the self-confidence and self-sufficiency of the Averrhoïsts, and contrasted the contradictions and the uncertainties of philosophy with the clearness and certitude of revealed religion. [22]

In this same year 1270 the Bishop of Paris, Etienne Tempier, solemnly condemned the thirteen propositions mentioned in Gilles de Lessines' letter to Albertus of Cologne. They were the doctrines being taught at the time by the two leaders of Averrhoïsm in the University, the Siger of Brabant just mentioned and Boëthius of Dacia.

Of Siger's works a number are extant. Two or three are concerned with the sort of logical conundrums popular among mediæval dialecticians or with theories of Aquinas and are orthodox enough, but the 'De aeternitate mundi' and the 'De anima intellectiva' contain the whole gospel of Averrhoës. [23] Their contentions are so completely a transcription of the 'great commentator' that it is unnecessary to do more than summarize them briefly.

For Siger, as for the Arabian, Aristotle is the one and only philosopher. Like Averrhoës too, Siger makes no attempt to reconcile Aristotle with revealed religion, but carries his teaching to its supposed logical conclusion. Both Albertus and Aquinas, Siger maintained, had perverted Aristotle. [24] Not they, but Averrhoës, was the true exponent of the Stagirite.

He proclaimed, then, in all boldness the doctrine of the unity of the intellect together with its inevitable corollary, the denial of personal immortality; the doctrine of the eternity of matter, which involved the negation of the Biblical story of creation, the intervention of providence, the free will and moral responsibility of the individual. [25]

Such were the fundamental conceptions of Siger's teaching and of the propositions condemned by the Bishop of Paris in 1270. The condemnation did not silence the Averrhoïst champion and his friends. For six or seven more years they continued to be possibly a small, but apparently an energetic and defiant, body among the masters of arts in the University.

Between 1272 and 1275 Siger was in open revolt against the authority of the rector, Amaury of Rheims. The Averrhoïsts separated themselves from the rest of the faculty; but the force and skill, perhaps the very audacity, of their leader attracted a large number of students to his lectures. [26]

The doctrinal controversy continued. It was one not so much concerning the truth or erroneousness of the Averrhoïst position as on the question of fact—was Averrhoës or Aquinas the more faithful interpreter of Aristotle? Aegidius Romanus triumphantly vindicated the Stagirite from the Averrhoïst deductions. [27]

On the other hand, there continued to be those to whom Aristotelianism and the expositions of Albertus Magnus and Aquinas were anathema. [28]

In the end the latter triumphed over their adversaries: Aquinas was canonized, Aristotle was vindicated, and the Alberto-Thomist principle tended to take the place of Platonic Augustinianism as the most authoritative philosophy of the schools.

It was far otherwise with the anti-scholastic faction of Siger. They, the literal slaves of Aristotle, accepting the Averrhoïst interpretations of him without emendation, refusing to accept

IV: AVERRHOÏST INFLUENCES

the idea of any compromising adaptation to suit the requirements of revealed truth, were accused of maintaining that the Christian faith, in common with all other religious creeds with their fables and errors, was an obstacle to scientific enquiry leading to the acquirement of exact truth. [29]

Here was Averrhoïsm naked and unashamed indeed; but it is difficult to believe that this accusation can be true. However that may be, the Paris Averrhoïsts—and Siger very outspokenly—asserted the collateral existence of two distinct truths, the religious and the philosophical.

It is remarkable that principles of this type should have been tolerated so long. In 1277 there came a change. In January of that year Pope John XXI addressed a letter to Etienne Tempier in which he bids him search out notable errors in doctrine, since it is deplorable to find the pure streams of Catholic faith, which it is the special function of the University to send forth, being grievously polluted. [30]

Thus commanded, Tempier set to work once more, and this time produced a list of no fewer than 219 errors. [31] Again an attempt was made to confound the Thomists with the Averrhoïsts, and the long list included many very petty points. But the principal errors enumerated are Averrhoïst and the list is obviously aimed chiefly against Siger and Boëthius. The Bishop not only produced the catalogue, but he fulminated a decree pronouncing excommunication against all those who harboured the opinions therein condemned.

Henceforward such persons were 'suspect' of heresy; and it is not surprising that either in November 1277 or 1278—probably the former—Siger and Boëthius were cited to appear before the inquisitor of France, Simon du Val, in the diocese of Noyon. [32]

The two Averrhoïsts seem to have appealed against the inquisitor direct to the court of Rome, probably on the grounds of the special privileges of the University of Paris, the peculiar solicitude of the papacy for the University, their own intrinsic importance as teachers of great reputation and their persistent declaration that they were true Catholics.

The circumstances of their latter days are obscure; but the strong probability is that they made their way to Rome to purge themselves from the suspicion of heresy, were tried before the inquisition of Tuscany, abjured their errors, were duly reconciled and then penanced with perpetual imprisonment. [33]

Siger died at Orvieto, certainly before 1300, since in that year Dante imagines a meeting with him in his journey through Paradise. How comes it that Dante places this heretic in Paradise?

Two possible conjectures have been put forward. The first that Dante did so in ignorance of Siger's true character, not being sufficiently well versed in the current philosophy of the time; the other, that he wanted to place in Paradise some one who should represent the philosopher *par excellence* as distinct from the theologian. It was not easy to find such a one; and of the possible candidates, Siger of Brabant was the most distinguished. [34]

Parisian Averrhoïsm, despite the condemnation of its chief exponents, did not die with Siger, Boëthius and the thirteenth century. In the next century a certain John of Landun or of Ghent was preaching Averrhoïst doctrine in the University and attacking the reputation of St. Thomas; and he had numerous followers. [35]

But by this time the chief centre of Averrhoïsm was tending to be Padua rather than Paris. Here the Averrhoïst school was founded by Peter of Abano, equally famous as physician, magician, astrologer and Averrhoïst, who only escaped the clutches of the Inquisition by dying an opportune natural death in 1316. [36]

The school there also admitted its direct indebtedness to the Parisian, John of Landun. From his days right down to the seventeenth century speculations of an Averrhoïst character continued to be discussed in northern Italy, especially in Padua.

In the late fifteenth and early sixteenth centuries there were two rival Aristotelian parties in Padua and Bologna, Averrhoïsts and Alexandrists (so-called after the Greek commentator, Alexander of Aphrodistias), who disputed academic-wise concerning the personal or impersonal nature of immortality.

Of the Averrhoïsts the most distinguished were Achellini, Augustino Nifo and Zimara; of the Alexandrists, Pomponazzi. Although an Alexandrist, this bold and lively thinker owed much to Averrhoës while it is an indication of the very academic nature of Italian Averrhoïsm that Nifo, it is true after somewhat

IV: AVERRHOÏST INFLUENCES

modifying his views, was commissioned by Leo X to prove as against Pomponazzi that Aristotle believed in the immortality of the soul. [37]

The most perfervid opponent of Latin Averrhoïsm in the Middle Ages was Raymond Lully, who made it his dominant object in life to combat Islam in all its shapes and forms. His schemes embraced the recovery of the Holy Sepulchre and the conversion of all Jews and Saracens; but he desired to attack not only the Koran, but Moslem heterodoxy also, and to rescue the truths of Christianity from the contaminations of the 'great commentator.'

To these ends he laboured untiringly and with an intense zeal. We find him approaching the Council of Vienne in 1311, with projects for the amalgamation of the great military orders, a new crusade against the infidel, the foundation of colleges for the study of Arabic so that Moslem errors may be the more easily confuted. Lully also desired the suppression of the works of Averrhoës in all schools, and the prohibition of all Christians from reading them. [38]

It is remarkable that the works of this great antagonist of Averrhoïsm should have themselves come under suspicion of heresy. It is probable that his followers, rather than Lully himself, were responsible for the damaging of his reputation, since some of them held opinions of a Joachite character. But it is clear that in his animosity to Averrhoïsm Lully went to the opposite extreme.

Condemning the tenet of the incompatibility of philosophy and revealed truth, he was moved to maintain that there was no difference between them, that there was no dividing line between the rational and the supernatural. [39] Therein was perhaps as great error as in the contrary opinion.

However that may be, Nicholas Eymeric determined to have Lully's memory condemned, and in the 'Directorium' is particularly venomous against him. In 1376 he exhibited a papal bull condemning no fewer than 500 Lullist opinions as heretical. The results were curious. These were in the days of the Schism; and the Aragonese acknowledged neither pope. Declaring the bull a forgery, perpetrated by the inquisitor himself, the Lullists secured his banishment, and Eymeric died in exile. [40]

A better known enemy of Averrhoïsm than Raymond Lully was Petrarch, who like Lully hated everything that savoured of Islam. He hated its medicine and its astronomy, but above all its philosophy. He makes the Averrhoïsts—of whom it is clear he must have known a number—targets of an indignant irony. They are men who make it a point of honour to deny Christ and the supernatural.

Petrarch, his inspiration drawn from the classics of paganism, a man who had witnessed and loathed the abominations of Avignon, who regarded Rome as 'the temple of heresy,' had no brief to defend the orthodox creed. But to him Christianity was endeared because of its humility, Averrhoïsm abhorrent because it was dogmatic, self-confident, pedantic. [41]

This to the mediæval mind is the outstanding characteristic of Averrhoïsm. It is insolent in the assurance of its denials. In the fourteenth century Averrhoës himself stands as the unique personification of the spirit of unbelief; and as such is bracketed with Antichrist and Mohammed. [42]

In this light he figures in the paintings of Orcagna and others. To Gerson he is the most abominable of all enemies of Christianity, to Petrarch a rabid dog ever raging against the Catholic faith. [43]

The famous phrase 'the three impostors,' which had first been attributed by Gregory IX to Frederick II, and the essential conception of which in book form was destined to be attributed to many others from Boccaccio to Erasmus, Rabelais to Milton, was fathered upon Averrhoës. [44]

He had declared—so it was believed—that Moses, Christ and Mohammed were three impostors who had deluded the world; also that of the three religions, Judaism, Christianity, Mohammedanism, the first was a religion for babes, the second a sheer impossibility, the third fit only for hogs. The Eucharist was the impossible feature of Christianity, and Christians were especially hateful because they ate the flesh of the God whom they professed to adore. [45]

Perhaps the most interesting fact connected with the story of the Islamic philosophy in Europe is the fact that it helped to familiarize Christendom with some of the features of another

IV: AVERRHOÏST INFLUENCES

religion. It was not, of course, the sole agency to do that; the Crusades played their part.

It is significant that many of the mediæval stories and mystery plays have as their central idea apostasy, which as a rule takes the form of conversion to Mohammedanism. Even the religious wars in Palestine did not breed exclusively antagonism to the faith of the infidel, and friendly intercourse with Saracen Spain and academic interest in Islamic philosophy produced a knowledge that was less critical than sympathetic. Such familiarity with the main conceptions of other creeds rendered feasible the comparative study of religion.

That was to be an achievement for a future age. Yet it needed no exact science of the subject to encourage the spirit of toleration. When other religions were discussed, were it only for the sake of attacking and refuting them, still the curious eye could not fail to be aware of their common elements. Not even in Marsiglio is the principle of religious toleration more notably set forth than in one of the tales of the 'Decameron,' the pithy parable of 'The Three Rings,' which inspired Lessing's 'Nathan the Wise.' [46]

Melchizedek in Boccaccio's tale emphasizes in his analogue the common elements in the three religions of Jew, Moslem and Christian, each claiming to be the sole truth, and no doubt one of them being in fact the truth, yet so alike that none can tell which that one is.

Boccaccio's attitude is one of sceptical indifference, and it is no far cry from that to the attitude of Pulci in the 'Morgante Maggiore,' in which the mood is one of complete levity and all the forces of ridicule are brought against the quips and quiddities of the theologian and the superiority of Orlando's God over Morgante's original deity is made to look exceedingly equivocal.

We must not allow ourselves to discover an Averrhoïst origin for all the outspoken language used in the thirteenth and fourteenth centuries, in which Christianity is regarded critically, objectively. [47]

It is no doubt true that Averrhoïsm was principally an academic force belonging to the universities, and that even there its adherents were never numerous.

On the other hand, there must inevitably have been some infiltration of Averrhoïst ideas through the general community. There must have been some dispersal through the agency of the scholars who thronged the seats of learning, who were more often than not wanderers from one school to another, from Spain to France, from France to England, from England to Italy, and who must have scattered abroad the influences under which they themselves were brought.

There were from the point of view of the Church two obviously dangerous features in Averrhoïsm.

First there was its anti-scholastic nature, its determination to follow philosophy wheresoever it might lead, regardless of whether it could be reconciled with Christian dogma or not, a determination which was accompanied by a bold insistence upon their incompatibility in point of fact. In the resolution to follow truth, untrammelled by religious dogma, there might at the surface appear to be something of that critical spirit which produced another anti-scholastic revolt, that of Roger Bacon.

But whereas in his case the inductive method gave promise of progress in knowledge, the possibility scarcely existed with philosophers who were just as completely persuaded as was the most orthodox mediæval saint that the truth had once and for ever been vouchsafed to mankind, with the sole difference that whereas the saint found the truth in the Bible, the Averrhoïst found it in the treatises of Aristotle.

But the fact that he did so find it—in pagan and not in sacred writ—was, one would have thought, radical enough and dangerous enough; while the actual doctrines he professed were as divorced from Christian belief, as wildly heretical as any that the most fiercely persecuted mediæval sect ever expressed. Nevertheless as a rule the Averrhoïst was not persecuted.

At first glance this appears very surprising. Yet the explanation is in reality simple enough. In the first place, the Church was no enemy of speculative thinking as such. The doctors, the masters and the students who debated so earnestly, so vehemently, abstract questions in philosophy as well as in theology were themselves clerics; the universities were ecclesiastical foundations; their studies were essentially sacred, not profane.

IV: AVERRHOÏST INFLUENCES

It was no part of the policy of the mediæval Church to stifle enquiry and discussion by those properly qualified concerning the ultimate truths of existence. Such work might well be to the glory of God and the permanent enrichment of the Church.

And if the Averrhoïsts did not, like Albertus Magnus and Aquinas and the great Franciscan Augustinians, convert their learning into Christian apologetics; on the other hand, they were not like the wandering sectaries, whom the Church did persecute, irresponsible unlearned laity, who spoke of mysteries they were not fit to understand, but they were themselves clergy under proper academic discipline and supervision.

Moreover, they did not attack the Church; on the contrary, they professed themselves the most devout true Catholics.

Their interest in philosophy was purely abstract; they had no ulterior motives, no remotest idea of propaganda with a view to shaking the authority of the Church or the filial allegiance to her of a single one of her children.

On the contrary, they repeatedly and most emphatically asserted that their philosophical tenets were exclusively academic and not intended to have any bearing upon life and conduct.

Thus the Averrhoïst postulate of a double truth, one philosophic, the other religious, stood its adherents in good stead.

We cannot to-day see into the minds of these Latin Averrhoïsts, cannot tell whether they persuaded themselves that they really were Christians, were sincere in their conception of two irreconcilable truths or adopted it merely as a convenient subterfuge and were flippantly cynical or sardonically insolent in their hypocrisy. The subterfuge served the Averrhoïsts; whether its acquiescence in the subterfuge served the Church is another matter.

While the obviously honest Waldensian and Beghard were harried to the stake, the obviously dishonest Averrhoïst was usually left at large. Was not the tendency of such discrepancy of treatment to place a premium upon mere lip-service and religious insincerity?

From the fourteenth-century Averrhoïst, with his idea of the double truth, it is but one step to the fifteenth-century humanist, openly indifferent to religion altogether, not troubling to consider whether such a thing as religious truth exists at all, seeking and discerning truth in the pagan world only.

---

[1] On the Scholastic Philosophy generally, see Taylor, *The Mediaeval Mind*, vol. ii, book vii, *passim*; M. de Wulf, *History of Mediæval Philosophy* (tr. P. Coffey, London, 1909), pp. 240-410 (*passim*); B. Hauréau, *Histoire de la Philosophie Scolastique* (Paris, 1880).

[2] Taylor, *op. cit.*, vol. ii, pp. 358-64.

[3] P. Mandonnet, S*iger de Brabant et l'Averroïsme latin au XIIIe Siècle* (Fribourg, 1899), pp. xxiii-xxvi; C. Douais, *Essai sur l'organisation des tudes dans l'ordre des Frères-Prêcheurs* (Paris, 1884), pp. 62 *et seq*.

[4] For Arabian Philosophy see the following: T. J. De Boer, *History of Philosophy in Islam* (tr. E. R. Jones, 1903); De Wulf, *op. cit.*, pp. 225-39; Hauréau, *Histoire de la Philosophie Scolastique*, vol. ii, pp. 15-53; Carra de Vaux, *Avicenne* (Paris, 1900), *Gazali* (Paris, 1902); S. Munk, *Mélanges de la philosophie juive el arabe* (Paris, 1859), pt. iii, especially pp. 352-83, 418-58.

[5] Alfarabi's work belonged to the first half of the tenth century.

[6] Avicenna, 980-1036.

[7] Ghazali, 1059-1111

[8] Ibn Roschd, or Averrhoës, was born in 1126 at Cordova; was entrusted by the Caliph, Abu Jacub Jusuf, with the task of making an analysis of Aristotle; in 1182 became physician at the court; but in 1195 was deprived of his office by the succeeding Caliph, Jacub Almansur, presumably owing to a fit of orthodoxy on the Caliph's part, and banished from Cordova. He died in Morocco in 1198.

[9] See Renan, *Averroës et l'Averroïsme*, pp. 107 *et seq*.

[10] See Renan, *op. cit.*, pp. 133-53 (*passim*); J. Owen, *Skeptics of the Italian Renaissance* (1893), pp. 67-72.

[11] Renan, *op. cit.*, pp. 209 *et seq.*, p. 291; De Wulf, *op. cit.*, p. 248.

[12] By the middle of the thirteenth century the University of Paris was in possession of practically all the Commentaries of Averrhoës, *ibid*. See also Renan, pp. 201-2, 'Un des phénomènes les plus singuliers de l'histoire littéraire du moyen âge, c'est l'activité du commerce intellectuel et la rapidité avec laquelle les livres se repandaient d'un bout à l'autre de l'Europe.'

[13] Mandonnet, pp. lxix *et seq*.

[14] 'Nec libri Aristotelis de naturali philosophia nec commenta legantur Parisiis publice et secreto, et hoc sub pena excommunicationis inhibemus.' This, and the subsequent prohibition of 1215 referred of course only to Paris.

IV: AVERRHOÏST INFLUENCES

See *Directorium* on the errors of Aristotle and his Arabian commentators, pt. ii, question iv, pp. 253-5. See Hauréau, *op. cit.*, vol. ii, pp. 83-107. On action of Gregory IX, *ibid.*, pp. 108-19.

[15] The tract was written against Averrhoës, not the Averrhoïsts. When, however, it was incorporated in his *Summa Theologica*, Albertus Magnus made mention of the fact that Averrhoïsm had made considerable progress and boasted a number of advocates. Mandonnet, p. lxxiii.

[16] *Ibid.*, pp. xcvii-ix.

[17] See *Fr. Rogeri Bacon Opera quaedam hactenus inedita* (ed. J. S. Brewer, 1859), p. 429. There are several contemporary poems on the troubles in the University of Paris, especially on the part played by William de Saint-Amour, in Rutebeuf, *Œuvres Complètes* (Paris, 1874), vol. i, pp. 178-213.

[18] See Mandonnet, p. cx.

[19] Salimbene, *op. cit.*, p. 108. 'Isti boni homines semper de scientia gloriantur, et dicunt quod in ordine eorum fons sapientiae invenitur.'

[20] *Registrum epistolarum fratris Johannis Peckham* (Rolls series, ed. C. T. Martin, London, 1882-5), vo1. Iii, p. 842. See also A. Little, *The Grey Friars in Oxford* (1892), pp. 72-5.

[21] See *Alberti Magni De Quindecim Problematicis* in appendix to Mandonnet, pp. 13-36.

[22] See Mandonnet, p. cxxvi.

[23] In appendix to Mandonnet, pp. 69-83, 83-115 respectively.

[24] In his tract *Contra praecipuos viros in philosophia Albertum et Thomam*. On Siger and St. Thomas, see Hauréau, vol. iii, pp. 131-7.

[25] See, *passim*, De Wulf, *op. cit.*, pp. 379-85; Mandonnet, pp. cxxviii-ccvi.

[26] De Wulf, p. 384; Mandonnet, p. ccxxi.

[27] The tractate, *De Erroribus Philosophorum*, is attributed to him. It is printed in appendix to Mandonnet, pp. 2-11.

[28] *Ibid.*, p. clxxvii.

[29] Mandonnet, p. ccvi.

[30] *Ibid.*, p. ccxxvi.

[31] *Ibid.*, pp. ccxxviii *et seq*.

[32] *Ibid.*, pp. cclxiv *et seq*.

[33] Mandonnet, pp. cclxx *et seq*. Mandonnet sees a reference to Siger and Boëthius in the words of Peckham: 'Nam eam (opinionem) credimus non a religiosis personis, sed saecularibus quibusdam duxisse originem, cuius duo praecipui defensores vel forsitan inventores miserabiliter dicuntur concluisse dies suos in partibus transalpinis, cum tamen non essent de illis partibus oriundi.'—*Registrum*, vol. iii, p. 842.

[34] For the former view, see Baeumker, *Die Impossibilia d. Siger von Brabant* (Münster, 1898), pp. 97 *et seq.*; for latter, see Mandonnet, pp. ccxciii-cccxx.

[35] De Wulf, pp. 441-4.
[36] Lea, vol. iii, pp. 440-1.
[37] See De Wulf, pp. 470-3; Owen, *op. cit.*, pp. 57-151, esp. 132-51.
[38] Renan, *op. cit.*, pp. 255-9; Lea, vol. iii, pp. 578-89.
[39] De Wulf, pp. 403-6.
[40] Lea, vol. iii, pp. 585-6; *Directorium*, pp. 272-8, 331-2. The text of the bull is given in the latter pages.
[41] Renan, pp. 328 *et seq.*; Owen, pp. 1 15-21; Petrarch, *Liber sine Titulo*, Epist. xviii.
[42] Renan, pp. 301-5.
[43] Lea, vol. iii, p. 565.
[44] *De Tribus Impostoribus* (ed. Philomneste Junior, i.e. G. Brunet, Paris, 1861).
[45] Renan, pp. 295 *et seq.*
[46] *Decameron*, Day I, Novel 3.
[47] Renan traced Averroïst influence in the Pantheism of the Spiritual Franciscans and the Illuminism of such German mystics as Ortlieb and Eckhart, *op. cit.*, pp. 259 *et seq.*; whereas the truth is that there was never the slightest sympathy between the Franciscans and Averroïsm, and German Illuminism had quite other origins.

V

Reform Movements of the Fourteenth Century and The Council Of Constance

The earlier heresies of the Middle Ages were of importance for their own day and generation only, leaving no permanent imprint on history. The Church was on the whole very successful in combating them, actually securing the destruction of the Albigenses and throughout western Europe generally keeping the danger well in check by the activities of the Holy Office.

The story of the Spiritual Franciscans, on the other hand, has a deeper significance, for it is intimately connected with momentous events which betokened the overthrow of the mediæval order, the rooting up of certain fundamental ideas associated with the matured conception of the Civitas Dei.

The one feature common to Waldensianism, Catharism and the other early mediæval heresies, which gives them any lasting importance, was their anti-sacerdotalism. Clerical, and in particular papal, pretensions tended to increase after the fall of the Hohenstaufen, which left the papacy triumphant as the result of its long struggle with the empire.

The high-water mark of those assertions was reached in 1300, when Boniface VIII declared himself to be not only Pope but also Caesar. [1] By two most important bulls Boniface sought to put his claims into practice, *Clericis laicos*, which denned the rights of the clergy to immunity from secular taxation, *Unam sanctam*, which declared unequivocally the absolute supremacy of the pope over the lay power, over every human creature in all respects.

The same uncompromising spirit was shown a little later on by John XXII, the oppressor of the Spirituals, an old man of immense vigour and a range of view which embraced even the minute concerns of the secular states of Europe. [2]

Unhappily for itself, the setting forth of the papacy's highest pretensions was coincident with the maturing of certain forces which tended to render those pretensions null and void. The most important of these was the force of nationality, the growth of nation-states, in particular under the strong royal houses of the Capets and the Angevins respectively in France and England.

In such nation-states the papacy was to find a more formidable obstacle to the realization of its temporal ambitions than the Empire had ever presented, especially as they had no such tradition of alliance with the papacy as was the heritage and indeed the technical origin and justification of the Holy Roman Empire. [3]

The distinction between the relation of the Pope to the Emperor and the relation of the Pope to the King of France is brought out forcibly in a work entitled 'An Enquiry touching the Power of the Pope,' by Peter du Bois, who in the year 1300 published a very remarkable treatise which advocated a modest proposal for uniting the whole of Europe under French sovereignty. The Emperor was dependent upon the Pope, because he had to be confirmed in his office and crowned by the Pope. No such necessity existed in the case of the French King. [4]

Certainly the conduct of Philip IV showed plenty of independence in his relations with the Roman pontiff. When Boniface in 1301 asserted that Philip held his crown of him and summoned him to appear at a council about to be assembled at Rome, the papal bull was solemnly burnt in the French capital.

The States-General was then convened to give national expression to a protest against the action of Boniface; and bishops and lesser clergy united with the people as a body, and most

V: REFORM MOVEMENTS AND COUNCIL OF CONSTANCE

important with the lawyers, to address letters of remonstrance to Rome. The civil law directly challenged the canon law.

In England the national feeling against papal exactions and interference was extremely bitter and vociferous under Henry III. Edward I gave a blunt answer to the claims of *Clericis laicos* in ruling that if the clergy were to be free of the law in respect of its duties they should be free of it also as regards its privileges and its protection, should be outlaws in fact.

The stand taken by the French and English kings on the subject of clerical taxation was so firm that Boniface was forced to nullify the bull *Clericis laicos* by the bull *Etsi de statu*. Not only the royal will, but popular feeling is evidenced under Edward III by the statutes of *Provisors* and *Praemunire*.

While in Germany the imperial dignity had much sunk in credit since the days of the Hohenstaufen, on the other hand the importance of a national sentiment there was revealed in the general support given to Lewis of Bavaria. It is true that he failed in his expedition to Italy, whither the German king journeyed in order to establish his imperial dignity, despite his excommunication by John XXII, by coronation at Rome, but in Italy his forces were recruited by adherents more valuable than armies in the General of the Franciscan Order, Michael of Cesena, and a yet greater Franciscan, William of Ockham.

The issue that had been joined was in reality one between papal and national sovereignty but in the lengthy war of words that ensued upon Lewis's failure in Italy the controversy appeared to be concerned with the theological question of the poverty of Christ, so that the feud between Spiritual and Conventual became a European question.

It now possessed a significance extraneous from, and much wider than, the original cause of quarrel: for in the doctrine of apostolic poverty could be focussed all the widespread anti-sacerdotal feeling which revolted at the secular preoccupations and ambitions of the clergy.

A heavy blow was struck at the overweening claims of the papacy by Philip IV's attack upon Boniface VIII, and, as it has been said, 'the drama of Anagni is to be set against the drama of Canossa.'[5]

But worse humiliations were to follow, when the papacy was brought under French tutelage by the 'Babylonish Captivity' of Avignon. Worse still, to the humiliation was added infamy. The corruption at the new papal court speedily became notorious. It surpassed all previous bounds, and the cost of its luxury and prodigality was defrayed by unparalleled extortion and simony. [6]

More powerful than ever, therefore, became the denunciation of the ugly materialism and spiritual decadence of the papacy. The scandal of Avignon was followed by one more deplorable still—the Schism. Christendom was presented with the unedifying sight of successive rival pontiffs, each anathematizing the other and reviling him in terms of vulgar scurrility. [7]

No mystic halo could remain undimmed, no sense of reverence unimpaired by a spectacle so profane. The resistance of princely prerogative, the emotion of national resentment against caste privilege and exemption were reinforced by a general consciousness of the violence done to men's ordinary sense of fitness, a consciousness mirrored in the literature, and particularly the polemics, of the day.

If disgust with the papacy led Dante in his 'De Monarchia' to find a solution of the world's troubles in a revival of the universal empire, of an effective imperial authority, his vision being one of a golden age in the past, in this respect he stood alone, and other writers looked forward to a radical alteration and amendment in the ecclesiastical polity.

It was indeed a radical innovation, but it was not so conceived by its authors, who regarded it as the true practice of the Church and were in some cases ready to denounce the Pope as a heretic for disregarding it.

The pulpits of the Grey Friars resounded to denunciations of John XXII as a heretic because he clave to earthly possessions and repudiated the doctrine of the poverty of Christ and His Disciples. But indeed the arguments of John's opponents were often so startling that it is in no way surprising that he with all honesty perceived in *them* the heretics.

Michael of Cesena, in a tract against the errors of the Pope, treated John as a mere heretic, and appealed from him to a General Council representative of the Catholic Church, since a

Pope might err both in faith and in conduct, as indeed many had erred before, while the Catholic Church was infallible, and its representative, a General Council, was necessarily endowed with the like infallibility. [8]

Of far greater weight than that of the Franciscan leader was the authority of William of Ockham in recommending the device of a General Council. Only, unlike the former, William of Ockham discerned infallibility in neither Pope nor General Council. All human beings are liable to err, whether individually or collectively, but the ultimate power in the Church must be the Church itself, the whole body of the faithful. [9]

In his enormous work, his 'Dialogus,' there are contradictions and qualifications which indicate that the author was perplexed by the manifold practical difficulties of the problem of how to reunite Christendom. [10] But as a Spiritual Franciscan he was clear that the Pope had no right to secular property, and as a philosopher preferred the Church Universal itself to its pontiff as the repository of truth.

Of much less influence and reputation in his own lifetime than Ockham, yet of infinitely greater originality, penetration and width of view, astonishingly farseeing and modern in his standpoint, was Marsiglio of Padua. The central argument of his 'Defensor Pacis' is that the cause of all the turmoil and disturbance of the world has been the bid for temporal power made by the clergy, and especially the papacy. [11]

Christ had definitely stated, 'My Kingdom is not of this world'; yet the clergy had become utterly immersed in affairs of the earth. Marsiglio equally combatted two sacerdotal contentions—the right to intervene in secular matters in despite of the spiritual office, on the one hand; on the other hand, the right of exemption from the ordinary payments and obligations of citizens in virtue of the same spiritual office.

He held that the clergy had one duty only, and that a spiritual duty—to attend to the welfare of the souls of their flock. They had no legitimate claim whatever, in his opinion, to special treatment from the lay authority. [12] Their spiritual character was relative only to their performance of spiritual functions; in so far as they performed any others they were on exactly the same footing as laymen. Their tenure of land should be on precisely the same conditions as that of the laity the civil obligations of the layman were incumbent upon them also.

Similarly, they had no right to special jurisdiction, involving the infliction of the same sort of penalties—fines and imprisonments for example—as appertained to the secular courts. Such jurisdiction was abhorrent to the spirit of the Gospel. [13] To counsel and to warn was within their province; to go beyond that was not.

This, according to Marsiglio, applied even to heresy. If a heresy were dangerous to society, it was for the civil authority to deal with it. Merely as wrong opinion it was not punishable at all in this world. [14]

While he thus restricted and narrowly denned the functions of the priesthood, Marsiglio in no wise narrowed the conception of the Catholic Church, but rather broadened it. For his outstanding argument is that the clergy have been narrowing that conception by arrogating to themselves a position and powers which belong to the whole community.

While perniciously extending the meaning of the word 'spiritual' to cover such essentially secular things as property and political power, they have as falsely contracted it to exclude from all control of the Church's destinies the mass of the laity. They also, although not in orders, are religious men, members of the Church; numerically they are by far the greater part of the Church.

Consequently, in a General Council, which is a representative of the entire Christian communion, and not merely a part—the fact of ordination not making the clergy any the less a fragment—in a General Council resides the ultimate authority of the Church. [15]

In these remarkable pronouncements of Marsiglio of Padua are contained the doctrines of democracy and of toleration: so also in the careful allocation of the clergy to purely spiritual functions is contained the suggestion of that precise differentiation between Church and State which perhaps more than anything else marks off modern from mediæval society.

The whole conception of the 'Defensor Pacis' was revolutionary. No heresy of the Middle Ages had been more dangerously subversive of the whole system of the Catholic Church as it then existed. The perverse absurdities of Catharism and other such half-crazed cults were abhorrent to all sane and healthily-minded men. But the doctrines taught by Marsiglio have commended themselves to many of the most sincere, the most devout and religious of men from his own day to this. [16]

Were these opinions heretical or not? They were declared to be so by John XXII; but amid the warring religious factions of the period it was no easy matter to say what was orthodox and what was not.

The controversy regarding mendicancy raged. The Minorites declared Pope John a heretic because he would not agree that mendicancy was enjoined by Scripture. The view of the Pope was shared and soberly argued by Fitzralph, Archbishop of Armagh. It was not only the worldly cleric necessarily that failed to find warrant for the contentions of the Spirituals in the Bible. [17]

A second new tenet of the time—the dogma of the Beatific Vision—John XXII, after first inclining to believe, latterly decided to reject; and in 1331 a certain English Dominican, for daring to assert that the souls of the righteous were immediately wafted into the presence of God and beheld Him without having to wait for the Day of Resurrection, was by the Pope's orders brought before the Inquisition, and was thrown into gaol.

John's political opponents in Germany and France, together with the Spiritual Franciscans, immediately asserted the truth of the doctrine he had denounced, the French King writing to point out that the Pope's ruling must seriously invalidate the belief in the invocation of saints and also all pardons and indulgences. John was forced to give way, and on his death-bed affirmed his adhesion to the doctrine of the Beatific Vision.

As he did not make a formal recantation, however, of his previous error, Michael of Cesena held him to have died a contumacious heretic. [18]

A third new doctrine, a little later on, after considerable and powerful opposition, gained a great triumph mainly through the instrumentality of the University of Paris, which forced Pope Clement VII to acknowledge its truth. This was the doctrine of the Immaculate Conception. It had been resolutely condemned by St. Bernard, Peter Lombard, and later by Thomas Aquinas. But the appeal to the popular imagination of Mariolatry was too strong, strong enough even to defeat the decision of the great Doctor. It became inconceivable to the popular imagination, which ever tended to prefer the sweetness and gentleness of the Virgin to the awfulness of the Trinity, to believe that she could have had any connection whatever with sin.

In 1387, when a certain Dominican professor at Paris preached a sermon maintaining that the Virgin was conceived in sin, there was a violent uproar, leading to Clement VII's consenting to declare all those who held this view to be heretics. [19]

The confusion as to the definition of orthodoxy and heresy, inevitably produced by the introduction of such new tenets as those just enumerated, was heightened by the decadent unreality of philosophy, when it permitted of the idea of a double truth, one theological, the other philosophical, and rendered it possible for a scholar to assert that even such cardinal doctrines as those of the Trinity, immortality, the resurrection, the efficacy of prayer might be true in theology, yet quite untrue in philosophy. [20] Such a disingenuous compromise put a premium at once upon scepticism and insincerity.

There was one great schoolman living against whom, despite the prolixity and barrenness of much of his logic, no charge of unreality or insincerity can be brought—John Wycliffe. Beneath the dialectical subtleties and sophistries common to all the works of the scholastic philosophers there was in his case a profound sense of the obligation to seek, and a zealous desire to discover, the absolute truth.

As with all great thinkers who have left a permanent mark on the history of religious and political opinion, there was in Wycliffe a great moral earnestness, an honest hatred of shams and impurities and all that is ignoble.

The scandals of Avignon and the Schism helped to form the creed of Wycliffe, as they did that of the most religiously-minded men of the fourteenth century. His teaching was the moral repercussion of a sensitive and powerful mind flung back from impact against the clerical abuses of the Church. Indeed, as in the case of Marsiglio, so in that of Wycliffe, his attack was primarily on the polity of the Church, only secondly on doctrine. Many of his writings are perfervid denunciations, in the violent language common to mediæval controversialists, of the ill-living, laxity and ostentation of the clergy. His diatribes against successive popes and the institution of the papacy became more and more unmeasured in the choice of epithets.

The writings of Wycliffe cannot be taken as a true description of the Church of his time, so great is the allowance that has to be made for the hyperbolical language of furious partizanship.

The constructive doctrine of Wycliffe is derived from his idea of Lordship. His theology is given a feudal structure, which cumbrously overweights it with technicalities and analogies of interest only to a feudal age. The whole of human society is conceived as holding from God, the suzerain of all creation. The essential characteristic which Wycliffe ascribed to it brings out of this feudal nomenclature no mere analogy but a pregnant idea.

Wycliffe postulated a fundamental distinction between spiritual and earthly tenure. The feudal system on earth was one of many gradations between the supreme overlord, the king, and the humblest holder of land. But between God and His subjects there were no such gradations: each man held directly of God. [21]

The consequences of this statement were radical. For one thing it was reinforced by the contention that dominion was founded in grace only (there was no other lawful claim to rule or possession) and that no man living in sin had any right to any gift of God, whether that gift be spiritual or secular in nature. For all other persons the right to such gifts was equal.

Thus the only test to a man's right to possession was a moral test. [22] These principles and their applications, elaborated in a work of immense length, 'Of Civil Lordship,' lead logically, on their political side, to Communism; while, on the religious side, they involve a democratic theory of the spiritual equality of all Christians, which was subversive of the claims of the priesthood, for whom the belief in the absence of any 'mediation' between God and man left no function. [23]

On the one hand, community of goods was regarded as essential to Christians; on the other—even more notably than in Marsiglio—the laity were accorded a novel and prominent place in the Christian fellowship. Clerical property was an abuse and the clergy ought to live on alms, tithes being recognized as such. [24]

Wycliffe did not exaggerate the theory of clerical poverty; he did insist that the clergy must live simply and possess nothing superfluous to ordinary needs. [25]

In accordance with the theory of 'grace' or merit it was laid down that such wealth as the clergy did enjoy should be taken away from the undeserving. Such money could with greater profit be given to the poor. It was for the secular power to deprive the unworthy clerk of his possessions. [26] This teaching regarding ecclesiastical property, the disposal of which he virtually assigned to the laity, was perhaps the most obnoxious element in Wycliffe's general scheme in the eyes of the Church in his day. [27]

For the regeneration of the Church Wycliffe turned from the hierarchy to the laity. That which makes a man a member of the Church is his own personal sanctity, and the Church therefore consists of those predestined to salvation, of none others. [28]

The mere fact of being a pope or a cardinal, for example, is nothing. The Church can dispense with bad popes. [29] They are antichrist. *Per contra*, a layman might be pope, however unlearned, even if unordained, so long as God had chosen him. [30] It is not man's appointment, but God's choosing—that is to say, spiritual excellence—that matters.

The extraordinarily radical character of these theories is obvious. They were subversive of the whole contemporary conception of the character of the Church. For a universal society Wycliffe substituted a small body of the elect. In all this he was emphasizing the spiritual nature of religion, as an inward force, the possession of the individual soul.

Confession, he declared, was superfluous for the contrite [31]; no man could be excommunicated unless he had first been excommunicated *by himself*, and no prelate ought ever to excommunicate anyone unless he knew that he had already been excommunicated by God. [32]

Like Luther after him, then, Wycliffe insisted upon the inner reality of religion, of which the individual is conscious in the depths of his own being. Like Luther also he insisted on the

V: REFORM MOVEMENTS AND COUNCIL OF CONSTANCE

necessity of appeal direct to the Scriptures, as to the supreme authority for the Christian life. As he looked to the laity to reform the Church, so it was necessary that they should be well acquainted with its text.

The translation of the Bible into the vulgar tongue became, therefore, an integral part of Wycliffe's scheme. There were extant in Wycliffe's day portions of the Scriptures in the vernacular. [33] He conceived the idea of translating all. Probably he himself translated only the Gospels, or perhaps the whole of the New Testament; one of his disciples did the translation of the Old Testament, and may have completed most of it before Wycliffe's own death. [34]

The significance of this great undertaking lies partly in its completeness; but even more in the intention with which it was adopted. The laity must be able to read the actual text of the Scriptures for themselves without the glosses of traditional interpretation and theologians' exegesis, so that they may know the gospel in its simplicity and view the realities of religion clearly for themselves.

To the Bible in the vernacular as such the Church had no objection, but there must be proper safeguards. The people must be taught how to read the Scriptures with understanding by their spiritual masters. The gospel of Christ had been entrusted to the clergy for them to 'administer gently' to the laity. Wycliffe's method meant that the 'gospel pearl' was 'cast forth and trodden down by swine.' [35]

Wycliffe was an idealist, and confessedly his entire conception of the Church and Society is an ideal conception.

In spite of its curiously matter-of-fact feudal foundations, Wycliffe's structure is not of the earth, but Utopian. His conclusions were indeed whittled down by certain important qualifications.

Thus, although ail men were ideally equal, the existing mode of society and government was sanctioned by God; and it was therefore unlawful to seek to gain by force the equality of possession which flagrantly did not exist—so that Wycliffe's communism, in so far as it was not spiritual only, was purely anticipatory of a new order in the future; so also it was unlawful to challenge the right to rule of the civil lord on the ground of personal unworthiness, for his power also is sanctioned.

As Wycliffe put it in a celebrated phrase, 'God ought to obey the Devil.' [36] Thus while the ideal theory of dominion 'founded in grace' is suggestive of antinomianism and revolution, Wycliffe's practical teachings were marked by devotion to the existing temporal order.

On the other hand, it is not surprising that both opponents and followers should have tended to fasten upon the former aspects of his tenets and give to them a revolutionary interpretation. And indeed the truly significant part of Wycliffite doctrine is revolutionary in the emphasis that it lays upon the individual and as time went on both the logic of events and the logic of the beliefs to which controversy drove him rendered Wycliffe more and more unequivocal in the essential radicalism of his attitude.

Anti-sacerdotalism led Wycliffe later on to attack a doctrine to which the clergy owed much of their hold upon the popular mind, whence largely came the peculiar veneration in which they were held—the doctrine of Transubstantiation. The miracle of the mass obtained a special note of awesome mystery from that doctrine and to the ignorant or superstitious mind it was natural to regard those who by the simple pronunciation of the prayer of consecration could transform bread and wine into the body and blood of the Blessed Lord as miracle-workers.

For the orthodox philosophy of Wycliffe's day, Nominalism, there was little difficulty in believing in such a transformation. Wycliffe was a realist, and to him the nominalist position seemed untenable altogether.

In the days of Abelard, and again in those of Thomas Aquinas, Realism had been the orthodox philosophy, and Aquinas in demonstrating that the abstract and general truths of Christianity were acceptable to the reason did the Church of his day a great service. But another realist had come after him, who had most trenchantly attacked St. Thomas, destroying all the reasonableness of the great Doctor's philosophic structure, and emphatically ousting the reason and substituting the authority of the Church as the only sure guide in the sacred mysteries of religion, the only sure foundation of faith.

V: REFORM MOVEMENTS AND COUNCIL OF CONSTANCE

There were action and reaction in the abstract thought of the Middle Ages, as indeed there have ever been in history. The reaction against the Realism of St. Thomas, apparent in Duns Scotus, grew intenser when the principles of Ockham became the popular, and were recognized as the orthodox, principles of Christian theology. It could easily be shown that Realism was apt to lead to exaggerations either heretical or absurd, very apt to end in Pantheism. [37]

The fact of the matter was that either school of the scholastic philosophy might be productive of heresy, by laying especial emphasis on one particular aspect of truth to the exclusion of others; that different generations, changing subtly in mental outlook and spiritual temperament, are susceptible to different phases of truth. It is not a matter of Yea or Nay, but simply a varying stress of mode or fashion.

But we do not look for recognition of such a fact on the part of any mediæval controversialist. There are no half lights and compromises with them; they have each his own vision of truth, and bitterly assail their opponents as enemies of the light.

So Wycliffe, beginning with a standpoint which could be shared, and in fact was shared, by many of the most orthodox catholics of his time, growing as he went on more profoundly conscious of, and convinced of, the rightness of his essential principles, became less and less compromising, more and more the opponent not only of practices but of the doctrines with which such practices were associated.

He became urgent against the reigning nominalist creed, but most especially against its theories of the Sacrament. For him space and time, matter and form were objective realities. The bread and wine were not a part of Christ and could not become so; they remained bread and wine in substance and could never be anything else, only Christ was present in them. [38]

The doctrine of identification between the bread and wine and the body and blood of Christ was pernicious. [39] Nothing could be more horrible than the notion that a priest had the ability to 'make' God daily. [40] The language of the service of the Eucharist was not literal, but figurative. [41] The literal interpretation was an invitation to mere idolatry, an encouragement to the ignorant to worship the Host itself. [42] Christ indeed was present in the Sacrament, and the bread and wine were not merely commemorative symbols; on the other hand, there was no miraculous transformation of the elements.

This is very much the same theory as Luther's doctrine of Consubstantiation. Wycliffe united with it the tenet that a priest living in mortal sin could not consecrate. [43]

The extent and nature of the influence of Wycliffitism in England is a difficult and somewhat controversial question. [44] The translation of the Bible certainly had its permanent influence; and the device of the Poor Preachers spread the new doctrines further afield than would have been possible in those days only with the aid of lecture, sermon and treatise.

Wycliffe's character does not appear to have been such as to have enabled him to become the leader of a great popular movement. He was too much of a schoolman; his method was too academic. [45] But the preachers—not to be thought of as crude, semi-educated men, for they were mostly clerks of Oxford, who had studied under Wycliffe—touched a wider public than their master himself reached. Clearly in popularizing, they also exaggerated his doctrines, making them more downright, more practical, more mundane, emphasizing their social tendencies, those communistic elements which had a natural popular appeal.

The Lollards prospered greatly at the first, being particularly successful in the capital itself, Norwich, Bristol, Leicester, Northampton and the larger towns generally. The protection of John of Gaunt and other nobles helped them, while Wycliffe's denunciation of the friars met with the support of public opinion generally. [46]

There seemed a prospect of Wycliffitism becoming really widespead. But separatist tendencies soon showed themselves, and already in 1392 Lollards in the diocese of Salisbury were undertaking ordinations.

The Lollards, then, soon showed a tendency to develop into a separate sect, and their hold on the country and their national influence decayed with extraordinary suddenness. This was partly due to the fact that the movement had owed much to the purely ephemeral factor of John of Gaunt's support; partly to

V: REFORM MOVEMENTS AND COUNCIL OF CONSTANCE

the fact that the favour that its social teachings had won among the peasants was more than counterbalanced by the conservative apprehensions of the larger population who viewed the activities of such men as John Ball with dismay; partly to the fact that the movement produced sharp divisions in families, between father and son, master and servant, and this sort of thing could not last beyond a generation. [47]

Extremists took possession of Lollardy and it began to betray a distinct iconoclastic character. But the orthodox zeal of Henry IV and Henry V forced it very much underground, and there were a number of recantations. [48]

Lollardy survived into the days of the Tudors, in small communities in country districts, such as the Chilterns, and there was certainly a measure of Wycliffite leaven in the nation; but it is going too far to discover in Lollardy a direct and potent influence in bringing about the English Reformation.

The influence of Wycliffe was deeper and more lasting and vital outside England than within it—for there is a clear and very important connection between Wycliffitism and Husitism in Bohemia. On the other hand, it would be a mistake to regard Wycliffe as the sole parent of the movement inaugurated by Hus; for Hus had forerunners in Bohemia itself, earnest reformers, such as Conrad Waldhäuser, John Militz Kremsier, and Matthias of Janow. [49]

The two former were never accused of harbouring heretical opinions; they were simply protestants against clerical abuses. Matthias of Janow, on the other hand, was definitely interested in dogma, a professed theologian. He was notable in appealing directly to the simple people of Christ in his denunciation of the invocation of Saints and his insistence on the administration of the Communion in both kinds to the laity. [50]

The beginnings of the religious movement in Bohemia centre in the drama of the University of Prague, the struggle between the German and native parties—a national struggle which had its significant philosophic counterpart, for Teutonic Nominalism warred against Czech Realism. The struggle was decided in favour of the native party by the famous proclamation of Wenzel, which led to the German exodus from the University.

The departure of the German scholars from Prague was a momentous event. Hus and Jerome of Prague had been expounding the doctrines of Wycliffe; the German majority had pronounced these heretical. Wenzel's decision was therefore a triumph at once for Bohemian nationalism and for the reforming Husite party, a victory for Realism—for heresy.

Hus's satisfaction was great. [51] It was not only the religious issue that appealed to him strongly: he was an intense patriot as well as a religious reformer.

The spread of the Husite doctrines, however, naturally received a considerable impetus. The association of certain religious opinions with those national aspirations, to which the revolution at the University had given so marked an encouragement, inevitably converted Husitism into a popular movement. The cause of Husitism and the cause of Bohemian nationalism became so completely dovetailed the one into the other that they were inseparable.

Hus received a papal summons to appear at Bologna to answer for his heretical opinions, which were making Husitism an European question, a dangerous problem to the Church, as serious as Waldensianism and Catharism had been. [52] Hus did not go, appealing from the Pope to Christ.

The opinions of the great Bohemian leader were not original; and indeed his greatness is much more moral than intellectual. Starting his career solely as a protestant against sacerdotal abuses, he was led by the influence of the doctrines of Wycliffe, which the close association between England and Bohemia at the time made familiar in the latter country, into adopting many of the tenets of the Oxford heresiarch. [53] His 'De Ecclesia' is little more than a translation of Wycliffe.

On the whole, he remained distinctly more orthodox than his master. His writings abound in denunciations of the worldliness of the clergy, in particular of the papacy; denunciations of simony (which is heresy), of the claim of the papacy to overlordship of the Church, based on no better foundation than the death of St. Peter in Rome. [54]

Heresy, he also declared, was not triable by the Church. [55] But the really fundamental article of his questionable doctrines

V: REFORM MOVEMENTS AND COUNCIL OF CONSTANCE

was his conception of Predestination. Here he was following Augustine; but he was under the influence of Wycliffe's idea of 'dominion founded in grace,' which gave the right of lordship and possession only to the elect. [56]

This principle, involving the position that only the 'rule of the saints' is legitimate, had clearly a dangerous tendency, subversive of law and order in an imperfect world, both in the secular and the ecclesiastical spheres.

Yet the principal element of danger in Husitism was the simple fact of its success. So serious was this that when the remarkable attempt was made to heal the wounds of Christendom by means of General Councils, the fathers aimed at dealing with the problem of heresy together with those of the restoration of the unity, which had been broken by the Schism, and the reform of clerical abuses.

The Conciliar movement—a serious and important attempt to reform the Church from within—was brought about by the labours of certain moderate reformers, of whom Gerson, Peter D'Ailly and Zabarella are the most notable. Dietrich Niem represents a German influence but the main source of inspiration was the University of Paris, firmly orthodox and nominalist and immensely influential.

In 1394 the University invited its members to send in opinions as to the best means of ending the Schism. Thousands of answers were received; but the most outstanding members of the University were convinced that the summoning of a General Council was the only expedient that gave any hope of success. The ideas of Marsiglio and Ockham—more especially the latter—had borne fruit, and an age in which the idea of representation was 'in the air' decided to apply the principle to the Church for the urgent practical purpose of removing a notorious scandal.

The *apologia* for the scheme is to be found in the writings of Gerson and D'Ailly, and of Niem, if Niem is indeed the author of the tractate, 'De modis uniendi et reformandi Ecclesiam.' [57]

The *plenitudo potestatis* of the Church resided in its whole body, as represented in a General Council. [58] With the assent of such a council, the Church could even dispense with a pope. [59] It was legitimate for the civil authority to summon a General Council.

It was easy to cite the practice of Roman Emperors to that effect.[60] Christ, urged representatives of the University of Paris to the French king, had submitted to the authority of His mother and Joseph. Was the Pope greater than Christ that he should not submit to the authority of his mother, the Church?[61]

The proposition, so worded, seemed mildly reasonable, certainly most orthodox. In truth it was a democratic innovation of the utmost significance. 'Pisa,' wrote Gregorovius, referring to the first of the series of councils which provide the chief interest of the opening years of the fifteenth century, 'was the first real step towards the deliverance of the world from the papal hierarchy; it was already the Reformation'; while the decree of the second and most important of the councils, that of Constance, in which it declared its superiority to the Pope, has been pronounced to be 'probably the most revolutionary official document in the history of the world.'[62]

When brought up against the glaring abuse of the papal schism it was not only Wycliffe and Hus and their followers that became revolutionaries; Gerson, D'Ailly, Niem and their adherents became revolutionaries also. In the reforming programmes of Wycliffe and Hus there was much that might have been expected to gain the sympathies of the fathers who met at Constance: yet they condemned both as heretics and consigned Hus and Jerome of Prague to the flames.

The explanation is easy enough. It was precisely because their scheme was revolutionary that the cardinals and other clergy assembled at Constance were so anxious to make it clear to Christendom that such revolutionary practice was perfectly compatible with strict orthodoxy regarding the cardinal doctrines of the Christian faith, that they were the guardians of the unity and continuity of the essential life and identity of the Church.

A proof of this was urgently needed to safeguard a position which had precarious elements. The opportunity of dealing with Hus would probably have been welcomed for that reason alone. As to the fact of Wycliffe and Hus being dangerous heretics the fathers assembled at Constance had no doubt whatever.

Zealous for the reform of clerical abuses as many of them were, they could only see in the invectives against the hierarchy and the

V: REFORM MOVEMENTS AND COUNCIL OF CONSTANCE

doctrines concerning Predestination and the Eucharist, in which the English and the Bohemian teachers indulged, an attack upon the whole edifice of the Catholic Church. [63] Reconstruction they might desire; but the specific of Wycliffe and Hus seemed to be extensive demolition preparatory to the creation of a new structure.

Hus, therefore, came to Constance as one 'suspect of heresy,' virtually pre-condemned.

He answered the Council's summons, relying upon the security of Sigismund's celebrated safe-conduct, expecting to take part in a public debate, to receive a fair and courteous hearing for his defence of his theological views. Instead he found himself treated as a criminal, thrown into prison, to answer a formidable indictment before judges who were also prosecutors. The Council virtually resolved itself into an inquisitorial court and followed inquisitorial methods of procedure.

Compared indeed with an ordinary trial by the Inquisition that of Hus was remarkably lenient. He had powerful friends and the undertaking of Sigismund counted for something, although certainly not very much.

Sigismund has been arraigned as a monster of turpitude for allowing Hus to be tried, condemned and executed after he had granted him a safe-conduct.

It is certain that Hus, while clearly apprehensive of what might ensue from his bold step of entering the stronghold of his enemies, had implicit confidence in Sigismund's protection, and when despite the security promised by the man who was both Emperor and president of the Council, Hus was consigned to the stake, at first sight unmitigated baseness on the part of Sigismund would appear to be the only explanation. [64]

If he cannot be entirely exonerated, on the other hand, it is quite clear he never had any idea of protecting a heretic, and that he was overruled by the Council, who, arguing from the customary rules regarding heretics, could legitimately maintain that no guarantee could have any validity whatever in the case of one suspected of heresy, that Sigismund's safe-conduct might certainly apply to the empire and secular states, might be valid while Hus was on his journey, but had no validity as regards the Church. The heretic or a man suspect of heresy could enjoy neither rights nor privileges. This was good law, both ecclesiastical and civil; and once granted that the Council must regard Hus as suspect of heresy, it was legally unanswerable. [65]

The trial resolved itself into a dialectical duel between Hus and Cardinal D'Ailly, with divers interruptions and at times uproar. Against the uproar, with which his statements were sometimes greeted, Hus strongly protested; and the proceedings would appear to have been more seemly subsequently. [66]

He was accused of a large number of doctrinal errors and of such absurdities as that of claiming to be a person of the Trinity. [67]

Generally speaking, the object of his prosecutors was to show that his opinions were identical with those of Wycliffe, which had already been condemned as heretical by the Council. It was easy enough to show that Hus had inveighed against the organization and practices of the Church as then existing; it was not so easy to convict him of heretical dogma.

From the first Hus's attitude was perfectly consistent. He wished to argue his thesis; but that not being allowed, he declared himself perfectly willing to abjure all tenets which he had at any time avowed if the Council proved them from Scripture to have been erroneous, but he strongly protested against the ascription to him of statements he had never made and interpretations that he had never intended. [68]

The Council, on the other hand, contended that it was the duty of the suspect heretic to put himself unreservedly in the hands of the Council, making an entire submission to their ruling and a complete abjuration of all the heresies with which he was charged.

One doctor told him that if the Council told him he had only one eye, though he knew he had two, he ought to agree that it was so.

Hus replied: 'If the whole world told me so, so long as I have the use of my reason, I could not say so without resisting my conscience.' It is right to add that the doctor subsequently withdrew his remark, agreeing that he had not used a very good illustration. [69]

V: REFORM MOVEMENTS AND COUNCIL OF CONSTANCE

Where Hus gave his enemies their best opportunity was in his teaching with regard to the predestined. He had declared that no man living in a state of mortal sin had any right to exercise authority. By this ruling Sigismund himself would have been excluded.

Apart from that, as has been said already, the doctrine was undeniably of perilous implication. The King of the Romans could appreciate the seriousness of the political application at all events. He pertinently reminded Hus of the truth that no man lives without sin. [70]

But the decisive factor in the trial of Hus proved eventually to be his absolute sincerity. He refused to be false to himself, to commit perjury in order to save his life.

'Serene Prince,' said he to Sigismund, 'I do not want to cling to any error, and I am perfectly willing to submit to the determination of the Council. But I may not offend God and my conscience by saying that I hold heresies that I have never held.' [71]

As he put it again in a letter written shortly before his death, 'Assuredly it is fitting for me rather to die than to flee a momentary penalty to fall into the Lord's hand and afterwards, perchance, into everlasting fire and shame. And because I have appealed to Christ Jesus, the most potent and just of all judges, committing my cause to Him, therefore I stand by His judgment and sentence, knowing that He will judge every man not on false and erroneous evidence but on the true facts and merits of his case.' [72]

Hus died a martyr for no specific theological dogma, heretical or otherwise, but for the noblest cause for which a man can ever die—sincerity to the truth that is in him.

After the condemnation and burning of Hus, the Council proceeded to the trial of Jerome of Prague, who after a recantation repented of it and elected to die like his greater comrade. The proceedings against him were marked by great heat and acrimony, for he had made many personal enemies. Moreover, controversialist passions, which had indeed been apparent in the trial of Hus—for Hus was condemned as much because he was a realist as anything—flared up with still greater violence.

Among the interested spectators of the death at the stake of Jerome of Prague was the great Italian humanist, Poggio. Much struck by the martyr's eloquence and genius, he thought it was a great pity that he should have turned his attention to heretical ideas, and half pityingly, half uncomprehendingly, wondered that a man should be willing to die merely for the sake of an opinion.

This chance connection between Jerome, the ardent scholastic reformer, and Poggio, the cynical forerunner of the New Learning—between the old order and the new, is remarkable and prophetic. The movement towards change, which Jerome of Prague represented, whether it was a conservative movement as interpreted by Gerson and D'Ailly, or radical as it became in the hands of Wycliffe and Hus, definitely failed.

The mediæval system had indeed been challenged by that movement, which had resulted from the glaring scandals of Avignon and the papal Schism; but the system, though severely shaken, yet remained; and pontiffs such as Martin V, Eugenius IV and Pius II were able by politic means to bolster it up through a restoration of influence, mainly of a temporal nature, to the Papacy.

The Conciliar method of ecclesiastical reform failed for a variety of reasons—partly because of defects in organization and policy, still more because of a natural failure to recognize the great significance of national differences and the need, or at least the demand, for variety of treatment as between states, which produced the Pragmatic Sanctions of Bourges and Mainz, of the years 1438 and 1439 respectively; yet more, precisely because the attempted reforms were not sufficiently far-reaching and thorough in character, a tinkering, not a renewal.

The movements of Wycliffe and Hus were also abortive of really direct results. Lollardy certainly lived on, but, as has been already noted, probably did not have any considerable influence among the various forces which brought about the English Reformation. The influence of Hus in Bohemian history is far greater and the triumphs of Ziska and Prokop in the wars that are known after the name of the great heresiarch won national and religious independence for the Czechs up to the time of the battle of the White Mountain in the Thirty Years War.

V: REFORM MOVEMENTS AND COUNCIL OF CONSTANCE

It is true also that Luther expressed his own indebtedness to Hus, declaring, 'We have all been Husites without knowing it.'

Nevertheless, the decisive influences which brought about the complete overthrow of the mediæval system and the substitution of the modern belong to the later fifteenth and early sixteenth centuries.

These influences were the humanism, which in its Italian form became critical, pagan, drawing its influence from the Greek world to which all the 'ages of faith' had been as an opaque curtain; which in its German form had a theological bias and a moral aim, as interpreted by Reuchlin and the school of Deventer.

The other influence was the apotheosis of a cynical nationalism, whose exponent is Machiavelli, which produced the secularization of politics and the segregation of Church and State.

It is, therefore, fanciful and erroneous to trace back the causes of the Reformation and the break-down of the mediæval world-state to the mediæval heresies and movements of reform. [73]

On the other hand, to ignore them would be equally mistaken. They had a minor effect, but it was not insignificant.

It may be the violence of the storm that rends and tears away the structure; yet its havoc has been aided by the almost unseen, unheeded shifting of the sands.

---

[1] J. Bryce, *The Holy Roman Empire* (1903), p. 109.

[2] See H. B. Workman, *The Dawn of the Reformation* (1901, 1902), vol.; *The Age of Wyclif*, p. 71: 'Some seventy thousand documents in the papal archives bear witness to his world-wide labours. Few subjects escaped his notice—from the habit of the French King of talking in church, the misrule of Edward II of England, or the devices of sorcerers, to the weightier matters of theology and law.'

[3] R. L. Poole, *Illustrations of the History of Medieval Thought* (1884), p. 247.

[4] *Ibid.*, pp. 256 *et seq.*

[5] M. Creighton, *History of the Papacy* (1903), vol. i, p. 32.

[6] For Avignon, see E. Baluze, *Vitae Paparum Avenionensium* (1693). See works cited in Workman, *The Dawn of the Reformation*, vol. i, Append. A., p. 291; also Pierre D'Ailly, *De Necessitate Reformationis Ecclesiae*, in *Joannis Gersonii Opera Omnia* (Antwerp. 1706), vol. ii, pp. 885-902, esp. p. 889. Poole, *op. cit.*, p. 248, 'The universal authority of Rome became confined within the narrow territory of Avignon the means by which it was exerted became more and more secular, diplomatic, mercantile…'

[7] The extent of the feeling aroused by the schism in Christendom can be illustrated by the fact that contemporary miracle-plays represented Pope and anti-Pope burning in hell (see Workman, *The Dawn of the Reformation*, vol. ii, *The Age of Hus*, p. 41), and by the life-work of a simple uneducated girl, St. Catherine of Siena.

[8] Melchior Goldast, *Monarchia S. Romani Imp.* (Hanover and Frankfort, 1611-14), vol. iii, p. 1360.

[9] Goldast, *op. cit.*, vol. ii, *Opera Omnia de Potestate Ecclesiastica & Politica*, G. Ockham, esp. *Dialogus*, pp. 822-30. The chief conclusions of Ockham are summarized on pp. 396-7; also in S. Riezler, *Die literarischen Widersacher der Päpste zur Zeit Ludwig des Baiers* (1874), pp. 258-71. But see generally pp. 241-77.

[10] See Poole, *op. cit.*, p. 277, note.

[11] *Defensor Pacis*, Lib. 1, cap. xviii; in Goldast, *op. cit.*, vol. ii, pp. 86-9.

[12] *Ibid.*, Lib. 11, cap. viii, p. 212.

[13] *Defensor Pacis*, Lib. II, cap. ix, p. 213.

[14] *Ibid.*, cap. x, pp. 216-19, esp. p. 217. 'Nemo quantumcunque peccans contra disciplinas speculativas aut operativas quascunque punitur vel arcetur in hoc seculo praecise inquantum-hujusmodi, sed inquantum peccat contra praeceptum humanae legis.'

[15] *Ibid.*, Lib. 1, cap. xii, pp. 169-71.

[16] Workman, *op. cit.*, vol. i. 'Wyclif has been called the Morning Star of the Reformation, but the author of the *Defensor Pacis* might more justly claim the title.' *Cf.*, on modernity of Marsiglio's thought, B. Labanca, *Marsilio da Padova* (Padua, 1882), pp. 219 *et seq.*

[17] Fitzralph's treatise, *De Pauperie Salvatoris*, is printed as an appendix to Wycliffe's *De Dominio Divino* (Wyclif Society, 1890), pp. 259-476.

[18] For this whole subject, see Lea, vol. iii, pp. 590-4.

[19] *Ibid.*, pp. 596-9.

[20] See *supra*, pp. 68, 75.

[21] *De Dominio Divino* (Wyclif Society, 1890), p. 33. 'Ideo Deus non mediate per regimen vasallorum subserviencium, ut reges ceteri, dominatur, cum immediate et per se facit, sustentat, et gubernat omne quod possidet, juvatque ad perficiendum opera secundum usus alios quos requirit.'

V: REFORM MOVEMENTS AND COUNCIL OF CONSTANCE

[22] See Poole, *op. cit.*, p. 293.

[23] See Workman, *op. cit.*, vol. i, pp. 173-8.

[24] See *Fasciculi Zizaniorum Magistri Johannis Wyclif* (Rolls series, ed. W. W. Shirley, 1858), pp. 280-1.

[25] Wycliffe's *De Potestate Pape* (Wyclif Society, ed. J. Loserth, 1907), p. 84.

[26] *De Civili Dominio* (Wyclif Society, ed. R. L. Poole, 1885), vol. i, pp. 335-42; also pp. 265-74, ch. xxxvii. See also *Select English Works* (ed. T. Arnold, 1869-71), vol. iii, pp. 216-17.

[27] See *De Potestate Pape*, pp. 84, 238 *et seq.*, 378-9.

[28] *Ibid.*, pp. 145-6, 154-5. This idea is either explicitly or implicitly in all Wycliffe's later teachings.

[29] *Ibid.*, pp. 120 *et seq.*, 148, 212, 266 *et seq.* The whole book is indeed on this theme. Wycliffe does not scruple to call a bad pope '*horribilius monstrum.*' Cf. *Fasciculi Zizaniorum*, p. 278.

[30] *De Potestate Pape*, p. 272.

[31] *Fasciculi Zizaniorum*, p. 278.

[32] *Ibid.*, p. 279; D. Wilkins, *Concilia M. Britanniae et Hiberniae* (1737). vol. iii. p. 157.

[33] *Works of Thomas Cranmer* (ed. J. E. Cox, Parker Society), vol. ii. *Misc. Writings*, p. 119.

[34] See Wilkins, vol. iii, p. 350; *Chronicon H. Knighton* (Rolls series, ed. J. R. Lumby, 1889-95), vol. ii, p. 152.

[35] *Ibid.*

[36] See *Fasciculi Zizaniorum*, p. 278, from *Epistola Willelmi Cantuariensis super condemnatione haeresum Wycclyff in synodo*. See also extract from a sermon by Wycliffe on this subject, *ibid.*, introd., pp. lxiv-lxv.

[37] There was a tendency to Pantheism in Wycliffe. See Workman, *op. cit.*, vol. i, p. 137 n.

[38] *De Eucharistia* (Wyclif Society, 1892), p. 109, cap. iv.

[39] *Ibid.*, pp. 189-232, cap. viii.

[40] *Ibid.*, cap. i, pp. 15-16. 'Nichil enim horribilius quam quod quilibet sacerdos celebrans facit vel consecrat cotidie corpus Christi.'

[41] *Ibid.*, cap. iv, p. 109.

[42] *Ibid.*, Introd., p. liii; cap. iv, pp. 110-11.

[43] *Fasciculi Zizaniorum*, p. 278.

[44] See Foxe's *Acts and Monuments*, iv and v.

[45] Workman, *op. cit.*, vol. i, p. 229. 'Of the scholastic Lollards it may be written that logic makes no martyrs.' *Cf.* pp. 213-90.

[46] See popular ballads in J. S. Brewer, *Monumenta Franciscana* (1858), pp. 591-608.

[47] Knighton, *op. cit.*, vol. ii, pp. 184-7.

[48] *De Haeretico Comburendo* being frequently enforced from 1401.

[49] See Count Lützow, *The Life and Times of Master John Hus* (1909), pp. 17-62; J. Loserth, *Wyclif and Hus* (trans. M. J. Evans, 1884); A. H. Wratislaw, *Native Literature of Bohemia in the Fourteenth Century* (1878), esp. book ii, pp. 181-291.

[50] See Lutzow, *op. cit.*, pp. 47-62.

[51] *Documenta Mag. Joannis Hus* (ed. F. Palacky, Prague, 1869), pp. 347-9, 355-63. See Lützow, *op. cit.*, pp. 106-9. Wenzel's reasoned answer to the objections made by the Germans may have been Hus's work. For the contest at the University, see also H. Rashdall, *Universities of Europe in the Middle Ages*, vol. ii, pp. 212-32.

[52] Lützow, *op. cit.*, pp. 130-3, 159-60; Palacky, *Documenta*, pp. 464-6; *The Letters of John Hus* (ed. Workman and Pope, 1904), pp. 422-5.

[53] Due to the marriage of Wenzel's sister, Anne, to Richard II.

[54] Palacky, *Documenta*, pp. 289, 292.

[55] *Ibid.*, p. 293.

[56] *Ibid.*, p. 287; *Letters of Hus*, p. 217. Hus does not seem to have regarded the Utraquist question as of great consequence. See Creighton, *Papacy*, vol. ii, p. 86.

[57] See J. B. Schwab, *J. Gerson* (Würzburg, 1858), pp. 482-9; also Creighton, vol. i, appendix 2, pp. 365-8.

[58] D'Ailly in Gerson's *Works*, vol. ii, pp. 949 *et seq.*

[59] Gerson, *ibid.*, p. 72.

[60] *Ibid.*, p. 178. See also, generally, Gerson's 'De Unitate Ecclesiastica,' *Works*, vol. ii, pp. 113-14; Niem, Theodoricus de, *De Schismate* (1890). For full list of tracts, see *Cambridge Modern History*, vol. iii, pp. 867-8.

[61] See Creighton's *Papacy*, vol. i, p. 143.

[62] F. Gregorovius, *Hist. of the City of Rome in the Middle Ages* (trans. A. Hamilton, 1894-1902), vol. vi, p. 606; J. N. Figgis, *From Gerson to Grotius* (1907), p. 35.

[63] See Gerson's exhortation to the Archbishop of Prague to extirpate the heresy in Bohemia, Palacky, *Documenta*, pp. 523-6.

[64] *Letters of Hus*, pp. 146-9, 149-51. These are letters written by Hus at the time of his setting out for Constance. One of them, he instructs, is only to be opened in the event of his death.

[65] See Gerson, *Works*, vol. ii, p. 572; H. v. der Hardt, *Magnum oecumenicum Constantiense concilium* (Frankfort, 1697-1742), vol. iv, p. 521; Palacky, *Documenta*, p. 284; Lea, vol. ii, pp. 467-8. 'The explanation of the controversy over the violation of the safe-conduct is perfectly simple. Germany, and especially Bohemia, knew so little about the Inquisition and the systematic persecution of heresy that surprise and indignation were excited by the

V: REFORM MOVEMENTS AND COUNCIL OF CONSTANCE

application to the case of Hus of the recognized principles of the canon law. The Council could not have done otherwise than it did without surrendering those principles.'

[66] *Letters of Hus*, p. 216.

[67] Lützow, p. 249.

[68] Palacky, *Documenta*, pp. 308, 310. Like Wycliffe before and Luther after him, Hus would acknowledge no other authority than Scripture. The Council wanted him to acknowledge the authority of the Church and of itself as the Church's representative.

[69] *Letters of Hus*, p. 226.

[70] *Ibid.*, p. 217.

[71] *Ibid.*, p. 224.

[72] *Letters of Hus*, p. 239. See also his letter addressed to all the people of Bohemia, pp. 230-3; also pp. 275-6, and Palacky, *Documenta*, p. 323. See Creighton, *Papacy*, vol. ii, p. 51: '...It is the glory of Hus that he first deliberately asserted the right of the individual conscience against ecclesiastical authority, and sealed his assertion by his own life-blood.'

[73] See, however, J. Mackinnon, *A History of Modern Liberty* (1906), vol. i, p. 162: 'The defiance of the Council was the prelude of the modern Reformation. It was a distinct intimation not merely of a solitary reformer like Wiclif or Hus, but of a body of men who claimed to speak in the name of a whole people, that they would not submit to traditional authority *per se*. It was a plea for fair discussion of matters of controversy, and a protest against the principle of stifling inquiry and dissent by such authority. Otherwise the reason and intelligence of the inquirer will revolt in the name of conscience, justice and religion.'

VI

The Magic Arts

(i) Sorcery

If such phenomena as the Flagellant and dancing manias, the acceptance of such persons as Guglielma and Segarelli as divine incarnations is evidence of the depth of credulous superstition among the ignorant lower orders, the great witchcraft and sorcery craze, especially in the fifteenth century, is proof of a much wider diffusion of such a spirit in mediæval society.

Christianity early accepted the belief in magic arts unquestioningly. The story of the Witch of Endor would have been sufficient evidence, even had it stood alone: which it was far from doing, for the Bible was full of references to magicians, demoniacs, and soothsayers.

Thus it was in disbelief in such things, not in belief, that heresy lay. Incredulity challenged the authority of Scripture. Nor was it to be argued that the existence of evil spirits in Old Testament history was no warrant of their existence now.

The mediæval world was profoundly conscious of the powers of Satan being abroad in the earth. It discerned the clear sign of their presence in the frequent occurrence of disaster to the undeserving, in the fits of the epileptic; it discerned them in the

VI: THE MAGIC ARTS

wizened features of the shrivelled old woman who muttered inarticulately as she gathered her herbs.

Given the combination of an ignorant and wondering fear of the bewildering riddles of nature and the cold strangeness of the stars with a sincere conviction of the reality of that evil potentate who is at war with God, causing disaster among men and having subtle communion with the human heart, inspiring to wicked deeds and hideous thoughts, it is small wonder that imagination peopled the world with sorcerers, magicians and witches.

And the evidence was so extraordinarily sound. No reasonable man could resist the force of it.

It was not only the proverbially superstitious Middle Ages that believed in occult arts; no one had a more wholesome faith in these matters than Luther, and no country surpassed Protestant Scotland in the savage cruelty of its witch-trials.

Richard Baxter, in his 'The Certainty of the World of Spirits,' was able to give numerous well authenticated cases from his own lifetime; and the sceptical man of science, Glanvill, showed that unreason, not reason, rejected the evidence for witchcraft.

All history was full of the exploits of these instruments of darkness, and not 'the easily deceivable vulgar only,' but 'wise and grave discerners' were first-hand witnesses, who had no interest 'to agree together in a common lie.'[1]

The magicians and witches being almost universally believed in, it followed as a corollary that they were punished for their nefarious practices; but whereas in the pagan Roman world they had been punished simply on politic grounds, the magician being punished 'because he injured man, not because he offended God,'[2] in the Christian era the offence was regarded as a much more heinous sin.

In days of polytheism the state could be tolerant of certain magic practices; not so Christianity, which regarded all pagan deities as emanations of the Devil. The punishments, save under the apostate Julian, were usually of a most ferocious character, reputed magicians being crucified or flung to wild beasts.[3]

But while thus zealous in punishing the magician, there is no doubt that Christianity itself became contaminated, and in the Dark Ages thaumaturgy became rife within the Church.

On the other hand, while in the Eastern Empire sorcery continued to be punished with severity, the Teutonic tribes in the west, who in their pagan days had been thoroughly imbued with magic beliefs, were more or less tolerant.

During the epoch of the Carolingian empire ecclesiastical lenience, tempered by occasional mob violence, was the rule; and such lenience or indifference continued in western Europe till the end of the twelfth century. [4] Roger Bacon, unlike learned philosophers of later and presumably more enlightened periods, gave it as his opinion that reputed sorcery was either fraudulent or a delusion.

There are instances of severity on the part of the secular authority in Spain, and the first mediæval legislation against sorcery was introduced in Venice in the twelfth century; yet the Church remained apparently indifferent. And when the Inquisition came into being, it was not given authority in cases of witchcraft and sorcery.

A change is to be traced from Alexander IV's bull, *Quod super nonnullis*, issued in 1257, which laid it down that inquisitors were not to be distracted from their all-important duties by other business and were to leave cases of simple sorcery to the ordinary ecclesiastical tribunals; on the other hand, in sorcery cases where heresy was clearly involved, they were to take cognizance. This became the Canon law under Boniface VIII. [5]

Now, when did sorcery clearly involve heresy? It was not difficult to argue that it invariably did. Sorcery was invoking demons, trafficking with Satan, and to do this a man must surely entertain heretical ideas about Satan and demons. Certainly, if a man dealt in such trafficking, holding it to be not sinful, he was a manifest heretic. [6]

Again, to seek to acquire knowledge of the future from Satan, the future depending solely on the Almighty, involved heresy. Under the title, sorcery, there came to be included astronomy's parent, astrology. [7] Some men of unquestioned orthodoxy gave their sanction and support to it, notably Cardinal D'Ailly; and it was not apparently definitely forbidden during the thirteenth and fourteenth centuries in ecclesiastical formularies.

But clearly, although there was no question of invoking

VI: THE MAGIC ARTS

demons in connection with astrology, on the other hand, the astrologer by maintaining that a man's destiny was controlled by the conjunction of stars and planets at his birth was denying the freedom of the will, questioning the omnipotence of God, consequently being guilty of manifest blasphemy and heresy. Accordingly, the astrologer was always liable to prosecution by the Inquisition.

The best security lay in the fact that belief in astrology was extremely widespread among all classes of society, among clergy as well as laity, of whatever degree of education.

In the fourteenth century there was a marked increase in sorcery. This was probably the direct consequence of persecution on the grounds of heresy—such persecution being in a way the highest possible testimony to its genuineness. For the Inquisition never dealt with a reputed magician as a charlatan; it dealt with him as one really in league with Satan. Otherwise there would have been no heresy involved.

The attitude of the Church towards sorcery—its attribution of heresy to the magician —actually put a premium upon sorcery. The sorcerer was the more in request because people were more than ever convinced that his claims were well founded, and he was able to make more out of his calling because it had become precarious.

For these reasons the extreme zeal of Pope John XXII against all workers of magic failed in its object. In 1317 he satisfied himself, on grounds good or bad, that several persons in his household had been plotting to take his life. Under torture they stated that they had first had recourse to poison, but that that ordinary humdrum method having failed, they had next invoked the assistance of demons to accomplish their purpose.

The Pope was roused to thorough and energetic action, and started a resolute campaign against the accursed race of magicians. Dissatisfied with the ambiguous terms of Alexander IV's directions to the Inquisition in matters of sorcery, he gave it direct authority in such cases and urged it to earnest efforts. [8]

Ten years later, however, for some reason or other, he withdrew this jurisdiction from the Inquisition; and it is to be gathered that there ensued a period of comparative immunity for sorcery until 1374, when Gregory XI once more entrusted the task of prosecuting magicians to the Holy Office.

The two most remarkable men to fall into the hands of the Inquisition as sorcerers were Peter of Abano and the Maréchal Gilles de Rais. [9]

The former, an astrologer, undoubtedly harboured speculations which were flagrantly heretical; but he escaped the stake by dying a natural death before his trial was concluded.

The latter—the original of the Blue-beard of the fairy-tale — had been the constant and intimate companion of Jeanne d'Arc during her leadership of the French armies. Of such military distinction as to be made a Marshal of France at the age of twenty-five, he was also a man of culture, of a restless curiosity and an intense love of things brilliant and beautiful, of rich colours and ornaments, of all that was costly, magnificent and ornate.

But beneath all the gorgeous external trappings of this æsthete was something much more pernicious than mere vulgar ostentation. A depraved voluptuary, he found that the ordinary modes of satisfying his sensuality soon palled, and they were succeeded by the most horrible unnatural lusts and the slow torture leading to murder of his victims, in the watching of which this monster eventually came to find his chief delight.

While he indulged himself in such enormities, de Rais' other great interest in life was the practice of the necromantic art, by which he hoped eventually to discover the philosopher's stone, which would place him in command of all the wealth of the world.

Notwithstanding the character of his favourite pursuits, the Marshal was at the same time particularly devout, showing an even perfervid faith, and now and again resolving to make atonement for his sins by going on crusade, never doubting that by this means he would wipe out all the stain of his misdeeds and eventually attain to salvation.

In spite of all this outward appearance of devotion, it is remarkable that de Rais succeeded in maintaining his abominable way so long without question.

But secrecy and immunity could not last indefinitely. Stories came to be bruited about of strange and loathsome happenings

VI: THE MAGIC ARTS

within the castle of Tiffanges, of children being slain in order that with their blood the sensualist magician might write a book of necromantic art. Even then, owing to the Marshal's high position, it was difficult to strike. But eventually the Bishop of Nantes took action, citing de Rais to appear before him on the charges of having gratified his lust on children, whom he had subsequently butchered, of having invoked a familiar spirit with atrocious rites, and of having committed other crimes also suggestive of heresy.

The trial that ensued was abnormal in several respects, the most notable being its publicity, public opinion being deliberately called into play, the fathers and mothers of the children, who had been spirited away into the monster's castle, being allowed to let loose their clamourings against the villain. [10]

Action was taken in a civil court contemporaneously with the ecclesiastical proceedings before bishop and inquisitors. In the ecclesiastical court he was found guilty on both counts —first, unnatural lust and sacrilege; second, heresy and the invocation of demons; but his death-sentence was pronounced in the civil court. The extraordinary man underwent the final penalty with a contrition, an assurance of salvation and an enthusiasm for God which must have been strangely edifying. [11]

(ii) Witchcraft

The great witchcraft craze did not seize upon Europe until the beginning of the fifteenth century.

It is true that for hundreds of years before this crimes, which became associated with the name of witchcraft, had been known and punished, but until the twelfth century we do not find the precise well-defined conception of the witch as a woman who has entered into an unholy compact with Satan, is in possession of certain miraculous powers and in particular that of transporting herself through the air to the so-called Sabbath, or rather Sabbat, where she and her kind meet together to renew their allegiance to the Prince of Darkness.

It is very likely that the idea of the omnipresence of the powerful and maleficent force of Satan took greater hold of western Europe than ever before in the twelfth century, that marvellous period of the earlier Renaissance, when men's minds were quickened to a new realization of the splendour and beauty of things of the earth, when heresy took a firm root, and doubt and hesitation sometimes usurped the place of a faith which had been childlike and unquestioning, a period of clashing between intellectual aspiration and the inflexibility of dogma, such that the timid and the ignorant were assailed by a vivid consciousness of the dangers pressing around the Ark of the Lord upon every side, of the sinister might of the dark powers arrayed against the Redeemer.

In such circumstances more insistent, more clearly denned became the conception of those evil beings going about in the world, who had sold themselves to the Devil and were assisting him in his fell purposes. [12]

At first the Church refused its sanction to the popular tales about witches, more especially to the tale of the Sabbat and the transportation of witches through the air, often over immense distances. The canonists, Ivo of Chartres and Gratian, dismiss this as a fiction: which to believe is pagan, an error in the faith—in short heresy.

But popular credence triumphed over the canonists. The reports of the activities of witches became so numerous, so determined and so circumstantial that it was wellnigh impossible to disbelieve. It became simply a question of how to reconcile well-authenticated facts with the canonists.

A way out of the dilemma was discovered in the fifteenth century, at a time when the craze had almost reached its height.

The witches meant by the canonists must have been a different order of being from those referred to by a later generation when they spoke of witches. It was merely a matter of nomenclature after all. Those responsible not only for guarding the purity of the faith but also for protecting the faithful from the assaults of the Evil One as delivered by witches could no longer allow their freedom of action to be curtailed, the powers of the Devil actually aggrandized by the misinterpreted ruling that belief in witches was error.

Accordingly, when a certain eminent lawyer named Ponzinibio dared to maintain the accuracy of the canonists and to assert that all belief in witchcraft and sorcery was a delusion, the master of

VI: THE MAGIC ARTS

the Sacred Palace, Bartholomew de Spina, wrote a vehement and momentous reply, in which he turned the vials of a righteous indignation against Ponzinibio and called upon the Inquisition to proceed against the lawyer as himself a fautor of heretics. [13]

The attitude of the Church had indeed made a complete reversal. What previously it had been heresy to assert it now became heresy to deny. The divine law was now discovered clearly to prove the existence of witches, and the Scriptures were reinforced by the civil code. [14] There no longer remained any room for doubt or equivocation.

Before the end of the century there appeared Sprenger's celebrated 'Malleus Maleficarum,' the most authoritative work in existence on witchcraft from the standpoint of credulity. [15] Sprenger was an inquisitor, so that in his compendium, as in other similar treatises, we have the conclusions regarding the nature and the practices of witches, as ascertained by the examination of supposedly authentic cases.

We learn in the first place the fundamental fact which explains the existence of witches—the inherent inferiority of the female sex to the male. Women are discontented, impatient creatures, who have a natural proclivity to evil. Woman is at the best a necessary evil. St. Chrysostom is quoted with approval on the subject of marriage. 'Quid est mulier nisi amicitiae inimica, ineffugabilis poena, necessarium malum, naturalis tentatio, desirabilis calamitas, domesticum periculum, delectabile detrimentum? …' [16]

Everything considered, it was not at all strange that women should be particularly prone to yielding to the corrupt wiles and solicitations of the Devil. Once bought by him, they received the sustenance for their infamous activities in the Sabbat, the great nocturnal assembly of the powers of darkness, held sometimes in the Brocken, sometimes in some unidentified spot east of Jordan, or indeed it might be in any spot chosen by Satan.

To the trysting-place, however distant it might be, the witches flew through the air. This aërial transportation to the Sabbat was in the opinion of Sprenger and other first-rate authorities certainly no illusion, it was a reality—only, according to Sprenger, the witch travelled in an aerial body, a vaporous part of herself, which issued out of her mouth and by the existence of which she was enabled to be in two places at one and the same time. [17]

At the nocturnal assemblage there took place the offering of unqualified allegiance to the Devil, feasting, dancing and sexual intercourse, either with Satan himself or some of his demons. [18]

Foul details occur in plenty in all the fifteenth-century treatises on witchcraft concerning the sexual abominations practised by 'incubi' and 'succubi' at the Sabbat. From such horrid intercourse, we are informed by our authors, proceed giants and wizards, such as Merlin, but never an ordinary human being. [19]

Bartholomew de Spina gives us a variety of circumstantial stories about women who had taken part in the witches' gathering. One or two may be taken as samples of a large class.

A respected burgomaster studied in his youth at Parma. Returning to his lodgings one night late, he knocked in vain at the door. He therefore let himself in by the window and went upstairs, where he found the maid-servant lying prone on the floor, naked and so inert as to appear dead. When she at last came to herself, she acknowledged that she had been to the Sabbat.

This case, comments Spina, proves that in the transportation to the Sabbat no corporal transference is involved. The body of the girl had lain all the time on the floor, only her aerial spirit had been absent. [20]

Again, a man one day finds his wife lying in an outhouse insensible, and on recovery she confesses to having been to the concourse. He is horrified, and, determined to rid himself of his atrocious spouse, gives information against her to the Inquisition, so that she may be burnt. The woman apparently escaped this fate by drowning herself. [21]

One suspects a somewhat simpler explanation than witchcraft of this tale of conjugal infelicity.

Another similar account is of a citizen of Ferrara, whose wife was in the habit of attending the Sabbat. One night he, pretending to be asleep, saw his wife rise, anoint herself and fly out of the window. As soon as she was gone he got up, and apparently succeeded in tracking her to the wine-cellar of a noble of the town, where he found her together with a number of witches. Directly he was seen, they all disappeared.

The unfortunate husband, however, could not get away and was there discovered by the servants of the house, who very naturally took him for a burglar. Happily he succeeded in giving satisfactory explanations to the owner of the house.

At the earliest possible opportunity he gave information against his wife, whom he handed over to the punishment she had deserved. [22]

Here again we get the hint that the charge of witchcraft might be a useful weapon in the armoury of a husband, should he desire for one reason or another to separate from his wife—for good. Another tale is of a girl who saw her mother rise out of bed, anoint herself and fly out of the window.

The girl did likewise, acquiring apparently the power of flight on the instant, and she found herself transported into her mother's presence. Then, being frightened, she called upon the names of Jesus and the Virgin, and thereupon found herself back in her bed. [23]

The witches, who entered into their unholy compact with Satan at the Sabbat, were there invested with various tremendous and abominable powers.

Unlike sorcerers and magicians, who occasionally used their black art to good purposes, witches could work nothing else but evil. They were particularly fond of interfering with procreation, where both men and women, because of the connection with original sin, were most vulnerable. They produced sterility in the one sex, impotence in the other. [24] Indeed it could be taken practically for certain that these two evils were invariably due to witchcraft.

Witches also produced abortion and interfered with the flow of the mother's milk. [25] They sometimes offered up infants at their birth to demons; were vampires and sustained themselves by sucking children's blood. [26] They were able to transform men and women into beasts, to create tempests and thunderstorms. [27]

Indeed they went about the world doing all manner of noxious damage, ranging in seriousness from the breaking of crucifixes to the destruction of human life. In their peregrinations they were much assisted by their being able to transform themselves into the likeness of animals, particularly of cats, so that it was very difficult to keep them out of any dwelling-house they cared to visit. [28]

Indeed so powerful and versatile were witches supposed to be, not only by vulgar report, but according to authoritative statement, that it may seem difficult to understand how it could be imagined that any human agency could ever get the better of them.

But something had to be done. The evil tended to grow so disastrously, in this helped as a matter of fact—as in the case of sorcery—by the Church's decision that the magic arts were no mere delusion but reality, and that while the practiser of them was a heretic, to believe that he or she was no charlatan but genuinely in league with the Devil was sound doctrine.

In this way were men and women encouraged, whenever ill-fortune befell them, to find a facile explanation for unmerited calamity in such an intrinsically innocent incident, for example, as that of a sinister-looking old woman with a hooked nose having peered in at their cottage window.

The simple fact of being found wandering alone in fields or woods after nightfall constituted legitimate evidence before the Inquisition. Or again, if an old woman said to someone who had injured her, 'You will repent of this,' and some misfortune subsequently occurred to the latter, the old woman might easily on such trivial grounds be suspect. [29]

One of the most interesting and remarkable phenomena of the history of witchcraft is that of the self-confessed witch, the woman who deliberately and of her own accord gave herself out to be possessed of supernatural powers in spite of the terrible peril incurred by such an announcement.

The explanation of this is partly economic—the law of supply and demand operating in the case of the occult arts as a marketable commodity, just as in any other—partly psychological.

Particularly when there was such unimpeachable authority for the reality and potency of the black arts, there were always people quite anxious to avail themselves of the means of fore-knowledge of, or avenging an injury, or discomfiting a rival, and to pay handsomely for the privilege.

VI: THE MAGIC ARTS

The demand existing, there were not wanting those willing to satisfy it, to accept the risk in view of the generosity of the remuneration.

Sometimes the reputed witch succeeded in persuading herself that she was one in very deed. Some curious coincidence, the desired object actually occurring after the utterance of spells and incantations, persuaded the superstitious mind, arguing 'post hoc ergo propter hoc,' that the spells and incantations held in them a miraculous power. The wretched woman would then with a vain pride or a trembling apprehensive awe perceive in herself a being supernatural. [30]

But clearly the greater proportion of witchcraft lore is founded upon confessions wrung by means of the rack from the supposed culprit when brought before a civil or inquisitorial tribunal.

We do not know definitely when the Inquisition was first employed against witchcraft; but certainly in 1374 it was determined by the papacy that the Holy Office was competent to try such cases. [31] In 1437 Eugenius IV called upon inquisitors everywhere to exert themselves against the evil. [32]

And there is no question that throughout the fifteenth century the tribunal carried on a crusade against witchcraft with great assiduity.

Although Sprenger was moved to confess that the extirpation of the pest seemed an impossibility, being inclined to lay the blame on the carelessness and inactivity of the secular authority [33], nevertheless the number of executions was terrible. We are told that in a single year the Bishop of Bamberg destroyed six hundred witches, the Bishop of Wurzburg nine hundred. [34] A thousand perished in the same space of time in the diocese of Como. [35]

The execution of witches, then, both in this century and the next, assumed great proportions, largely owing to the thoroughness of inquisitorial proceedings, though it must be added—despite Sprenger's animadversions upon its slackness—that actually the civil authority was responsible for many.

The Inquisition, therefore, must bear much of the blame for the spread of witchcraft, or rather —for it amounted to the same thing—for the witchcraft craze. Largely in its records were collected the great stores of indisputable evidence of the reality of that heresy which it had become one of the functions of the tribunal to eradicate.

By reason of its constitution and its methods of procedure the Inquisition was always a very effective court; but it was especially so in the case of witches, because in dealing with them the inquisitor felt that he was engaged in a personal combat with Satan himself, and that he had to exert all his powers in order to withstand, still more to overcome, so formidable an adversary.

Indeed it was very fortunate that he was able to comfort himself with the knowledge that he was impervious to the attacks of witchcraft. Nevertheless it was felt necessary to take special precautions. [36]

Torture was used thoroughly where witches were concerned, and no doubt the delirium thus occasioned, the victim being willing to put an end to her torments by saying what she knew her judge wanted her to say or imagined he would like to hear, was productive of many of the most marvellous witch stories to be found in inquisitorial archives.

But the severity of the torture administered in these cases was due to the extraordinary obduracy frequently shown by the victims. Such obstinacy was taken as proof positive of Satanic assistance afforded to these servants of hell, and the inquisitor was therefore goaded to greater and greater cruelty, because he felt himself put upon his mettle.

The silence of the accused thus became positive evidence of guilt, as damning as confession under the pains of rack or pulley —perhaps even more so. [37]

The gift of taciturnity, it was conjectured, might be due to the wearing of a charm somewhere on the person, so that as a preliminary to the application the alleged witch had to be divested of all her clothing for thorough investigation to be made. [38]

It was held that a witch was unable to shed tears under torment, whereas—as Sprenger urges sententiously—it is natural for women to weep. It was desirable therefore to adjure the accused to shed tears. [39] If this solemn exhortation was successful and the victim did cry and lament under torture, she was not necessarily the better off; for this might well be a device to deceive, a wile of

VI: THE MAGIC ARTS

the Devil's to defeat the ends of justice. The inquisitor, ever on the alert to discover such signs of Satanic intervention, was apt to disbelieve in the genuineness of the witch's tears accordingly.

Thus, whether it produced confession or only obduracy, lamentation or silence, torture was in any event practically certain to be successful. Indeed anyone defamed of witchcraft before the Inquisition became so inextricably enmeshed in the toils that escape from conviction was hardly possible save in the event of being able to prove that the accuser was actuated by mortal enmity. [40] And even the most persistent silence must, one imagines, practically always in the end have been overborne.

A sufficiently prolonged continuance of torture must have produced the desired result—answers to leading questions about the Sabbat, detailed descriptions culled from the imagination of demon orgies, confessions as to the invocation of evil spirits and malpractices carried on by their help, finally the incrimination of others.

So the witchcraft legend grew in substance, in precision, in lurid picturesqueness. From the lips of the witches themselves came the authentic particulars of the Sabbat, the flittings through the air on broomsticks, the blasting of human lives by foul spells, the inculpation of ever-increasing numbers in the guilt and the heresy of witchcraft.

There is a most striking illustration of the astonishing efficacy of inquisitorial methods in effectively defeating their purpose, and actually producing the spread of the witchcraft craze, in the famous case of the Vaudois or witches of Arras in the years 1459-1460, when the arrest of a single alleged witch led to the inculpation of one after another, each new victim in her torments naming others, including many of the wealthiest and most important as well as the humblest citizens, so that at length a positive panic was created. [41]

Not a single member of the community in Arras could feel himself or herself secure. No one dared leave the city for fear that that innocent act might be seized upon as a confession of guilt, and no one cared to enter for fear of falling into the hands of the tribunal, thus busily engaged in investigating an outburst of heresy of such alarming proportions.

To such a pass did things come that the material prosperity of Arras was seriously prejudiced, as people became afraid of having any dealings with the city. One dangerous source of economic disturbance was that all creditors demanded instant payment of their dues, fearing that their debtors might be among those arrested, seeing that conviction involved the confiscation of the victim's property, and in such a case the creditor was held to have no claim on any part of it.

In producing such results as these the inquisitor was no doubt ever most sincere and disinterested, genuinely aghast at the magnitude of the evil he was charged to suppress, wholly blind to the fact that its magnitude was mainly of his own creation. And in the feeling that there could be no security so long as the witch remained alive, he only shared the popular view.

It was simply the universal conviction that the appropriate punishment of witchcraft and the only sure remedy against it was death by fire.

Nor was the inquisitor alone in bringing offenders to the stake. The civil courts and the ordinary episcopal courts were no more lenient than the Holy Office. Even in Protestant countries, where there was no Inquisition, the lot of the supposed witch in the sixteenth century was no more tolerable than in those countries where the Inquisition still continued to flourish.

The belief in the reality of witchcraft had taken firm root everywhere, and Catholic and Protestant were alike in their literal interpretation of the terrible words of Scripture, 'Thou shalt not suffer a witch to live,' which seemed to afford all-sufficient sanction for the inexorable judgments of all tribunals, whether clerical or lay.

At the same time the part played by the Inquisition forms one of the most important chapters in the history of witchcraft, as it was the most efficient and energetic tribunal engaged in the prosecution of the heresy in its earlier days, inasmuch especially as it contributed so much to the spread of the belief by the convinced fanaticism of its members and those methods of obtaining evidence, which not only led to sure conviction and constant incriminations, but actually provided the raw material of supposed fact on which credulity was based.

VI: THE MAGIC ARTS

The voluminous records of the holy tribunal, the learned treatises of its members are the great repositories of the true and indisputable facts concerning the abominable heresies of sorcery and witchcraft.

---

[1] J. Glanvill, *A Blow at Sadducism* (1688), p. 5. *Cf.* pp. 32-3: 'But to reserve all the clear circumstances of Fact, which we find in well attested and confirmed Relations of this kind into the power of deceivable imagination, is to make fancy the greater Prodigy; and to suppose, that it can do stranger feats than are believed of any other kind of function. And to think that Pins and Nails, for instance, can by the power of imagination be conveyed within the skin; or that imagination should deceive so many as have been witnesses in objects of sense, in all the circumstances of discovery; this, I say, is to be infinitely more credulous than the assertors of sorcery and Demoniack Contracts. And by the same reason it may be believed that all the Battels and strange events of the world, which our selves have not seen, are but dreams and fond imaginations.'

[2] W. E. H. Lecky, *Rationalism in Europe* (1904), vol. i, p. 18.

[3] See W. E. H. Lecky, *Rationalism in Europe* (1904), vol. i, pp. 34-5.

[4] See Lea, vol. iii, pp. 422-9.

[5] See *ibid.*, p. 434.

[6] Sprenger, *Malleus Maleficarum* (Frankfort ed., 1582), vol. i, pp. 488-9: 'Et eodem modo de adorantibus Daemonē & sacrificantibus ei quia si hoc faciunt, credentes Divinitatem esse in Daemonibus, vel credentes quod cultus latriae sit ei exhibendus, vel quod omnino ex exhibitione talis cultus, assequantur quod requirunt a Diabolo, non obstāte Dei prohibitione, seu etiam permissione, tales essent haeretici. Sed si ista faciunt non ita sentientes de Daemone; sed ut aliquo pacto cum Daemone facilius per ista exequantur ab ipso quod intendunt, tales non sunt haeretici natura rei, licet gravissime peccent.'

[7] A. Albertini, *De Agnoscendis assertionibus Catholicis in Zilettus, Tractatus Universi Juris*, vol. xi, pt. ii, pp. 65-6. *Cf.* J. Simancas, *De Catholicis Institutionibus* in Zilettus, *ibid.*, p. 144 (Tit. xxi).

[8] Lea, vol. iii, p. 454: 'Inquisitors... began to insert a clause renouncing sorcery in all abjurations administered to repentant heretics, so that in case they should become addicted to it they could be promptly burned for relapse.'

[9] For Peter of Abano, see *supra*, pp. 69, 70, and Lea, vol. iii, p. 440; for Gilles de Rais, *ibid.*, pp. 468-89.

[10] Ordinarily inquisitorial trials were secret. Another abnormal feature in this case was the presence of a prosecutor; the third was that the court was really a joint one, being in part the bishop and inquisitors sitting together as a tribunal of the Holy Office to hear the charge of heresy, in part the bishop sitting as president of the ordinary episcopal court, the inquisitors not included, to hear the charge of unnatural lust with which the Inquisition was not competent to deal.

[11] *Cf.* Lea, vol. iii, p. 486: 'The morning saw the extraordinary spectacle of the clergy, followed by the whole population of Nantes, who had been clamouring for his death, marching through the streets and singing and praying for his salvation.'

[12] Lecky, *Rationalism in Europe*, vol. i, pp. 47-53.

[13] See *Bart. Spin, in Ponzinibium de lamiis Apologia prima in Malleorum quorundam Maleficarum tam veterum quam recentiorum authorum tomi duo* (Frankfort, 1582), vol. ii, pp. 623 *et seq*.

[14] *Ibid.*, vol. i, pp. 1-8 in Sprenger's *Malleus Maleficarum*.

[15] For a critique of Sprenger's work, see J. Michelet, *La Sorcière* in *Œuvres Completes* (Paris, 1893-9), pp. 481-96.

[16] Sprenger, vol. i, p. 94; also Michelet, *op. cit.*, p. 321.

[17] Albertini, *op. cit.*, in Zilettus, vol. xi, pt. ii, p. 85; also Sprenger, etc., vol. ii, pp. 262-4, and, generally, pp. 250 *et seq.*, *De modo quo localiter transferuntur de loco ad locum*.

[18] Frédéricq, *Documents*, vol. i, p. 371. 'Et illecq leur remontra comment ils avoient esté en ladite vaulderie, et fait tout ce que dessus ai dit, et mesme que aulcunes d'icelles, qui estoient la presentes, avoient esté cognues carnellement du diable d'enfer, l'une en forme de lièvre, l'autre en forme de renard, l'autre en forme de thor, l'aultre en forme d'homme et autant en forme de quelques bestes'—from *Mémoires de Jacques du Clercq*.

[19] Sprenger, pp. 40 *et seq.*, p. 773. See also in vol. ii. of *Malleorum... tomi duo, Tractatus utilis et necessarius per viam Dialogi, de Pythonicis mulieribus*, pp. 56-7.

[20] Sprenger, etc., pp. 458-9 in Bartholomew de Spina's *De Strigibus*.

[21] *Ibid.*, pp. 459-60.

[22] Sprenger, p. 546.

[23] de Spina, pp. 544-5.

[24] Sprenger, pp. 103-25, 267 *et seq.*; also in vol. ii of *Malleorum tomi duo, De Pythonicis mulieribus*, pp. 42-3.

[25] Sprenger, pp. 152 *et seq.* and 354.

[26] *Ibid.*, pp. 152 *et seq.*, 341 *et seq.*; de Spina, in vol. ii, p. 502.

[27] Sprenger, pp. 141 *et seq.*, 296-301, 360 *et seq.*; *De Pythonicis mulieribus*, in vol. ii, pp. 65 *et seq.*

VI: THE MAGIC ARTS

[28] Sprenger, p. 310; *De Pythonicis mulieribus*, in vol. ii, p. 75.

[29] See Sprenger, p. 581. Cf. Lea, vol. iii, p. 508.

[30] A very effective play based upon this idea is that of H. Wiers-Jenssen, of which the English version is *The Witch*, by John Masefield.

[31] It was so decided by Gregory XI, when the right of the French inquisition in the matter was challenged. Papal commissions issued to inquisitors early in the fifteenth century specifically enumerate sorcery and witchcraft among offences with which they are to deal.

[32] See Sprenger, pp. 492-3. Innocent VIII gave a great impetus to persecution of witches in 1485 by his bull, *Summis desiderantes*, in which all the malignant powers of the witch were enumerated. It was this bull that gave authority to Jacob Sprenger, the author of *Malleus Maleficarum*. It was supplemented by others of a similar character issued by Julius II and Alexander VI.

[33] Sprenger, pp. 172-82.

[34] See Lecky, *op. cit.*, vol. i, p. 3; Michelet, *op. cit.*, p. 10.

[35] *Malleorum—tomi duo*, vol. ii, p. 520.

[36] Sprenger, p. 214. *Inquisitoribus Maleficae non possunt nocere*. 'In oppido nempe Ravenspurg, cum a consulibus Maleficae incinerandae interrogarentur, cur nobis inquisitoribus aliqua maleficia, sicut aliis hominibus, non intulissent, Responderunt: Licet pluries hoc facere attentassent, non tamen potuerunt. Et de causa inquirentibus, respondebant se nescire, nisi quod a Daemonibus informatae fuissent.' Nevertheless, *ibid.*, p. 559, inquisitors should be careful not to allow themselves to be touched by wizards and witches.

[37] Sprenger, p. 549.

[38] *Ibid.*, pp. 552-3.

[39] *Ibid.*, p. 557. The adjuration was by the bitter tears of Christ shed on the Cross for the sins of the world, by the tears shed by the glorious Virgin Mary, by those shed by all the saints and elect of God on earth.

[40] Such enmity had to be really mortal and well authenticated for the inquisitorial point of view was that of necessity a witch always would excite a great deal of enmity. Allegations of enmity must, therefore, always be carefully sifted. See Sprenger, pp. 542 *et seq*.

[41] For the whole remarkable story, see Lea, vol. iii, pp. 519-34.

Part 2: The Inquisition

I

Attitude of the Church Towards Heresy Prior to the Institution of the Inquisition

The literal and fundamental meaning of the word Heresy is *choosing*. The heretic is the man who selects certain doctrines, discards others, giving rein to individual preference in the realm of religious belief. Such an attitude is essentially incompatible with the conception that the truth has once and for all been delivered to the saints, that the faith is indivisible and unalterable, to be accepted in its entirety.

It is easily understood that eclecticism should be regarded as a danger in the earliest days of a new religion by its adherents. The first proselytes are anxious to define those distinctive features which mark it off from other religions: for all religions have certain elements in common.

It was thus in the early stages of Christianity, which shared certain characteristics with such beliefs as Mithraism, Gnosticism, Neoplatonism. The idea of man's need of a mediator with heaven was abroad in the Roman world before the Messiah was proclaimed to it. There thus existed a danger of confusion, that alien shoots of dogma might be grafted upon the pure and original stock of Christianity. The influence of such extraneous sources is apparent in the fourth gospel.

Even in the very earliest days when the body of Christian belief consisted of little more than the disciples' recollections of the sayings and actions of their Founder, when the simplest conception of pure and undefiled religion was being taught [1], even then the faithful were warned to beware of 'false prophets,' 'false teachers' who 'privily shall bring in damnable heresies.' [2]

As the fabric of dogma began to be woven, the note became vehement. St. Paul denounces 'false apostles, deceitful workers, transforming themselves into the apostles of Christ.' [3] In another place he declares, 'But though we, or an angel from heaven, preach any other gospel unto you than that which we have preached unto you, let him be accursed.' [4]

So far, however, even the idea of what constitutes heresy is vague, and the spirit of tolerance and of brotherliness is strong. The offender is not to be counted as an enemy, but admonished as a brother. [5]

The fact is that the flock is so small and the pagan world outside so powerful that internal dissensions cannot be permitted. But the new faith surviving, doctrine becomes more stereotyped, the feeling of later generations more confident. Polycarp finds the heretic to be antichrist, who belongs to the Devil and is the oldest son of Satan, [6] and Tertullian in one passage recommends the employment of compulsion against the heretic. [7]

Such language is not common among the early Fathers. They are themselves members of a society liable to persecution, and they do not preach coercion. Lactantius urges that the only weapon for Christians to use is their reason; they must defend their faith not by violence, but persuasion. [8]

The Church in those days had not the opportunity to use force, even if it had wished to: and this fact must be borne in mind in connection with Tertullian's enunciation of the principle of tolerance, when he declares that the selection of his mode of worship is a man's natural right, the exercise of which cannot be either harmful or profitable to his neighbour, and that it is not the part of a religion to compel men to embrace it. [9]

In the (only apparent) contradiction between this ruling and the counsel given regarding the treatment of heretics, Tertullian laid down a principle of momentous consequence for the future,

I: ATTITUDE TOWARDS HERESY PRIOR TO INQUISITION

namely, that while force should not be applied to the unbeliever, its use is legitimate in the case of the man who has once accepted the faith and erred in it.

With the accession of Constantine, there dawned a new era for the Christian Church. Till then the Roman state had been neutral, when not actively hostile; from this time onwards, with one brief interval, it was an active supporter. The Church became possessed of all the enormous power of the imperial authority.

The civil order is definitely Christian, and one of the prime duties of the Emperor, lord of the world, is the protection of the Church. Constantine speedily showed himself anxious to take a leading part in ecclesiastical matters. He had recourse to torture, confiscation of property, exile and possibly the death penalty also in harrying the Donatists. [10]

Donatism was a small thing in comparison with Arianism, which shook the Christian Church to its foundations. When the fathers of Nicaea decided the intricate metaphysical question of 'consubstantial,' the Emperor proclaimed exile for all who did not accept the Council's decision. Against this determination to root out their enemies, to establish one interpretation of truth by force, the Fathers made no protest, but accepted the intervention of the secular authority on their behalf. There was no thought of the possible consequence of such a pact in the future. [11]

The triumph of the orthodox was short-lived. The Arians were victorious later on and in their turn persecuted the Trinitarians. The Christians, said Julian the Apostate, treated each other like wild beasts. The punishments inflicted by one party upon the other included imprisonment, flogging, torture, death. To such a pass had doctrinal differences already brought the adherents of a religion which proclaimed peace and goodwill among men.

The tradition of persecution had been thoroughly established. The laws of Theodosius II and Valentinian II enumerate as many as thirty-two different heresies, all punishable, the penalties being such as deprivation of civil rights, exile, corporal punishment and death. But the heresies are carefully differentiated, the severest penalties being reserved for Manichæism, which had been punished by the Roman state in its pagan, polytheistic and tolerant days, because of its anti-social tendencies. [12]

But now orthodox emperors persecuted Arians, Arian emperors persecuted followers of Athanasius, simply because they had taken sides in a theological controversy.

What view did the Church take of the activities of the lay power? Was it actively approving or disapproving, or passively acquiescent? We find some of the Fathers still preaching the old doctrines of tolerance.

Athanasius, himself at the time persecuted, declared that persecution was an invention of the Devil.

To Chrysostom heretics are as persons diseased, nearly blind, assuredly to be led, not forced. He comments on the parable of the tares, and urges the necessity of being very careful, lest the godly be destroyed together with heretics. [13]

Jerome remembers that the Church was founded upon persecutions and martyrdoms and on the whole seems to inculcate lenience in treatment of heretics, though a remark to the effect that Arius, at first only a single spark, not being immediately extinguished, set the whole world on fire, and that corrupted flesh must be cut off, points to a different opinion. [14]

The most significant of the later Fathers is St. Augustine. In his case there is a notable change of front with regard to the treatment of heretics.

By temperament he was an advocate of toleration, and at first, like Chrysostom, he appeals to the parable of the tares in justification of tolerance. Heretics should be allowed the opportunity to correct themselves and to repent. They are to be regarded as lost sheep. He is afraid that persecution might lead to those who were in reality heretics becoming hypocritical Catholics. [15]

But later on he altered his opinions. He had found that the weapons of persuasion and eloquence were not strong enough to break down the obduracy of his enemies the Donatists. He had been too optimistic. The methods of force employed by the secular power were after all salutary and necessary.

'He therefore, who refuses to obey the imperial laws, when made against the truth of God, acquires a great reward; he who refuses to obey, when they are made for support of the divine truth, exposes himself to most grievous punishment.' [16]

I: ATTITUDE TOWARDS HERESY PRIOR TO INQUISITION

He rejoices, therefore, in a Christianized state. The death penalty he indeed strongly reprobates as contrary to Christian charity, but he approves both banishment and confiscation of property. [17] These later opinions of St. Augustine were largely accepted after him.

An important episode in the history of the Church's attitude to heresy is the execution of the Spanish heretic, Priscillian, by the Emperor Maximus. Priscillian's teachings, akin to Manichæism, were denounced by several bishops, and it was upon their complaint that the Spaniard was brought before the imperial tyrant.

The action of the bishops, who had thus involved themselves in the guilt of blood, wittingly or unwittingly, was severely condemned by St. Ambrose and still more by Martin of Tours, who refused to have any communion with them. This happened in 385. [18]

In 447 it seemed that heresy was reviving in Spain, and Pope Leo I expressly commended the act of Maximus. He feared lest, if such damnable error was not crushed, there should be an end to all human and divine law; and if he did not ask for the death sentence, he was quite willing that the Church should acquiesce in the state's severity and reap the advantages resulting from it. [19]

Thus to welcome the results of the shedding of blood in cases of heresy, while refusing to accept the responsibility for it, constituted a most dangerous attitude.

For centuries after the days of Leo I heresy almost ceased to be a problem for the Church at all. Western Christendom entered into the gloom of the Dark Ages, its history the arid record of barbarian invasions and the rivalries of Childerichs and Chilperichs. The human intelligence was dormant: consequently heresy ceased to be a force. When there is no mental activity, no education, no discussion, there may be faith, there can never be heresy.

When the darkness lifted a little, heresy once more became a problem. In 1022 thirteen Cathari were burnt by order of, and in the presence of, King Robert II of France. The punishment of heresy by fire was an entire innovation. There was no existing law to sanction it. The stake had been used by Roman emperors to punish parricides, slaves who attempted their masters' lives, and incendiaries, and it still existed as a punishment for sorcerers and witches. The stake may have been used on this occasion because it was an impressive and theatrical death and, a choice being demanded between abjuration and death, it was considered the latter should be specially terrifying. [20]

Another execution of Cathari, this time by hanging, took place in 1051 at Goslar in Saxony in the presence of the Emperor Henry III. As in France, so in Germany, the law knew neither the offence nor the punishment. The Emperor was acting simply in the public defence. [21]

It is important to note the part played in the treatment of heretics at this period by the populace. In both the cases just cited the secular prince had in his action the full approval of the people. It is particularly noticed by the chronicles of the first incident that the deed was 'regis jussu et universae plebis consensu.' [22]

And Henry strengthened his position in the absence of any written law by securing the agreement of his subjects. [23] Nothing could be better attested than the crowd's hatred of the heretic in the eleventh and twelfth centuries, as far as northern Europe was concerned. [24]

In the south it was different. There are several instances of the feeling in the north in the late decades of the eleventh and early decades of the twelfth century.

For example, in 1076 at Cambrai a Catharan who had been condemned by the bishop as a heretic (no sentence pronounced) was seized upon by the bishop's officers and the mob, who placed him in some sort of cabin, which they burned with the prisoner inside it. It is said that the recantation of Roscellinus was due to the threat of death at the hands of the populace. [25]

In 1114 certain heretics having been placed provisionally in prison by the Bishop of Strassburg were in the bishop's absence forcibly seized upon by the crowd, who, the chronicler states, feared clerical lenience. They were led out of the town and there burnt alive. [26]

A similar event happened in Cologne in 1143; whilst two years later at Liége the clergy only just succeeded in rescuing

I: ATTITUDE TOWARDS HERESY PRIOR TO INQUISITION

the crowd's victims from its clutches. Lawless violence against heretics continued to evince itself in France into the following century, there being instances of it in Troyes, Nevers, Besançon, Paris, even at a time when the secular power, under Philip Augustus, was active in bringing heretics to the stake.

What was the attitude of the clergy in this period, during which it seems evident that in northern Europe secular princes and public opinion were united in thinking heresy deserving of death, even by burning? There is the evidence of the mob fearing clerical lenience in one case cited, of the clergy actually intervening against the crowd in another.

When the heretics were burnt at Cambrai in 1076 Gregory VII protested and ordered the excommunication of the inhabitants. [27]

And there is a very notable protest against the use of force by Wazon, Bishop of Liége (1042-8), who in answer to a query of the Bishop of Châlons as to whether he should yield up heretics to the secular arm or not, referred to the parable of the tares in support of lenience. [28]

His successor, Theoduin, on the other hand, is found counselling Henry I of France to mete out punishment to the followers of Berengar of Tours [29], and about the same time we find the Archbishop of Milan giving some supposed Manichæans the choice between abjuration and the stake. [30]

The fact that most clearly emerges from the consideration of rather conflicting evidence in this period is the absence of any law regarding heretics. The mob, secular princes and clergy are all acting irregularly, taking measures in self-defence in the absence of written rulings. Generally speaking, it would appear that there is a prevailing idea that heresy merits the extreme penalty. At the same time some attempt was made at various ecclesiastical councils to standardize procedure against heresy.

A Council at Rheims in 1049 spoke only of excommunication as a punishment; one at Toulouse in 1119 did the same, but also called upon the secular arm to render aid. [31]

The middle of the twelfth century saw a great revival of both Roman and Canon law and the publication of the Decree of Gratian.

The Decree did not put all uncertainty at an end. It certainly laid down a clear ruling regarding the confiscation of property. The heretic, being outside both human and divine law, could not hold property. But regarding the death penalty there could be no plain direction, because on this subject Gratian's authorities were contradictory and remained so despite his efforts to reconcile them. [32]

Further efforts at definition were made by ecclesiastical councils during the century. One sitting at Rheims in 1157 demanded banishment and branding for those who simply professed Catharism, for proselytizers perpetual imprisonment; but it seems to hint at the death penalty in the veiled phrase: 'carcere perpetuo, nisi gravius aliquid fieri debet visum, recludentur.' [33]

Another Council at Tours in 1163, presided over by Alexander III, reiterated the demand for incarceration and also ordered the confiscation of goods. [34] The second Council of the Lateran of 1179, lamenting the marked spread of heresy, commended the use of force by the secular arm and proclaimed a two years' indulgence to all who should take up arms against heretics. [35]

The first secular law in the Middle Ages dealing with heresy is English. In 1166 two Cathari were brought before Henry II at Oxford, whipped and branded with a red key and banished. [36] Shortly afterwards in the same year appeared the clause in the Assize of Clarendon, forbidding the sheltering of heretics on the pain of having one's house destroyed. [37]

Other severe secular legislation soon appeared in other countries. In 1194 the Emperor Henry VI ordered the confiscation of the property, and the destruction of the houses, of heretics and inforced fines on communities and individuals who neglected to assist, when they had the opportunity, in the arrest of heretics. [38]

The same year Alfonso II of Aragon, aiming at expelling all Manichæans and Waldenses from his dominions, issued an edict declaring all heretics public enemies and banishing them. [39] The ineffectiveness of this edict is demonstrated by the appearance of a severer one three years later issued by Alfonso's successor, Pedro II, famous as the victor over the Moors at Las Navas de Tolosa, equally notorious for his warlike prowess, his religious zeal, his prodigality and licentiousness.

I: ATTITUDE TOWARDS HERESY PRIOR TO INQUISITION

Once again banishment is decreed, but it is added that if any heretics remain in defiance of the edict after a specified date they shall perish at the stake and their effects be confiscated. [40]

Whatever may have been the case earlier, there seems good evidence of the zeal of the clergy against heretics in the latter part of the twelfth century, which saw so much more precision in the declarations of ecclesiastical councils and secular laws on the subject.

In 1167 we find the Abbot of Vézelai, when several heretics were before him, appealing to the people to give sentence, and accepting their demand for a death of torture.

Some years later at Rheims we find the Archbishop and clergy in agreement with the nobles that two Catharan women should be burnt. [41]

Hugh, Bishop of Auxerre (1183-1206), is a busy prosecutor of heretics, causing many to be burnt or exiled. More notable than such isolated instances of clerical activity is the co-operation between Pope and Emperor which led to the important bull entitled *Ad abolendam*. [42]

In 1184, Lucius III and Frederick Barbarossa met at Verona, and as the result of their conference this bull was promulgated, which (among other provisions) fixed rules for the prosecution of suspected heretics, the visitation of infected areas and the assistance of all civil authorities. The Emperor for his part placed heretics under the ban of the empire. [43] The decree of Henry VI, already referred to, was plainly based on this action of his predecessor's.

Towards the end of the twelfth century, then, we have clear evidence of secular and ecclesiastical authorities working hand in hand for the suppression of heresy.

To the former, heresy seemed equivalent to rebellion; to the latter, equivalent to murder, being the murder of the soul. When Pedro II issued his harsh edict against the Cathari of Aragon, he claimed that he was actuated by zeal for the public welfare and a desire to obey the canons of the Church. [44] There was no order in the canons that heretics should be burnt to death; but otherwise, Pedro's appeal to Canon law was justified: and besides the canons, there were the various edicts of ecclesiastical councils during the century, all of them calling upon the secular authority to use its utmost efforts towards the eradication of heresy.

It has been urged that the attitude adopted by the Church was a most unwilling attitude, forced upon it by influences too powerful to resist, that the main motive power of persecution came not from the Church, but from the lay authority and from public opinion. The theory is advanced that during the period, roughly from 1000 to 1150, when the position of the heretic was a matter of legal uncertainty, the clergy opposed the violence evinced against heretics, and in eventually yielding they submitted to the strength of a custom which constituted a sort of *jus non scriptum*.[45]

But there is not much force in this plea. To acquiesce in a *jus non scriptum* argues either indifference or impotence: and the Church in the eleventh and twelfth centuries was neither indifferent nor impotent. Nor is the opposition of the clergy to mob violence an argument to the point. A dislike for mob law and lynching does not necessarily betoken disapproval of capital punishment.[46]

It is true—and this is very important—that spontaneously, without any direct incitement from the clergy, the people regarded the heretic with intense abhorrence.

We ought probably to add that in the absence of written law on the subject there was a rather vague idea, shared by the mob and their rulers, that not only death, but a particularly terrible kind of death, was an appropriate punishment for the heretic— this idea being perhaps derived from the fact that Roman law had at different times meted out this doom for certain kinds of heretics, particularly Manichæans, and other offenders, such as sorcerers and witches.

It is true also that the heretics upon whom the mob turned were generally Manichæan. Yet no one who has any knowledge of the position of the mediæval Church can honestly maintain on these grounds that the Church had no responsibility for the rigour displayed towards the heretic. The heretic was regarded as an offender against society, because it was a Christian society.

Heresy, being error in the faith, was investigated and recognized by the Church. The clergy, not the mob, discovered the heresy

I: ATTITUDE TOWARDS HERESY PRIOR TO INQUISITION

and the heretic; for such discovery could not be made without theological knowledge, of which the mob were ignorant. And such knowledge as they possessed, were it reasoned understanding or merely half-assimilated fragments of doctrine, was derived solely from clerical instruction. It was difficult for any sort of knowledge to come from any other source.

Heresy was regarded as dangerous to the community, because, to begin with, the Church had found it dangerous to itself. The intellectual and spiritual atmosphere with which Christendom was permeated was of the Church's making.

The attempt, therefore, to absolve the Church from responsibility for the measures taken against heresy in these centuries—by whomsoever they were taken—involves a wholly erroneous, indeed an absurd, under-estimate of the authority of the Church.

In 1198 there came to the papal throne perhaps the greatest of the whole pontifical line, Lothario Conti, Innocent III.

High in resolve to strengthen Church and Papacy, he at once gave his attention to the problem of heresy. But though zealous, in some respects he showed a commendable moderation. He was anxious that the innocent should not be confounded with the guilty in the impetuosity of the perfervid clerk or the impatience of the mob; and for the first ten years of his pontificate he made trial of a pacific programme. [47]

But in one part of Christendom the problem of heresy had by this time become acute. In the lands of the Count of Toulouse, Catharism was as rampant as were clerical abuses. The pleasure-loving, prosperous inhabitants of Provence, of Narbonne, of Albi felt the authority of the Church to be an obnoxious incubus upon their worldliness, their careless independence. The clergy were hated and despised. The troubadour made pleasant ridicule of the sacraments and every doctrine of the Church, however sacred.

The death-bed repentance scheme of the Catharan system, its denial of a purgatory and a hell, were popular. Still more so was the pretext afforded by its anti-sacerdotal precepts for despoiling the Church. [48]

So the nobles and the rich bourgeoisie and merchants received heretics into their houses, clothed them and fed them, while they were exempted from taxes. So great was the hold of heresy in his lands, that Count Raymond V of Toulouse declared himself to be wholly unable to resist it. [49]

His successor, Raymond VI, had no wish to resist it, being of the same stuff as his people and seeing no call to disturb them at the bidding of priests. Thus when a Council at Montpellier in 1195 anathematized all princes failing to enforce the Church's decrees against heretics, he paid no heed.

A couple of months after his accession Innocent III sent two commissioners into Languedoc, one of them being subsequently entrusted with legatine powers, to tackle a situation so serious that the whole of that country seemed on the point of slipping away from its allegiance to the Catholic faith and communion. They were instructed that obdurate heretics were to be banished, their property confiscated; and the secular authority was to see to it that their measures were carried out under pain of interdict. The efforts of these two commissioners were entirely fruitless.

In 1204 their successors were entrusted with increased authority, which gave them a complete dictatorship over the ecclesiastical dignitaries of Languedoc, who were bitterly reviled for their incapacity. Yet neither these measures nor lavish bribes to secular rulers proved efficacious, and even the iron resolution of the commissioners, Pierre de Castelnau and Arnaud of Citeaux, was breaking down beneath the weight of persistent failure, when a certain Spaniard, Diego de Arzevedo, Bishop of Osma, suggested to the legates the scheme of an evangelistic enterprise.

This was adopted, and bare-footed missionaries were sent forth to re-convert the erring by simple preaching and exhortation. Among the preachers was St. Dominic himself. This laudable scheme also failed.

There is a legend that Dominic, stung by his ill-success, predicted what the upshot of such deplorable obduracy must eventually be. There was a saying in Spain, he quoted, that a beating may work where a blessing won't. The towers of the cities of the fair land would have to be laid low, its people reduced to servitude. [50]

The actual signal for a complete reversal of policy was the murder of Pierre de Castelnau in circumstances which recall the murder

I: ATTITUDE TOWARDS HERESY PRIOR TO INQUISITION

of Becket. The legate had exasperated the Count of Toulouse; one of the latter's knights slew the priest. Innocent called for vengeance upon the blood-guilty Count; and the Albigensian Crusade, which Innocent had ere this been preaching in vain to Philip Augustus of France, was the immediate consequence. The first crusading army, an international force, assembled at Lyons in June 1209. [51]

The ensuing wars are memorable for the men who took part in them—Pedro of Aragon, the zealous catholic, now intervening on behalf of Count Raymond and perishing on the field of Muret, Simon de Montfort, the 'athlete of Christ'! Never was there Christian warrior purer in his motives than Simon, more whole-hearted in his enthusiasm, or more utterly inhuman in his fanaticism.

These wars are also memorable for their political issues and consequences.

From the outset purely political interests were intermixed with the religious. The great nobles who led the forces of the Cross united with their pious zeal an at least equally genuine and powerful hatred and jealousy of the rich and bountiful southern land which harboured a culture so different from their own, more Saracen than European.

The wars were wars of the north against the south, of one civilization against another. The astute and calculating Philip Augustus seized with avidity the opportunity of bringing under his direct control a province of France, which had been practically an independent kingdom; and the crusade is, therefore, of first-rate importance as a big contribution to the unification of the French kingdom.

If to many who took part in them the original purpose of these religious wars was altogether subsidiary, that purpose was none the less most horribly accomplished. The peculiar civilization of Languedoc was blotted out, its beauty and fragrance being utterly extinguished by the onslaught of the crusaders.

With the civilization went the heresy that it had harboured. Catharism indeed continued to exist in the devastated region, but all its vital power of expansion had been destroyed when the conditions that fostered it vanished.

The Albigensian wars were the most successful attempt to extirpate heresy known in history. They were successful because they were utterly ruthless and included wholesale massacres. When the town of Béziers fell, it is said that twenty thousand of its inhabitants were slaughtered.

There were good catholics as well as Cathari among the populace of the place; but the story goes that when Arnaud of Citeaux was asked whether the catholics were to be spared, in his anxiety lest a single heretic should escape by pretending orthodoxy, he replied, 'Kill them all, for God knows His own.'[52]

When the crusaders appeared in Languedoc, toleration vanished out of western Christendom. There was no asylum left where the heretic could feel assured of safety from the persecutor. The power of the Church against the disobedient had been mightily asserted. The ruler who had dared to disregard her order to purify his land of its contaminators had been brought low.

From every country the papacy had been able to bring together doughty warriors to uphold the unity of the faith by spilling the blood of the perverse wanderers from the fold. The policy of force had been triumphantly vindicated by the amplitude of its success.

---

[1] James, i, 3.
[2] 2 Peter, ii, 1.
[3] 2 Corinth., xi, 13.
[4] Galat., i, 8. See also *ibid.*, iii, 1, 3.
[5] 2 Thessal., iii, 15. *Cf.* Galat., iii, 1, 3.
[6] Polycarp, *Epist.* § 7, in *The Apostolic Fathers* (ed. J. B. Lightfoot, 1891), pp. 171, 179.
[7] 'Ad officium haereticos compelli, non illici dignum est. Duritia vincenda, non suadenda.' Tertullian, *Opera omnia* (ed. Migne, *Patrologia latina*), vol. ii, col. 125.
[8] Lactantius, *Divin. Instit.*, lib. v, cap. 20 (ed. Migne), vol. i, p. 615.
[9] Tertullian, *Opera omnia*, vol. i, col. 699. *Liber ad Scapulam*, cap. 2.
[10] See De Cauzons, *op. cit.*, vol. i, p. 150.
[11] *Ibid.*, p. 154.
[12] See Philippe à Limborch, *History of the Inquisition* (trans. S. Chandler, London, 1731), vol. i, p. 8; L. Tanon, *Histoire des Tribunaux de l'Inquisition*

I: ATTITUDE TOWARDS HERESY PRIOR TO INQUISITION

en France (Paris, 1893), pp. 127-33; De Cauzons, vol. i, pp. 163-8; *Cod. Theod.*, i, xvi, leges 3, 8, 12, 30, 33, 34, 35; C. Moeller in *Revue d'histoire ecclésiastique* (Louvain, 1913), vol. xiv, pp. 728-9, *Les bûchers et les autos-da-fé depuis le moyen âge*.

[13] *The Homilies of St. John Chrysostom* (Oxford ed., Pusey), Homily xlvi, on Matt. xiii, pp. 630 *et seq.*

[14] Letter 82 to Theophilus, Bishop of Alexandria, in *Nicene and Post-Nicene Fathers* (ed. P. Schaff), 2nd series, vol. vi, pp. 170 *et seq.* See Limborch (Chandler's ed.), pp. 29-30. It has been averred that St. Jerome was in favour of the death penalty, on the score of *Epist.* 109 *ad Ripar.* See Lea, vol. i, pp. 214-15, and rejoinder of H. Maillet, *L'Église et la répression sanglante de l'hérésie* (1909), p. 15.

[15] 48th Epistle to Vincentius.

[16] 50th Epistle to Boniface.

[17] Epistle 185, n. 26. Also Epistle 93, n. 10.

[18] See Lea, vol. i, p. 213; Maillet, p. 17, and De Cauzons, vol. i, pp. 186-8.

[19] See Lea, vol. i, p. 215; Maillet, pp. 17 *et seq.*; Vacandard, pp. 27-30. 'Nor were they (the bishops) content with merely accepting it (the aid of the secular arm). They declared that the State had not only the right to help the Church in suppressing heresy, but that she was in duty bound to do so.' See also De Cauzons, vol. i, p. 189 n., and P. Frédéricq, *Les récents historiens catholiques de l'inquisition en France*, in *Revue historique* (vol. cix, Jan.-April, 1912), p. 314.

[20] This suggestion is made by J. Havet in his *L'Hérésie et le Bras séculier au Moyen Âge* in *Œuvres* (Paris, 1896), vol. ii, p. 131.

[21] See *ibid.*, p. 138.

[22] Vacandard, *op. cit.*, p. 33.

[23] Havet, pp. 129-34.

[24] *I.e.* in the *langue d'oïl* of France, in Flanders, Germany, Burgundy.

[25] De Cauzons, vol. i, p. 235.

[26] See Havet, p. 135.

[27] See De Cauzons, vol. i, pp. 233-4.

[28] Frédéricq, *Corpus*, vol. i, pp. 6-7, No. 3, gives Wazon's letter. See also Frédéricq in *Revue historique*, already cited, p. 320; also Maillet, *op. cit.*, p. 34. On the strength of this instance he declares: 'Nous voyons assez souvent les évêques s'opposer aux exécutions'; whereas this episcopal protest is unique.

[29] Havet, *op. cit.*, p. 133. See Maillet on the whole subject in *op. cit.*, ch. ii. He argues that Theoduin had no particular punishment in view and that, therefore, one cannot say he approved the execution of heretics. But as the Bishop must have known very well the sort of punishment customarily inflicted by the State at this time, the argument is not very sound.

[30] See De Cauzons, vol. i, p. 260.

[31] J. D. Mansi, *Sacrorum Conciliorum nova et amplissima Collectio* (Paris, 1901-13), vol. xxi, p. 718, and Frédéricq, *Corpus*, vol. i, No. 31.

[32] See De Cauzons, vol. ii, pp. 271-2; Tanon, p. 454.

[33] Frédéricq, *Corpus*, vol. i, No. 34; Maillet, p. 55; Frédéricq, in criticism of Maillet in *Revue historique*, p. 321.

[34] Frédéricq, *Corpus*, vol. i. No. 39; Mansi, vol. xxi, p. 1177; Havet, pp. 151-2.

[35] Mansi, vol. xxii, p. 231; Frédéricq, *Corpus*, vol. i, No. 47.

[36] See De Cauzons, vol. i, p. 269.

[37] Stubbs, *Select Charters of English Constitutional History* (Oxford, 1890), pp. 145-6, § 21 of the Assize.

[38] See De Cauzons, vol. 1, p. 277.

[39] J. A. Llorente, *Histoire critique de l'Inquisition d'Espagne* (Fr. trans, from the Spanish, Paris, 1818), vol. i, p. 30; Eymeric, *Directorium*, p. 298.

[40] Ludovico à Paramo, *De Origine et Progressu Officii Sanctae Inquisitionis eiusque dignitate et utilitate* (Madrid, 1598), p. 90; Havet, p. 167; De Cauzons, vol. i, p. 283. This is the first secular law of the Middle Ages prescribing the penalty of the stake. But it only refers to Waldenses in a particular country, and the stake is only to be had recourse to in the event of banishment (the penalty primarily enjoined) being incomplete. The legislation of general significance is that of the Emperor Frederick II, between 1220 and 1239.

[41] For particulars of a rather interesting case see Lea, vol. i, pp. 111-12. The charge of heresy was mainly based on the obduracy of a young girl in repelling the licentious advances of a young canon of Rheims.

[42] Mansi, vol. xx, p. 476; Frédéricq, *Corpus*, vol. i. No. 56.

[43] See Havet, p. 154.

[44] Vacandard, p. 56.

[45] This is the argument of Maillet, *op. cit.*, p. 49.

[46] See Frédéricq, *Revue historique*, p. 320.

[47] A. Luchaire, *Innocent III; la croisade des Albigeois* (Paris, 1905), pp. 58-9.

[48] *Ibid.*, pp. 17, 27.

[49] *Ibid.*, pp. 7-8; Tanon, p. 21.

[50] Luchaire, *op. cit.*, p. 103.

[51] J. C. L. Sismondi, *History of the Crusades against the Albigenses* (Eng. trans.), p. 53.

[52] Lea, vol. i, p. 154. See, however, Lord Acton in his review of Lea's work in *The History of Freedom of Thought and other Essays* (1909), p. 567. The chronicler, Caesarius Heisterbach, does not relate a fact, but tells a story, which may or may not be fact.

II

The Beginnings of the Inquisition

Originally jurisdiction over heresy belonged to the ordinary ecclesiastical courts, heresy being classed with such other offences as adultery and breach of contract, which came under ecclesiastical purview. [1]

The special tribunal of the Inquisition came into being because these courts proved defective for the trial of heresy. In the first place, the new offence became so frequent that the ordinary courts were unable to support the large additional burden without impairing their efficiency in the performance of their original duties.

How, then, did it happen that whereas heresy had become a formidable danger in the twelfth century, the institution of the special tribunal did not take place until the thirteenth? The suggestion appears plausible that there must have been some other cause besides the mere spread of heresy to account for the birth of the Inquisition at that date. [2]

The answer is that it took time for heresy to be recognized as sufficiently serious to warrant the creation of an entirely new organization, and before the magnitude of the task of repressing religious error was fully apprehended. [3]

In the second place, the papacy during this period was much preoccupied with more pressing concerns, particularly the investiture question, which involved the supreme issue as to the pre-eminence of secular or spiritual authority in Christendom.

When once attention had been thoroughly arrested by the problem, the deficiencies of the existing spiritual courts for the new work became apparent. Overwork was by no means the only drawback. The character of the judges was at fault. Even after the Hildebrandine reforms, bishops still remained feudal barons with many inevitable secular distractions; archdeacons and other lesser officials were often venal and incapable. [4]

In any case the very nature of diocesan authority militated against success. It was too purely local to be effective against offenders who could easily migrate from one part of the country to another. Even more serious was the lack on the part of the existing officials of special training and knowledge, especially in theology, which were found necessary, since heretics often evinced diabolical familiarity with the text of Scripture. [5]

Lacking such special equipment and being badly pressed for time on a diocesan visitation, the bishop was apt to come to a hurried and arbitrary judgment, frequently falling back upon the device of the ordeal when the defendant pleaded 'not guilty.' Both the Councils of Rheims of 1157 and of Verona of 1184 ordered that suspects of heresy should be submitted to this test. But the method was never felt to be satisfactory, was strongly condemned by Ivo of Chartres and Alexander III, and so emphatically denounced by the Fourth Council of the Lateran in 1215 that it disappeared from the practice of lay as well as spiritual courts.

Another disadvantage under which the episcopal courts laboured in dealing with heresy was their procedure, that of Roman Law.

There were two systems—those of *denuntiatio* and *accusatio*. In the former some person in authority—in ecclesiastical cases the archdeacon—brought forward a charge founded upon his own personal knowledge. In the latter the charge was based on information tendered by a private individual to the authorities.

Owing to the fact that the archdeacon was a very busy man, the Church was largely dependent on the second method in the

II: THE BEGINNINGS OF THE INQUISITION

prosecution of heresy. But the average person had no inducement to lodge a charge. He was in danger of private vengeance if he did so; equally important, by Roman Law he was expected to prove his case, being in the event of failure liable to the same penalty which he had himself alleged against the accused. Seeing that, should he prove his case, he was entitled to the property of the prisoner either in whole or in part, this stipulation was a salutary and indeed necessary check, not only on malice but cupidity. [6]

This mode of procedure, which though indicative of its origin in the rudimentary idea of private justice was certainly equitable, did not commend itself to the Church, once it had become determined upon the extirpation of heresy. The difficulty of obtaining convictions greatly increased when, instead of small isolated communities, the Church was faced by a great organization like Catharism, widespread and secret in its movements. It was clear that episcopal jurisdiction must be strengthened.

The Edict of Verona was an attempt in this direction. It was resolved to make use for prosecution of common report, the public opinion of the locality.

Archbishops and bishops were to visit in person, or through their archdeacons, once or even twice a year every parish in which heresy was supposed to exist, and were to compel men whom they thought of trustworthy character or, if they thought fit, all the inhabitants of the neighbourhood, to denounce those whose manner of living differed from that of good catholics. Such bad characters were to purge themselves by a solemn oath on the gospels before the bishop (*purgatio canonica*); if they refused—and Cathari were likely to be unwilling owing to their views regarding oaths—their refusal was to be construed as tantamount to a confession of heresy. [7]

We have here a method of enforced delation, the bishop proceeding upon the evidence so obtained (*diffamatio*) without the formalities of the *accusatio*. In other words the bishops are to make an *inquest*, so that from this date, 1184, we have in existence an episcopal inquisition. [8]

The decree does not appear to have been very effective, and after the Albigensian Crusades—it being necessary to follow that success by the institution of systematic prosecution of heresy for fear of the recurrence of trouble [9] – similar regulations were made by Councils, sitting at Avignon in 1209 and at Montpellier in 1215, also in the Fourth Council of the Lateran of the latter year. There was a new feature in the introduction of a priest in addition to a trustworthy layman as informer against heretics. [10]

The Council of Narbonne (1227) went a step further in ordering the bishops to appoint in each parish *testes synodales*, to make diligent enquiry concerning heresy and other matters and give information to their bishops. [11]

The phrase 'synodal witness' is new, though it may easily designate the same persons as those nominated by the previous councils. However this may be, the 'synodal witnesses' are entrusted with a new duty. They are not merely to inform, but to search out. This advance was to be anticipated; the informer easily blossoms out into the detective. Here we have a system of local inquisition, which is enjoined again by a Council sitting at Toulouse two years later, which requires the synodal witnesses to visit all suspected houses and hiding-places. [12]

It is doubtful whether the orders of these two Councils were ever acted upon. In any case, not even the most well-intentioned reform of their procedure could make the episcopal courts satisfactory for the trial of heresy. The bishops are repeatedly urged to bestir themselves even on pain of deprivation. [13] The fact was that some special machinery had to be devised.

On the other hand, the authorization of the system of inquisition was of the utmost importance. It was fully recognized by Innocent III, who in his Decretals carefully distinguished it from the two other judicial methods of *accusatio* and *denuntiatio*. [14]

Innocent was not thinking only, or perhaps mainly, of heresy in introducing a new judicial method—but of clerical reform. Even when the offence of a prelate was a matter of common notoriety it was difficult to bring the crime home to him when the system of *accusatio* required the concurrence of seventy-two witnesses. That system sheltered the high in office; and it was therefore, from the reformer's point of view, defective.

The greatest of the popes had given his imprimatur to a system, which beginning in the ecclesiastical courts, was, owing to its manifest advantages, destined to make a triumphal progress in

II: THE BEGINNINGS OF THE INQUISITION

the temporal courts also, eventually supplanting the system of *accusatio* altogether.

The definite starting-point of the Inquisition has been attributed to many dates. One enthusiast went as far back as Creation, finding the first inquisitor in the Almighty Himself, and successors to Him in Jacob, Saul, David, Eli, Jesus Christ, John the Baptist and St. Peter among others. [15] Less ambitious authorities, content to go no further back than the Middle Ages, have discovered the starting-point in the legatine commission entrusted by Innocent III to Pierre de Castelnau, Arnaud of Citeaux and their colleagues. [16]

Whether they, with their lieutenant St. Dominic, were inquisitors or not turns on the interpretation of the word. [17] In the loose general sense of searchers out, certainly they were—as others had been before them. The plain fact is, there were inquisitors before the Inquisition existed. But in the strict technical sense of officers of a tribunal specifically set apart for jurisdiction over heresy, they clearly were not. [18] The tribunal of the Inquisition was not in existence in the pontificate of Innocent III.

On the other hand, we have by this time advanced a considerable distance on the road to the formation of a new tribunal. Heresy has been recognized as so dangerous as to justify the organization of a crusade against it. The bishops' courts have been found so defective in dealing with heresy that the device has been adopted of sending special commissioners to try to do what they have failed to do. The method of judicial procedure by *inquisitio* in place of *accusatio* has been officially approved. It wants but one other step to bring us to the foundation of the permanent delegacy for the prosecution of heretical pravity, which is the Inquisition.

This step was taken by Pope Gregory IX, who may therefore legitimately be said to have founded the Inquisition. Both the episcopal courts and the experiment of the occasional legate had been insufficient.

Gregory made use of a powerful weapon which came readily to hand in the two great Mendicant Orders. Recognizing their potential utility, Gregory, herein followed by Innocent IV, showered upon them all manner of special privileges and exemptions and bound them by this means peculiarly to the service of the papacy. They were preeminently fitted, as it happened, for the special service of prosecuting heresy. They were still young in the first white heat of a new enthusiasm, while their zeal and their purity made them both influential and popular.

They were also often endowed—especially the Dominicans—with high intellectual gifts and early acquired a great reputation as subtle and learned theologians. Thus while their poverty, their single-mindedness and their good works were an answer to anti-sacerdotal attacks, their theological attainments enabled them to combat the dialectical arguments of the heterodox.

The uniformity and permanence of inquisitorial practice came largely from the selection of the two orders of the Friars to undertake the jurisdiction over heresy. In so far, therefore, as the choice of a particular date or incident for the commencement of an institution can be otherwise than arbitrary, it is legitimate to fix upon the delegation by Gregory IX of jurisdictional powers almost exclusively to the members of the Franciscan and Dominican orders as marking the beginning of the Inquisition as an organized tribunal.

Actually the first delegation made by Pope Gregory in regard to heresy was made neither to a Franciscan nor a Dominican, but to a man notorious for his extraordinary relations with Saint Elizabeth of Hungary, namely Conrad of Marburg. Whatever his status to begin with, he certainly became a delegate possessed of very wide powers eventually.

He was in fact an inquisitor in precisely the same sense as Pierre de Castelnau and Arnaud of Citeaux had been inquisitors; and the question of his precise authority has exactly the same bearing on the question of the beginnings of the tribunal of the Inquisition as the question of their authority—no more. [19]

Eight days after the bestowal of the commission upon Conrad, namely on June 20, 1227, Gregory entrusted another inquisitorial commission to a Dominican. This, however, is not the significant date. The decisive event is the addressing of two bulls to France in April 1233, the first to the bishops, the second to the Preaching Friars.

II: THE BEGINNINGS OF THE INQUISITION

The first explains that owing to 'the whirlwind of cares' and 'the presence of overwhelming anxieties,' under which the bishops labour, the Pope has thought it well to divide their burdens and has decided to send the Preaching Friars against the heretics of France. The bishops are earnestly exhorted to treat the Brothers kindly and lend them all assistance in the fulfilment of their office.

The second, and by far the more important bull, addressed to the Friars, empowers them 'to deprive clerks of their benefices for ever, and to proceed against them and all others without appeal, calling in the aid of the secular arm if necessary, and coercing opposition, if needful, with the censures of the Church, without appeal.' [20]

Some have detected in these bulls an apologetic tone indicating uncertainty on Gregory's part as to whether the bishops would acquiesce in this invasion of their powers, and it is also no doubt true that 'the character of his instructions proves that he had no conception of what the invasion was to lead to.' [21]

On the other hand, there is here the clear evidence of a matured conception, based upon the experience of the multiplication of special commissions to individual legates, of a permanent delegation. [22] By 1235 this system had penetrated not only through France, Toulouse and Burgundy, but also Lombardy, Sicily, Aragon, Brabant, Germany. [23]

The inquisitorial commissions entrusted to the Friars, it is important to note, did not involve the extinction of episcopal jurisdiction in matters of heresy. In 1234 Gregory is found threatening the bishops of the province of Narbonne, if they do not show due energy against heretics, and making no mention of the new authority. [24] As yet the friars-inquisitor are regarded only as a more efficient supplement to the ordinary ecclesiastical tribunals.

Gregory intended that bishops and inquisitors should work together, and bishops had to concur in the friars' sentences. Plainly there was not unnatural antagonism, bishops wishing to treat inquisitors simply as expert advisers, inquisitors aiming at becoming the real judges. In 1247 Innocent IV treats the bishops as the real judges: yet in the numerous sentences of the celebrated inquisitor, Bernard de Caux, recorded between 1246 and 1248, there is no trace of episcopal concurrence. [25]

In 1248 the Council of Valence had to bring pressure upon bishops to observe the sentences of inquisitors. [26] Between 1250 and 1254 the director of the proceedings of the Carcassonne inquisition who makes the interrogations and imposes the sentences is a bishop: but it is not certain whether he was acting in his episcopal capacity or as a special papal commissioner.

Such commissions were rarely given to bishops, as the popes much preferred, as a rule, to use the friars. The root fact was that to perform his special duties efficiently an inquisitor needed to devote his entire time and attention to them: and thus, as it became more and more apparent that heresy was no mere ephemeral menace which could be stamped out once for all, but a lasting trouble which had constantly to be met, so the Inquisition, first regarded as a temporary expedient to deal with an emergency, developed into a permanent institution.

So also the efforts of the bishops, either to retain the jurisdiction over heresy in their own ordinary courts or to superimpose their authority over the inquisitor in his extraordinary court, were alike doomed to failure. As a matter of fact, probably the average bishop was too much immersed in other cares and interests to trouble to secure his prerogative in the matter of heresy. [27]

Thus it was that before the end of the thirteenth century the Inquisition had come to be an intrinsic part of the judicial organization of the Church.

The pontificate of Gregory IX is in more ways than one a critical period in the history of the repression of heresy. It saw the first clear authorization of the death penalty for the obdurate heretic.

Capital punishment had at times been shown to be the popular remedy for heresy; it had sometimes been adopted by the secular arm, sometimes approved by the clergy. But it had not been legalized in the empire, formally sanctioned by the temporal law of the world, as the general rule of Christendom.

The first public law of Europe enjoining it was the work of the Emperor Frederick II. That the most extraordinary member of the house of Hohenstaufen, being a man who despite a curious

II: THE BEGINNINGS OF THE INQUISITION

strain of superstition in him was a rationalist and a sceptic, should have been responsible for this legislation may at first sight appear astonishing.

An Italian, not a German, brought up among the half Greek, half Saracen influences of Sicily, drawing his inspiration rather from Averrhoës and Arab free-thought than from any Christian source, amazingly versatile, poet, lover of learning, statesman, diplomatist, his outlook upon the world was altogether individual, his intellect powerful and singular, untrammelled by convention.

He was a medley of strange contradictions: he protected Jews and Mussulmans; he persecuted heretics. The Averrhoïst heretics from Islam interested him, the heretics from Catholicism not at all.

On November 22, 1220, Frederick produced his first constitution for Lombardy. [28] This repealed the penalties of Frederick Barbarossa in his edict of 1184, confiscation of property and outlawry, penalties severe enough, because outlawry in the Middle Ages was a terrible punishment, putting the culprit at any man's mercy. This first constitution appears to have been inspired by Honorius III. [29]

A second constitution of March 1224, published at Catania for the whole of Lombardy, first introduced the death penalty—death at the stake; but at the discretion of the judge, the loss of the tongue might be substituted. [30]

In 1231 in the Constitutions of Melfi, which applied indeed only to Sicily, this element of choice was no longer included, and the penalty was made absolutely death by fire. In 1238 this regulation was extended to the empire, being afterwards introduced into the Sachenspiegel and Schwabenspiegel of Germany. [31] Thus death by fire became the recognized punishment for heresy in the empire.

In 1226 Louis IX issued ordinances prescribing severe punishments for heretics but at the time the use of the stake was general in France, and it was formally accepted as the legal punishment in the *Etablissements* of Louis IX in 1270. [32]

In view of what Frederick II did in his Constitutions, some historians have placed upon his shoulders the full responsibility for the horrors of the stake. This is both unfair and unhistorical.

The blame attaches to no single man. The fact of first giving sanction in civil law to death by burning is certainly important, but the importance can easily be exaggerated.

Frederick was only giving legal recognition to the actual practice of France and Germany; only introducing what was customary elsewhere into Italy, where tolerance had on the whole been general.

Some importance should also be attached to the revival of the study of Roman Law, which showed that Manichæans had suffered death in days before Constantine. In the part played by Frederick II we shall be wise to recognize not something catastrophic but rather a link among very many in a lengthy chain of development. [33]

Nor must we forget the significance of the order that burnings are to take place 'in conspectu populi.' This is surely an answer to a popular demand that the execution of heretics should be made a public example, a salutary spectacle? The examination of the force of public opinion is almost always more fruitful than that of the motives of individuals, however powerful.

What was the attitude of the Church in its crusade against heresy towards the action of Frederick? Being crucial, the question is exceedingly controversial. There have been apologists for the Church who have argued that the whole blame for the burning of heretics rests with the secular power, that Gregory IX had a positive aversion to the idea, that Frederick II's laws against heretics are to be regarded as an attempt to humiliate the Pope and wrest from the Church jurisdiction which properly belonged to it. This argument makes the establishment of the Inquisition a measure of self-defence, a strategic blow delivered in the great war between the secular and ecclesiastical anthorities. [34]

This ingenious theory will not stand close examination.

There is in the first place the prima facie probability that an unorthodox emperor, anxious to utilize the question of heresy in a conflict with the papacy, would rather protect than prosecute it.

In the second place, there is really no evidence for discovering in Frederick's action an elaborate Machiavellian device; while we have sufficient evidence that Gregory did approve the burning of heretics. [35]

II: THE BEGINNINGS OF THE INQUISITION

There seems clearly to have been clerical influence behind the constitutions. The constitution of 1224 has been ascribed to the influence of a certain German prelate, Albert, Archbishop of Magdeburg, imperial legate in Italy, who wanted to see heretics treated in Italy as they were in his own country, and who therefore induced the emperor to give legal sanction to the death penalty. [36]

Even more significant would appear to have been the part played by the Spanish Dominicans, Guala and Raymond of Peñaforte. Guala was Bishop of Brescia in 1230, and Brescia was the first town to place among its municipal laws the Lombard Constitution of 1224. The Bishop was in constant communication with Gregory, and when Rome followed the example of Brescia, it is surmised, though it cannot be proved, that Guala was responsible for this, as also for the Constitution of 1231. [37]

This is conjecture, and so is the alternative theory which attributes the legal establishment of the death sentence not so much to Guala as to Raymond. [38] Whatever may be the truth concerning clerical influence prior to the promulgation of the Constitutions, the question of the subsequent attitude of the Church towards them is not a matter of conjecture.

In his bull, *Excommunicamus*, Gregory orders that heretics, condemned by the Church, shall be handed over to the secular arm and punished by the merited penalty ('puniantur animadversione debita').

What this punishment is, is not expressly mentioned, but inasmuch as all other possible penalties are mentioned by name — imprisonment, excommunication, infamy, deprivation of civil rights etc., we are left by a process of elimination with the death penalty as the only conceivable end for the obdurate heretic abandoned to the secular arm. [39] Only wilful blindness can misinterpret the phrase 'animadversione debita,' especially as its meaning seems to be forcibly illustrated by the practice of the Senator Annibaldi who ruled Rome in Gregory's name.

In 1231 he issued a decree, introducing the imperial constitution into the city and establishing that each senator, on admission into office, must pronounce the ban of the city against all heretics in it, seize upon all who are pointed out as heretics by the inquisitors and punish them within eight days from the passing of sentence. Here Annibaldi used the Pope's euphemism, 'merited penalty.' The same year several heretics were seized in Rome, some imprisoned, but the obdurate burnt. [40]

If it may still be felt that there is some doubt regarding the personal feeling of Gregory IX about Frederick II's action, there can be no doubt at all as to his successor, Innocent IV, who gave complete pontifical sanction to the Constitutions by inscribing them *in extenso* in a bull entitled *Cum adversus haereticam pravitatem*, issued in 1245. [41]

The Church did more than simply give its formal approval to secular legislation against heresy: it saw to it that the lay authority put its legislation into practice. It was for the Church to seek out, arrest, examine and condemn the heretic; it was the function of the State to free the Church from the guilt of blood by arranging for the actual execution of the impenitents, the canon thus being reconciled with harsh necessity. Apportionment of its duties in the matter of heresy to the State by the Church was no new thing in the days of Gregory and Innocent.

The resolutions of earlier councils had referred significantly to the danger of popular revolutions, did not the secular authority play its part, and had threatened that disobedient lords might find their lands and goods given away to other more zealous or more prudent. [42]

The decree of Verona (1184) had claimed excommunication as the penalty for failure to execute the imperial laws (at that time those of Barbarossa) against heretics; and the Fourth Council of the Lateran, enjoining an oath upon all secular rulers that they will banish all heretics from their lands, declares their vassals to be absolved from fidelity in the case of non-compliance. [43]

Already, before the days of Innocent IV, it had been made perfectly plain that the Church not only desired and expected the execution by the secular authority of its own laws against heretics, but that it was prepared to use all available means to compel it to do so.

Innocent IV placed the coping-stone upon this system by his famous bull issued to all the lay rulers of Italy in 1252, known as *Ad extirpanda*. [44] This bull is remarkable for the thorough and

II: THE BEGINNINGS OF THE INQUISITION

systematic nature of its provisions. To the end that the pest of heresy may be uprooted, all lay rulers are to swear to carry out the laws against heresy on pain of fine and of being held an infamous perjuror and fautor of heretics. [45]

Every civil magistrate within three days of his entrance into office is to appoint twelve good catholics, two notaries, two senators, two friars from the Prædicants, two from the Brothers Minor, whose duties are to search out heretics, seize their goods and hand them on to the bishop. These officials are to enjoy a variety of privileges and to be free from all interference in their work.

The civil magistrate is to hand over all heretics within a fortnight of their capture either to the bishop or the inquisitors. [46] Those condemned are within five days of sentence to be dealt with by the secular arm in accordance with the Constitutions (of Frederick II).

The secular authority is also required to inflict torture on those heretics who refused to confess or inculpate their confederates, to see to the exaction of fines and destruction of heretics' houses, to keep lists of those defamed of heresy. [47]

These statutes, and all others which might subsequently be added against heresy, are to be religiously preserved in the statute-books of every city, on pain of excommunication for any non-compliant official, of interdict for any recalcitrant city. No attempt must be made to alter these laws or to observe any other laws which may be found to be in contradiction to them. [48]

Various slight alterations and modifications were subsequently made in the terms of this all-important fulmination. But with only insignificant revisions it was reissued by Alexander IV in 1259, and in 1265 by Clement V, who, however, inserted the word 'inquisitor' in places where previously only bishops and friars had been designated.

In the main the bull remained unaltered, a lasting monument both to the Church's power in that age and of its attitude towards secular action with regard to heresy. It was for the Church to command where her interests were concerned; she expected to be obeyed and, in case of defiance, had the necessary force to compel obedience.

Excommunication and interdict in those days were no empty words. To be placed outside the communion of the Church was even more than being outlawed from the Empire, equivalent to being placed outside civilization; it was to be deprived of all rights, made any man's legitimate prey.

And if excommunication was more injurious to the simple citizen than to the prince or noble, still the latter had much to fear. The ban of the Church relieved his vassals from their allegiance and was an invitation to his enemies to march to his despoil. In the eyes of the believer excommunication entailed something very much worse than even such material trouble and loss; it meant the exclusion from the greatest of means to salvation on earth, the imperilling of salvation in eternity.

There was, as a matter of fact, no reluctance on the part of the state to the task of persecuting heretics, as the secular legislation of Henry II of England, Barbarossa, Alfonso II and Pedro II of Aragon abundantly testifies. But few secular magistrates would be willing to incur so great a material and spiritual risk as excommunication merely for the sake of a few fanatical schismatics.

The argued justification of the now well-established system of persecution, of which *Ad extirpanda* is the coping-stone, we find in Thomas Aquinas.

In the Church's procedure in respect of heretics he sees proof of her deep mercy and charity. Her aim is the retrievement of the prodigal, his penitence and return to the fold. She aims not at punishment, but forgiveness. For the penitent all is well, only for the obdurate and those who have relapsed after reconciliation is there punishment. It is meet that these should suffer, for in her kindness to the individual the Church must not jeopardize the welfare of the whole community. Heresy is the most terrible of all offences. To corrupt the faith is a far worse crime than to corrupt the coinage. [49] The latter is an aid to our temporal existence, the former an absolute necessity for the eternal life of the soul. If then the coiner be deemed worthy of death, how much more the heretic!

The argument of analogy is fortified by the text of Scripture. The methods of the Inquisition are found to be justified by

II: THE BEGINNINGS OF THE INQUISITION

Christ's words: 'If a man abide not in me, he is cast forth as a branch, and is withered, and they shall gather them and cast them into the fire and they are burned.'

Thus the sayings of the Founder of Christianity were made to sanction a system of cruelty utterly abhorrent to the whole tenor of His teaching. [50]

---

[1] The *potestas inquirendi* handed down from Christ to St. Peter has been annexed to the episcopal dignity. See Ludovico à Paramo, *op. cit.*, book ii, p. 89.

[2] C. Douais, *L'Inquisition; ses origines, sa procédure* (Paris, 1906), pp. 45-6.

[3] Sometimes a new heresy was not at once recognized as one at all. Gregory VII was indulgent to Berengar of Tours and Alexander III congratulated Peter Waldo. See Luchaire, *op. cit.*, p. 38.

[4] See De Cauzons, *op. cit.*, vol. i, p. 333.

[5] Simancas, *op. cit.*, Tit. xxv, p. 150, 'De Episcopis.'

[6] See Lea, vol. i, p. 310; De Cauzons, vol. i, pp. 378-80. See also A. Esmein, *Histoire de la Procédure Criminelle en France, et spécialement de la Procédure inquisitoire* (Paris, 1882), pp. 66-78; in English version, *A History of Continental Criminal Procedure*, Continental Legal History Series, vol. v (Boston, 1913), pp. 3-11, 78-94.

[7] Mansi, *op. cit.*, vol. xxii, pp. 476-8.

[8] See De Cauzons, vol. i, p. 393.

[9] At first sight it may appear as though the completeness of the success of the Albigensian Crusade rendered further action unnecessary. This would appear to be the implication in Douais' *L'Inquisition*, pp. 45-6. As a matter of fact it was rather a case of following up an initial advantage.

[10] Mansi, vol. xxii, p. 785.

[11] *Ibid.*, vol. xxiii, p. 24, § xiv. '*Ut sint in omnibus parochiis, qui de haeresi & manifestis criminibus inquirant.*'

[12] *Ibid.* p. 194. § i.

[13] Mansi, vol. xxii, pp. 989-90.

[14] See De Cauzons, vol. i, p. 395; P. Fournier, *Les Officialités au Moyen Age* (Paris, 1880), pp. 266-9.

[15] Ludovico à Paramo, pp. 27, 31, 49.

[16] Luchaire, *op. cit.*, p. 71. 'En 1204, il enleva aux évêques, pour la donner aux légats, la juridiction ordinaire en matière d'hérésie, première esquisse du procédé d'où sortira l'Inquisition.' To which M. Douais rightly retorts: 'Il n'est pas exact de dire que le Pape enleva aux évêques la juridiction ordinaire en matière d'hérésie. Il ne leur enleva rien.' *L'Inquisition*, p. 67. See, however, De Cauzons, vol. i, p. 414. 'Sans enlever donc aux évêques le droit de juger les hérétiques, les rescrits romains constituaient, à côté de leur tribunal, un pouvoir, pouvant juger lui aussi, avec des juges d'une juridiction plus étendue que le leur, ayant le droit d'exiger des chefs des diocèses l'obéissance à leur autorité. Il suffisait d'assurer à ce tribunal nouveau les moyens d'exécuter ses sentences et de le rendre permanent, pour avoir l'Inquisition.'

[17] For claim that Dominic was the first inquisitor, see Ludovico à Paramo, pp. 95-6; Douais, *L'Inquisition*, pp. 25-6; De Cauzons, vol. i, p. 421 n. Dominic was certainly more than a missionary preacher; he examined and condemned heretics. See Acton, *op. cit.*, p. 554.

[18] It has been said, truly, that it is neither the crime, nor the procedure, nor the penalty that makes the inquisitor in the strict sense; but his character as a permanent *judge-delegate* for the cause of heresy. Douais, *L'Inquisition*, pp. 37-8.

[19] For text of commission to Conrad, see Frédéricq, *Corpus*, vol. i, p. 71, No. 72. '…diligenter et vigilanter inquiras heretica pravitate infectos in partibus memoratis, ut per illos, ad quos pertinet, zizania valeat de agro Domini extirpari.' Douais on this comments (*op. cit.*, p. 53 n.), 'Si Conrad eut été inquisiteur, c'est à lui que ce soin eût d'abord incombé comme juge.' The argument is invalid. The appeal to the assistance of the secular arm is normal and certainly does not prove Conrad not to have been an inquisitor. See Lea, vol. ii, p. 319, 'This was in effect an informal commission as inquisitor-general for Germany'; and De Cauzons, vol. i, p. 449.

[20] For text of the bull, *Ille humani generis*, see Mansi, vol. xxiii, pp. 74-5; Frédéricq, *Corpus*, vol. i, No. 83, pp. 82-3. The Friars are urged to demolish the heretics who 'sicut cancer serperent in occulto, & velut vulpes latentes niterentur vineam Domini Sabaoth demoliri.'

[21] Lea, vol. i, p. 328. *Cf.* Tanon, *op. cit.*, p. 175, who considers that Lea does not attach sufficient importance to these bulls.

[22] The first bull delegating inquisitorial powers to the Brothers Minor in collective fashion is apparently one issued by Innocent IV, Jan. 13, 1246. See Frédéricq, *Corpus*, vol. i, No. 122.

[23] See De Cauzons, *op. cit.*, vol. i, p. 446 n. 'La transformation des inquisitions épiscopaux en juges pontificaux, a été la vraie fondation de l'Inquisition; telle qu'elle est connue et louée par certains, abhorrée par d'autres. Or, cette transformation s'est faite progressivement, par tâtonnements autour

II: THE BEGINNINGS OF THE INQUISITION

des années 1230-1233, non par édit général, plutôt par rescrits spéciaux. Les dominicains ont été l'occasion d'un bon nombre de ces rescrits, mais non de tous.'

[24] See Lea, vol. i, p. 330.

[25] *Ibid.*, p. 339.

[26] *Ibid.*

[27] Tanon, *op. cit.*, pp. 177-80.

[28] *Historia Diplomatica Friderici Secundi*, Huillard-Bréholles (Paris, 1852-61), vol. ii, pt. i, pp. 4-6; *Monumenta Germaniae historica*, G A. Pertz (Hanover and Berlin), vol. iv, pp. 242-5; Frédéricq, *Corpus*, vol. i, pp. 70-1, No. 71.

[29] See Maillet, *op. cit.*, ch. ii; Frédéricq in *Revue historique*, p. 310. This edict was drawn up five days before the coronation ceremony by the Curia and sent to receive the imperial signature, so that it might be published in the Emperor's name in St. Peter's. For Frederick's promise to assist the Pope against heresy, see Frédéricq, *Corpus*, vol. i, p. 70, No. 70.

[30] Huillard-Bréholles, vol. ii, pp. 421-3; G. A. Pertz, vol. iv, p. 252. 'Presenti edictuli constitutione nostra in tota Lombardia inviolabiliter de cetero valitura duximus sanciendum ut quicumque per civitatis antistitem vel diocesanum in qua degit post condignam examinationem fuerit de haeresi manifeste convictus et hereticus judicatus, per potestatem, consilium et catholicos viros civitatis et diocesis earumdem ad requisitionem antistitis illico capiatur, auctoritate nostra ignis judicio concremandus, ut vel ultricibus flammis pereat, aut si miserabili vite ad coercitionem aliorum degerint reservandum, eum lingue plectro deprivent, quo non est veritas contra ecclesiasticam fidem invehi et nomen Domini blasphemari.'

[31] Huillard-Bréholles, vol. i, pp. 5-8; Pertz, vol. ii, p. 242; Mansi, vol. xxiv. pp. 586-8.

[32] Havet, *op. cit.*, pp. 169-70.

[33] For arguments ascribing the responsibility to Frederick, see Havet (passim) and J. Ficker, *Die Gesetzliche Einführung der Todesstrafe für Ketzerei in Mittheilungen des Instituts für oesterreichische Geschichtsforschung* (1880), pp. 177-226, 430-1. See also C. Moeller in *Revue d'histoire ecclésiastique* (Louvain, vol. xiv, 1913); *Les Bûchers et les Autos-da-fé de l'Inquisition depuis le Moyen Age* (pp. 720-51), esp. pp. 725-6; Maillet, *op. cit.*, p. 87, and De Cauzons, *op. cit.*, vol. i, pp. 293-7: 'La théorie qui met sur le dos de Frédéric II la responsabilité des mesures de répression sanglante, du bûcher en particulier, est née de tendances apologétiques mal comprises, car vouloir concilier l'Inquisition avec nos idées modernes est une chimère.' Also Tanon, *op. cit.*, p. 462. These laws 'n'en sont pas moins en une grande importance pour le temps où elles ont été rendues, en présence des difficultés que l'Eglise

rencontrait, en Italie aussi bien qu'en France, de la part des autorités laiques, pour assurer la répression de l'hérésie, en donnant à cette répression la sanction nouvelle de l'autorité impériale elles devaient aider puissamment l'Eglise à vaincre ces résistances.'

[34] See Maillet, *op. cit.*, in ch. ii; Douais, *L'Inquisition*, ch. 5, esp. pp. 141-2; also De Cauzons, vol. i, pp. 296-7 n., and Moeller, *op. cit.*, pp. 727-8.

[35] Lea, vol. i, pp. 227-8. 'We can imagine the smile of amused surprise with which Gregory IX or Gregory XI would have listened to the dialectics with which the Comte Joseph de Maistre proves that it is an error to suppose, and much more to assert, that Catholic priests can in any manner be instrumental in compassing the death of a fellow creature.'

[36] Havet, p. 174; Douais, *L'Inquisition*, p. 122.

[37] Havet, p. 176; Acton, *op. cit.*, p. 555.

[38] Acton, *op. cit.*, p 557. 'The five years of his abode in Rome changed the face of the Church... Very soon after Saint Raymond appeared at the Papal court, the use of the stake became law, and the inquisitorial machinery had been devised and the management given to the priors of the order. When he departed he left behind him instructions for the treatment of heresy, which the Pope adopted and sent out whenever they were wanted... Until he came, in spite of much violence and many laws, the popes had imagined no permanent security against religious error, and were not formally committed to death by burning. Gregory himself, excelling all the priesthood in vigour and experience, had for four years laboured, vaguely and in vain, with the transmitted implements. Of a sudden, in these successive measures, he finds his way, and builds up the institution which is to last for centuries. That this mighty change in the conditions of religious thought and life, and in the functions of the order was supported by Dominicans, is probable. And it is reasonable to suppose that it was the work of the foremost Dominican then living, who at that very moment had risen to power and predominance at Rome.'

[39] See De Cauzons, vol. i, pp. 301-3.

[40] Frédéricq, *Corpus*, vol. i, pp. 78-80, No. 80, *Capitula Senatoris Annibaldi et populi Romani edicta contra Patarenos*. See Gregorovius, *City of Rome*, vol. vi, pt. 1, pp. 156-61. Heretics were at this time numerous in the States of the Church, Viterbo, Perugia and Orvieto also in Lombardy. Some of these, the Arnoldists at any rate, were also Ghibellines. 'The Inquisition now became another instrument in the hands of the Pope for the subjection of the people.'

[41] Mansi, vol. xxiii, pp. 586 *et seq.*

[42] Council of Rheims, 1148, Frédéricq, *Corpus*, vol. i, No. 31; Montpellier, 1162, *ibid.*, No. 35; Lateran, 1179, *ibid.*, No. 47.

[43] Verona, 1184, Frédéricq, *Corpus*, No. 56; Montpellier, 1195, *ibid.*, No. 58; Fourth Lateran, 1215, *ibid.*, No. 68. See also Mansi, vol. xxii,

II: THE BEGINNINGS OF THE INQUISITION

pp. 987-8; Eymeric, *Directorium*, pt. ii, question 46, p. 378.

[44] In Mansi, vol. xxiii, pp. 569 *et seq.*

[45] § 1.

[46] §§ 3, 5, 12-15.

[47] §§ 24, 25, 31.

[48] § 37.

[49] *Summa*, 2, 2, qu. 11, arts. 3 and 4. 'Multo enim gravius corrumpere fidem, per quam est animae vita, quam falsare pecuniam, per quam temporali vitae subvenitur. Unde si falsarii pecuniae vel alii malefactores statim per saeculares principes juste morti traduntur, multo magis haeretici statim ex quo de haeresi convincuntur, possunt non solum excommunicari, sed et juste occidi.' Vacandard (p. 176) answers: 'Such reasoning is not very convincing. Why should not the life-imprisonment of the heretic safeguard the faithful as well as his death? Will you answer that this penalty is too trivial to prevent the faithful from falling into heresy? If that be so, why not at once condemn all heretics to death, even when repentant? That would terrorize the wavering ones all the more. But St. Thomas evidently was not thinking of the logical consequences of his reasoning. His one aim was to defend the criminal code in vogue at the time. That is his only excuse. For we must admit that rarely has his reasoning been so faulty and so weak as in his thesis upon the coercive power of the Church and the punishment of heresy.' St. Thomas's logic is sounder than his apologist's, if his humanity is less! It is not St. Thomas's logic that is at fault, but the standpoint of mediæval Christianity, which it is vain to seek to harmonize with modern humanitarianism.

[50] St. John, xv, 6. Vacandard, p. 177. 'To regard our Saviour as the precursor or rather the author of the criminal code of the Inquisition evidences, one must admit, a very peculiar temper of mind.' So judged, again by modern humanitarianism.

III

The Spread of the Inquisition through Europe

By the willing labours of the two Mendicant orders the Inquisition was introduced into most of the countries of Europe during the course of the thirteenth century.

Sometimes the two co-operated, as for example in Aragon, Navarre, Burgundy and Lorraine. But there was a good deal of jealousy between them, and sometimes friction, so that it was generally found expedient to assign Franciscans and Dominicans to different areas.

Thus the former were given the eastern portion of France south of the Loire; the latter the western. Italy was also divided, each order being allotted carefully defined districts by Innocent IV in 1254. Northern France, Germany and Austria were entrusted to Dominicans; eastern countries, Bohemia and Dalmatia, to Franciscans.

The tribunal met with varying measures of success in the different countries of Europe, and in early days encountered considerable opposition and other difficulties in each.

In Languedoc the way for the Inquisition had been well prepared by the Albigensian Crusade: yet even so it was far from smooth. The zealous proceedings of Guillem Arnaud and

III: SPREAD OF THE INQUISITION THROUGH EUROPE

his assistants provoked the bitterest popular resistance. [1] An assistant, Ferrer, was expelled from Narbonne; Arnaud himself from Toulouse. But his unconquerable spirit, assisted by Gregory IX's support, triumphed over popular hatred.

Particularly in 1241 and 1242 the inquisitors were exceedingly active, so much so that in desperation certain Cathari set upon Arnaud and several others and did them to death. Not by such means could the Inquisition be worsted.

The Count of Toulouse, who had been planning to reassert his independence, was forced to become completely reconciled to the papacy, and as an outward and visible sign of submission to take up arms against his own subjects by besieging the last fortress of Catharism in the land, the fortress of Montségur. The fall of Montségur and the holocaust of heretics which followed it, together with improved organization, enabled the Inquisition to make better headway.

A new difficulty, however, arose in 1290 in the shape of strong protests against the alleged cruelties and injustices of two inquisitors, Nicholas d'Abbeville and Fulk de Saint-Georges. The complaint that Nicholas had condemned the innocent and wrung false confessions by cruelty was laid before Philip IV.

There was particularly strong feeling aroused by the posthumous proceedings taken against a noted citizen of Carcassonne, a great friend of the Franciscans, named Fabri, who was accused of having been hereticated on his death-bed. The defence of Fabri's memory was undertaken by a remarkable man, a Franciscan, named Bernard Délicieux.

The inquisitors represented Délicieux as a deliberate adversary of their tribunal but when in 1301 Philip sent two representatives into Languedoc to inquire into the causes of trouble, they called to their assistance the resolute Franciscan, who suggested the suspension of the inquisitors pending investigation.

The case was argued out before the King, who came to the conclusion that the complaint had been justified, that the inquisitors had been guilty of grave excesses, of lawless exactions and the manipulation of evidence, and took the unprecedented step of removing both Nicholas d'Abbeville and Fulk de Saint-Georges.

At the same time he deprived the inquisitors of the right to make arbitrary arrests. Philip's attitude towards the activities of the tribunal in Languedoc was not based upon principle, but was dependent upon the varying circumstances of his quarrel with Boniface VIII. Thus when, as at this time, French king and pontiff were quarrelling, it was demonstrated that the Inquisition in France existed only on sufferance and that its peculiar privileges, derived from the papacy, automatically ceased during such disagreement.

On the other hand, in 1304, when a reconciliation between the combatants had been effected, a compromise was arranged: whereby it was settled that royal officials should give every assistance to the inquisitors, when called upon to do so; but on the other hand these officials were to visit the inquisitorial prisons, and to prevent abuses, and independent action on the part of inquisitors without the co-operation of the bishops was to cease.

It was not long before complaints against the Inquisition were renewed—the most important charge being that good catholics were forced into pleading guilty to heresy by the use of torture and imprisonment. [2]

This time an appeal was made to the Pope, Clement V, who sent two cardinals to investigate at Carcassonne and Bordeaux. [3] They seem to have discovered many abuses in the management of the prisons and to have become satisfied of the genuineness of some at any rate of the allegations against the tribunal; and Clement made a praiseworthy attempt at reform.

In 1312 the Council of Vienne [4] issued a number of canons to this end, known as Clementines, which required that in the infliction of torture the inquisitors must have the concurrence of the bishop, also in the supervision of prisons. Excommunication was threatened against any who should abuse his power in order to satisfy personal animus or greed. The restrictions imposed on inquisitorial action by the Clementines were most bitterly resented by the great inquisitor Bernard Gui. [5]

With the death of Clement such vexation disappeared. The Clementines were indeed republished by John XXII, but it was at once clear that he had no desire to interfere with the Inquisition.

III: SPREAD OF THE INQUISITION THROUGH EUROPE

The feeling of freedom enjoyed by the Inquisition in Languedoc is evidenced by its triumph over its former enemy, Délicieux. During the days of Pope Clement he had been suffered to live in peace; now he was charged with having impeded justice and with having compassed the death of Benedict XI by poison. Overcome by repeated tortures, he threw himself upon the mercy of the court; found guilty on the first charge, he was condemned to perpetual imprisonment.

This event in 1319 marked the victory of the Inquisition in Languedoc. Now without fear of opposition it could prosecute its labours in persecution, systematized, unremitting, relentless. Heresy was extirpated, the finishing touch to the Albigensian Crusades supplied, and the distinctive features of southeastern France, as far as possible, blotted out.

The irony of the situation is that in accelerating this process the Inquisition was unconsciously assisting the aggrandizement of the royal power of France, with whose centralizing policy the existence of so powerful an independent tribunal was eventually found to be incompatible.

The beginnings of the attempt to extirpate heresy north of the Loire are associated with the hated name of Robert le Bugre who, armed with a somewhat vague authority from Gregory IX, is found active from the year 1233 in La Charité, Péronne, Cambrai, Douai, Lille, his aim—it has been said—'not to convert but to burn.' [6] He aroused the jealousy of the bishops, who informed the Pope that heresy' was non-existent in their provinces.

The results of Robert's enthusiastic labours convinced Gregory that the episcopal assurances had been misleading, that heresy was in reality rampant, so that he entrusted his delegate with a special commission and ordered the bishops to support him. Thus fully recognized, the inquisitor traversed Flanders, Champagne, Burgundy in a passion of religious energy, finding many victims and producing widespread consternation. But his career was a short one: found guilty of numerous excesses, he was deprived of his commission and relegated to prison.

After this we do not hear of holocausts. There was, in reality, little heresy in northern France, and the Dominicans, to whom the scouring of heretics in the country was entrusted, had not a great deal to do. Their labours, however, received the wholehearted support of Louis IX, who liberally supplied them with money; their tribunal was well organized, the officers vigilant.

The first *auto-da-fé* recorded to have taken place in Paris occurred in May, 1310, when a woman called Marguerite la Porète was the principal victim. She had written a book, the thesis of which was that the sanctified soul could without sin satisfy all the cravings of the flesh. Her followers would appear to have been the chief prey of French inquisitors in the latter part of the century.

There are illustrations during this period of the efficacy of the Inquisition even against powerful personages, most notably perhaps Hugh Aubryot, *prévôt* of Paris [7] and builder of the Bastille, who, incurring the animosity of the University of Paris, found himself brought up on a flimsy charge and condemned to perpetual imprisonment; but in France the Inquisition did not rest on very secure foundations.

It might be useful when heresy was rife and the proceedings of inquisitorial confiscations brought money into the royal exchequer; but success in coping with heresy, that is to say efficiency on the part of the tribunal, rendered it no longer an object of solicitude to the crown. [8]

By far the most notable fact concerning the Inquisition in France was its dependence on the crown. An interesting illustration of its subordination was given in 1322, when the tribunal absolved a certain abbot from the charge of heresy.

The *procureur-général* was not satisfied with this finding and appealed against it, not to the Pope, but to the Parlement. The matter was one clearly coming within the province of a spiritual, not a temporal court, yet the Parlement calmly assumed jurisdiction at the instance of the royal officer.

A yet more outstanding case arose in 1330, when Philip sent a representative, de Villars, to redress encroachments by ecclesiastical courts upon royal courts in Toulouse. Being ordered to produce his registers by de Villars, the inquisitor of Toulouse appealed not to the Pope but to the King.

In 1334 Philip, making known his royal pleasure that inquisitors shall enjoy their ancient privileges, makes it clear that they are to

III: SPREAD OF THE INQUISITION THROUGH EUROPE

be regarded as derivative from the crown. The inquisitor is looked upon as a royal official. [9]

The two most noteworthy inquisitorial trials in France were both of a political nature, the state making use of inquisitorial machinery for its own ends, those of the Templars and Jeanne d'Arc.

The great Schism, and still more the Pragmatic Sanction of Bourges, by weakening the hold of the papacy, enlarging the independence of the Gallican Church, and aggrandizing the Parlement still further weakened the position of the Inquisition.

Not only the Parlement but the University of Paris was a formidable antagonist and rival. The latter arrogating to itself a supremacy in theological matters, regarding itself as arbiter in all matters of doctrinal speculation, acquired the authority which the Inquisition lost.

The tribunal was still active in the fifteenth century, but it was finding the question of expenses a difficult problem, and the growth of indifference to the penalty of excommunication made its task harder. An effort was made by Nicholas V in 1451 to restore the former powers of the Inquisition and a wide definition was given to its authority. In France, however, it had lost too much in prestige to allow of its being revivified. [10]

When Protestantism entered the country in the sixteenth century it was not the Inquisition that was employed against it, but the University of Paris and the so-called *chambre ardente* of the Parlement—national institutions under royal control. The days of the Inquisition in France were over.

The history of the Inquisition in Germany opens with the careers of Conrad of Marburg and Conrad Tors, who carried on a fanatical crusade against Waldenses and different pantheist sects, of which the Amaurians and Luciferans were the chief, the methods of their persecution being purely arbitrary and leaving the accused practically no opportunity of defence. Conrad of Marburg's execrated existence was terminated by his murder in 1233. [11]

That inquisitors were working in Germany through the latter part of the thirteenth century we know; but they do not appear to have accomplished much.

After the publication of the Clementines, however, new efforts were made to suppress the Beghards and similar unauthorized associations, but the work seems to have been carried out rather by episcopal courts than by friars specially deputed by the pope. It was not until 1367 that, with the appointment by Urban V of two Dominicans, a thorough attempt was made to organize the papal inquisition in Germany.

Pressure was brought to bear upon the Emperor Charles IV, and in 1369 he issued edicts extending the fullest possible authority to the papal delegates with a view to the eradication of the Beghards. Under threat of severe punishment all prelates were enjoined to obey the orders of the inquisitors with a good grace, while in order that their privileges might be secured certain high nobles were appointed to protect the inquisitors and to deal with any complaints they might make. Later on, Charles IV entrusted the Inquisition with a new power, that of censorship, for the Beghards derived much of their influence from the circulation of pamphlets in the vernacular.

Fortified by the imperial favour, Kerlinger, the principal delegate, displayed great energy at Magdeburg, Erfurt, Mühlhausen, etc.; and notwithstanding the occasional opposition of a jealous episcopate the Inquisition had made such good progress by 1372 that it had apparently succeeded in driving its enemies out of northern and central Germany. These were the days of the Flagellants and of the dancing mania as well as of Beghards and the Brethren of the Free Spirit.

There certainly seemed to be no less need of organized repression; nevertheless the Inquisition in Germany after the days of Kerlinger tended to lose ground.

Complaints made against its recent proceedings were found on investigation by Gregory XI to be well founded, and the papal disapprobation armed the episcopate against their rivals. As in France, so in Germany, the Schism had the effect of still further reducing the influence of the Inquisition. Persecution of Brethren of the Free Spirit continued late into the fifteenth century: but heresies far more formidable than the mystic antinomianism which had been the characteristic heresy of Germany were about to dawn.

III: SPREAD OF THE INQUISITION THROUGH EUROPE

The intellectual force in men such as Johann Wessel, Reuchlin and Erasmus had infinitely greater power than a perverted pantheism. And when Lutheranism took hold upon Germany, there was no powerful Inquisition to check it. Had there existed in Germany such a tribunal as had stamped out Catharism in Languedoc, it might, so far as we can tell, have succeeded in silencing Luther, while he was still an unknown monk of Wittenberg, before he had come to apprehend the full significance and the ultimate developments of his famous theses.

But when the hour came of the Church's greatest danger from heresy in Germany, the weapon which it had used with such tremendous effect in earlier days had been hopelessly blunted.

The publication of Frederick II's Constitutions and the activities of Gregory IX introduced a new era of intolerance into Italy, where apparently tolerance had hitherto been the rule. Inquisitorial activity started in Florence and in Rome; it was carried further afield by several perfervid champions, of whom the best known was Peter Martyr, the scene of whose labours was first Milan, then Florence.

In Florence persecution had become so menacing that a formidable rising was provoked. This was the occasion of Piero's coming to Florence, where he at once formed a company on the model of one he had created in Milan for the protection of Dominicans, giving it the title of the *Compagnia della Fede*.

The Florentine inquisitor, with this protection, proceeded with his persecutions and a bloody conflict was provoked, which was as much one between Guelph and Ghibelline as between orthodox and heretic. Peter Martyr led the banners of the faith with such good effect that the forces of heresy were badly beaten and the city reclaimed for Pope and Inquisition. He was next engaged as inquisitor in Cremona and again in Milan. Though there is no record of his proceedings there, that he was as ardent a persecutor as before seems proved by his assassination at Milan in 1252.

As a practical memorial of the martyr's enthusiasm a voluntary association similar to those which Piero had himself founded in Milan and Florence was formed among the upper classes of the principal Italian cities, the name *crocesegnati* being given to them, for the protection and assistance of inquisitors. As devoted and determined a champion as even Peter Martyr had been was found in Rainerio Saccone of Vicenza, who undertook the task of combatting heresy in Lombardy, where it was very strong owing to large migrations from Languedoc. Reorganizing and strengthening the Lombard Inquisition, he achieved considerable success with the assistance of Innocent IV, who at this time issued the bull *Ad extirpanda*. [12]

With the accession of Alexander IV activity in Lombardy was still further increased. The number of inquisitors was doubled, and Rainerio announced that hitherto he had shown incomparable mildness, henceforth he would be rigorous.

The chief obstacle—a formidable one—to the complete success of the tribunal in Lombardy was the power of the two great Ghibelline nobles, Eccelin da Romano and Uberto da Pallavicino, into whose territories not even a determined inquisitor dared enter. A crusade against the former, organized by Alexander, after varying fortunes proved successful, and the March of Treviso, hitherto closed to the Inquisition, was laid completely open.

A yet greater success was achieved by the Holy See in 1266, when Charles of Anjou triumphed over the Ghibellines at Benevento and the kingdom of Sicily passed into full obedience to the papacy.

Two years later the last of the Hohenstaufen in a futile attempt to regain Italy for his house perished on the field of Tagliacozzo, and with him the last chance of the imperial faction. Uberto had espoused the cause of Conradin and the young prince's failure involved the downfall of the Lombard noble.

The story of the fortunes of the Inquisition in Italy being largely that of the fortunes of Guelph in the strife with Ghibelline, this Guelph triumph naturally gave a great impetus to the Inquisition. It had now practically no political obstacle to face, and it immediately extended its operations into all Ghibelline territories, and although there were occasional outbursts against it, as in Parma in 1279, when the populace attacked the convent of the Dominicans and burned the registers of the Inquisition, still the setbacks were not serious.

III: SPREAD OF THE INQUISITION THROUGH EUROPE

Ghibelline districts were particularly attacked, and it was said that in such centres it was impossible to feel safe, as in the eyes of the Church Ghibelline was apt to mean heretic. [13] It should, on the other hand, be noted that even during the period of the Inquisition's greatest ascendancy in Italy, there are instances of papal lenity in mitigation of the full rigour of the tribunal's practice. [14]

In certain parts of Italy the Inquisition did not thrive as in Lombardy and the Papal States. When Charles of Anjou established himself in the Neapolitan kingdom, one of his first proceedings was to plant the Inquisition there, and he gave it his own personal assistance in prosecuting its labours. On the other hand, it remained somewhat dependent on the crown and did not enjoy the whole-hearted support of the local magistrates. Perhaps more serious was the natural obstacle presented by the mountainous character of the country. In the island of Sicily the Inquisition had at no time much influence.

In another Italian state the Inquisition never succeeded in obtaining a thorough hold—Venice, ever zealous for its independence of outside control. When Gregory IX started his campaign against heresy, the republic held aloof; the Constitutions of Frederick II were not incorporated in its laws. Persecution indeed existed and the ordinary bishop's court existed as elsewhere in Christendom; but the Council, a secular body, maintained a supervision in cases of heresy. The Inquisition was not permitted to enter, and in consequence Venice became an asylum of refuge for heretics from other parts of Italy.

But in 1288 Nicholas V ordered the *signoria* to respect the laws of Pope and Emperor and facilitate the work of the Inquisitor of Treviso in whose province Venice ought to come. [15]

According to the recognized principles of the age, the attitude of the republic was indefensible. Venice, accordingly, gave way, but was able to effect a compromise, whereby the Inquisition was admitted, but on the other hand the edicts, imperial and ecclesiastical, were still not placed among the statutes of the city and the republic supervised the financial arrangements, defraying the expenses of the inquisitors, but at the same time receiving the profits of confiscations.

Thus one of the most prolific sources of inquisitorial abuses was cut off, and at the same time the power of the purse retained supreme control for the state, the imposition of such important restrictions allowed the Inquisition no such prestige in Venice as it enjoyed in Lombardy. We find it at times being deliberately ignored by the *signoria*, and by the middle of the fifteenth century it had almost entirely lost such influence as it had possessed after the compromise of 1288.

In spite of its obtaining only partial ascendancy in certain states, the Inquisition achieved its purpose in Italy with marked success.

Catharism lasted longer there than in Languedoc, being found in Piedmont in the late years of the fourteenth century; but it was harried energetically, and early in the next century it was to all intents and purposes extinct.

Waldensianism lasted longer, having a much greater hold over the country. In 1352 we find that the Waldensian Church in Turin is nourishing and its numbers so great that no attempt is made at concealment. Gregory XI made special efforts to suppress the sect in Piedmont, but without complete success.

The next century saw another strenuous effort made by Yolande, the regent of Savoy, who with the co-operation of the inquisitor of Dauphine undertook a campaign for the extermination of the Waldenses, all her officials being by the Duchess's orders placed at the disposal of the inquisitors. For a time the persecuted in Savoy were under the aegis of Louis XI's protection; but on his death persecution was carried on assiduously.

In 1488 an attempt was made to put down the Waldenses by force of arms, but the 18,000 men to whom the task was entrusted met with a crushing defeat. The respite thus secured did not, however, last long, and in 1510 we find the Inquisition strengthened by the loan of troops by the secular power and using every means in its power against the heretics.

In the Alpine valleys the sect was never stamped out by the Inquisition and remained in existence there until the terrible Vaudois massacres of 1655. But as a result of the persistent persecution, emigration on a considerable scale was continually taking place, the majority of those who took flight finding a

III: SPREAD OF THE INQUISITION THROUGH EUROPE

refuge in Calabria and Apulia, where the arm of the tribunal scarcely ever extended.

The great Schism was disastrous in weakening the respect felt in Italy not only for the papacy, but the Church as a whole, and the Inquisition inevitably suffered in consequence.

The fame of the Inquisition in the Spanish peninsula has been so great that it has almost wholly eclipsed its fame anywhere else in Europe, and its history has been in every way peculiar.

It acquired an altogether unique position there; enjoyed an extraordinary prestige and unexampled success. It earned an undying notoriety. It became, as nowhere else in Europe, a national institution, closely identified with the monarchy, but also popular, a possession of which the people were proud. It was a terror to the foreigner; it made the name of Spaniard feared all over the world. It had played a great part in welding the Peninsula together, in driving out alien elements, producing national homogeneity. It played, then, a large part in Spanish history, and obtained a very marked influence on the national mind and character.

But the Inquisition which is so famous or infamous in Spain was the creation of Ferdinand and Isabella. It was a quite distinctive institution, much more monarchical than papal, and it was not directly the offspring of the tribunals that had existed in the Peninsula in the Middle Ages.

The most remarkable fact concerning the Spanish Inquisition is that this country in which the Inquisition most abundantly flourished, the country which won for itself easy pre-eminence for its close fidelity to the Church, its zealous and implacable intolerance of any sort of dissent, was originally equally pre-eminent for its tolerance.

The ardour of persecution in Spain was not due to something ingrained in the national character; it was to a very large extent the offspring of the methods pursued by the Holy Office; and the deep implanting of the Holy Office was due to deliberate policy on the part of the Spanish monarchy from the days of Ferdinand the Catholic and Isabella. [16]

In the Middle Ages the civilization of Spain was very largely Saracen. From such sources south of the Pyrenees came that distinctive culture of Languedoc, out of which heresy had so luxuriantly sprung. From a non-Christian people came the philosophy, the mediæval, astronomical, botanical knowledge, the art and fancy and the industrial skill and trading enterprise of the country. Moreover, Jew and Christian met and did business together.

So long as such intermingling of different races, religions, civilizations continued, the soil was not favourable to the success of such an institution as the Holy Office.

Heterogeneity is productive of tolerance. The Inquisition's day could only come with the determination to drive out the other elements and to make the Peninsula European in race, Christian in religion and ideas. The success of that policy had to wait for the union of the two crowns of Aragon and Castile. Prior to that, the Inquisition obtained success in Aragon only, being unknown in Castile and Leon, while in Portugal, though there were inquisitors in the country from 1576 onwards, they appear to have been singularly inactive.

In Aragon [17] persecution was originally organized by the state, both Alfonso II and Pedro II promulgating severe legislation against heresy, though a sort of inquisition, consisting partly of clergy, partly of laity, was established by a statute issued at Tarragona in 1233.

The real beginnings of the Inquisition in Aragon are, however, to be traced from the intervention of the redoubtable Raymond of Peñaforte, a year or two after this. He was instrumental in introducing members of his own order to deal with heresy; and in 1238 Gregory IX entrusted the prosecution of heretics to the Mendicant orders in Aragon.

In 1242 a very important Council held at Tarragona formulated rules of procedure for the guidance of inquisitors. [18] The Aragonese inquisition did not, however, show great activity until the opening of the fourteenth century. Its activity then produced popular protest, and in 1325 the Cortes, with the royal assent, prohibited inquisitorial methods of torture. It is doubtful if this was intended to apply to ecclesiastical as well as lay courts. If it was, it had no lasting results, as can be seen from Eymeric's 'Directorium.' [19]

III: SPREAD OF THE INQUISITION THROUGH EUROPE

This very remarkable inquisitor assumed office in Aragon about 1360. With the most genuine and most exalted conceptions of the dignity and importance of his position, he put forward the utmost claims for the Holy Office; yet from the internal evidence of his treatise itself, it does not seem to have flourished in Aragon in his day. He makes loud complaints of its poverty. But the fact that so little came into its exchequer from confiscations and that so ardent and active an inquisitor should apparently have accomplished so little seems mainly to prove that heresy was not a serious menace in Aragon at this time.

In the next century the history of the Aragonese inquisition is neither interesting nor important, and the end of that period brings us to the era of Torquemada and the organization of a great inquisition for the united kingdoms of Spain.

In Eastern Europe [20], the Inquisition never succeeded in obtaining much of a foothold. The main stronghold of Catharism was in lands east of the Adriatic, but here the papacy possessed but scant authority. A practically abortive attempt was made to deal with the heretics in 1202; but in the twenties the Mendicants in their untiring zeal, using Hungary as their base and with the armed support of Calomar, Duke of Croatia and Dalmatia, waged successful warfare against the Bosnian Cathari until the retirement of the crusaders in 1239.

Their withdrawal meant that no effectual result was achieved, and Catharism remained powerful not only in Bosnia, but Dalmatia, Bulgaria, and Roumania. The bishops of Bosnia found themselves compelled to leave the country.

In 1298 an attempt made by Boniface VIII, to establish an inquisition in the lands south of Hungary from the Danube to Macedonia, came to nothing. But in 1320 an inquisitor named Fabiano, with the assistance of the king of Hungary, made some progress against the heretics, and a further effort was made in 1336 by Dominicans with the co-operation of the Hungarian king. Though in 1378 Urban V congratulated Louis of Hungary and the friars on having restored two thousand heretics to the fold, four years later that monarch himself complains that practically all his subjects are Cathari, good Catholics being very sparse in numbers.

In 1407 Sigismund made an attempt to establish himself in Bosnia, his cause obtaining papal recognition as a crusade against Turks and Manichæans; but his attempt ended in failure.

In 1432 an Observative Franciscan, Giacomo della Marca, already well known as a stalwart persecutor of heretics in Italy, embarked upon a missionary enterprise in Slavonia, and is said by his eloquence to have made numerous converts; but his success was short-lived, as he was recalled by Sigismund to help in the religious troubles of Bohemia.

After the days of Sigismund there was little chance of success for missionary or inquisitor beyond the Adriatic. The flow of the Ottoman advance swept over the Balkans, and the Cathari were converted not to Catholicism but to the faith of Islam.

The Inquisition did not make its appearance in Bohemia until late, the first inquisitors being appointed in 1318, when they were also appointed for Poland, Cracow and Breslau. There is hardly any record of what they did. In 1335 Benedict XII made fresh efforts, and between 1350 and 1380 there was considerable activity against heretics, but it was the activity of the ordinary episcopal courts, not of a papal inquisition.

There was a large diffusion of Waldensianism in the country; apparently early in the century there had been a certain number of Luciferans. With the Church in Bohemia in a low state of efficiency and the rise of the anti-sacerdotal movement which led to Husitism, the task of repression was a difficult one, and there was no inquisition. One of the causes of the indignation of the Czechs at the treatment of Hus at Constance was the fact that Bohemia had had virtually no experience of the Inquisition and was ignorant of its methods and procedure.

After the silencing of the two great heresiarchs, the Council commissioned the Bishop of Litomysl with inquisitorial powers for the extirpation of heresy in Bohemia; but as the Czechs were ravaging the Bishop's territories at the time he dared not show face.

The next expedient of the Council was the arrangement that Husite heretics should appear before special inquisitors in the Roman Curia. As it was in the highest degree unlikely that any Husites, particularly after the fate of Hus and Jerome, would quit

III: SPREAD OF THE INQUISITION THROUGH EUROPE

their own country to answer charges of heresy, this was a futile proceeding, as was the next—a formal citation to 450 nobles, who had signed a protest against the burning of Hus, to appear before the Council on the charge of heresy. It was evident that no inquisition could exist in Bohemia as long as the country remained rebellious, predominantly schismatic.

The success of the Inquisition invariably required the support of popular opinion, magisterial acquiescence, or armed force. Neither of the first two being forthcoming, the last expedient had to be tried. A crusade was preached against the heretic people, to which only one upshot was anticipated. But the anti-Husite crusade ignominiously failed, and the Czech people kept the Inquisition from entering their borders.

In Scandinavian lands the Inquisition never penetrated, and it only once, for a very brief period, made its appearance in the British Isles. This was in connection with the suppression of the Templars. At first when the horrible accusations which led to the undoing of the great military order were bruited about, Edward II refused to credit them, the record of the order in England giving no colour to the charges.

When, however, Clement V issued his bull, *Pastoralis praeeminentiae*, in which he stated that the heads of the order had made confession of the crimes imputed to the iniquitous knights, and called upon the potentates of Europe to take action for their suppression, the English king ordered the apprehension of the Templars in England and the sequestration of their property. No further action was taken.

But in September 1309 two papal commissioners, who had been appointed more than a year previously, made their appearance. Instructions were issued that all Templars not yet seized should be brought to London, York, or Lincoln, where the commissioners with the co-operation of the bishops of the respective dioceses were to hold inquiries. Similar orders were also dispatched to Scotland and Ireland, where the inquisitors appointed delegates.

The proceedings in London began on October 20, 1309. The Templars, on examination, one and all protested the innocence of the order; outside witnesses, as a whole, gave the same testimony.

The object of the inquisitors being conviction, this was most unsatisfactory. Progress was much better on the Continent, where torture was employed; torture they must use also in England, therefore. They obtained from the King an order to the custodians of the prisons to allow the inquisitors to do with the bodies of the Templars what they pleased, in accordance with ecclesiastical law.

Still only meagre results were obtained and Clement became indignant. He wrote to Edward saying that he had heard that he had refused the use of torture as being contrary to the laws of his kingdom. No law could be permitted to over-ride the canon law, and in interfering with the work of the Inquisition the King had been guilty of a very serious offence. He was offered remission of sins if he would withdraw his prohibition of torture.

Thus urged, Edward again sanctioned the use of 'ecclesiastical law,' but this time mentioned torture expressly, explaining that he gave his sanction in deference to the wishes of the Pope. Even thus the inquisitors could not make headway. They were on alien soil in England; the country took ill to the special tribunal and its methods. All that they achieved was that the knights eventually confessed themselves so 'defamed' for heresy as to make it impossible for them to make the 'canonical purgation,' and therefore undertook to perform any penances enjoined upon them. Such were the total results attained by the Inquisition in England.

Persecution of heretics there had been before, under the Assize of Clarendon; persecution in plenty there was after, under *De Haeretico Comburendo* and in the days of the Tudors; but the persecuting authority was always the State—no such international, papally-controlled tribunal as the Holy Office.

Mary Tudor might have achieved a large measure of success in her Romanist policy had she been able to make more use of those international agencies, of which Jesuit propaganda and the Holy Office were the two chief, which provided the sinews of the Counter-Reformation movement.

As it was, the British Isles remained free from inquisitorial influence; their judicial customs and principles of justice being uncontaminated by those methods of procedure by *inquisitio*,

III: SPREAD OF THE INQUISITION THROUGH EUROPE

by the use of torture, which the example of the Holy Office introduced into so many civil courts on the Continent.

---

[1] Tanon, pp. 52-3. To be carefully distinguished from Arnaud of Citeaux, Archbishop of Narbonne, the former papal legate in Languedoc.

[2] Vaissete & Devic, *op. cit.*, vol. iv, p. 118. 'Clamor validus et insinuatio luctuosa fidelium subditorum, processus suos inquisitionis negotio a captionibus, quaestionibus, et excogitatis tormentis incipiens personas quas pro libito asserit haeretica labe notatas, abnegare Christum... vi vel motu tormentorum fateri compellit.'

[3] See Douais, *Documents*, vol. ii, pp. 303-27. for particulars of this commission.

[4] The bull, *Multorum querela*, incorporated in the decrees of this Council. See Frédéricq, *Corpus*, vol. i, No. 170.

[5] *Practica*, p. 188.

[6] Tanon, p. 116.

[7] See Tanon, p. 119. Also the case of the Sieur de Partenay, the most powerful noble of Poitou. Lea, vol. ii, p. 124.

[8] Lea, vol. ii, p. 130.

[9] Lea, vol. ii, pp. 130-2.

[10] *Ibid.*, p. 140.

[11] Lea, vol. ii. p. 341.

[12] Lea, vol. ii, p. 221. For Peter Martyr, see Ludovico à Paramo, pp. 108-9.

[13] Lea, vol. ii, p. 236.

[14] Lea, vol. ii. p. 236. Notably Honorius III in 1286, who, in consideration of the fidelity of the people of Tuscany, relieved them of the penalties of heresy, save in the case of the relapsed, so that the children of heretics could enjoy the property confiscated from their parents.

[15] *Ibid.*, p. 251.

[16] Ludovico à Paramo attributes the tranquillity of Spain to the beneficent influence of the Inquisition, *op. cit.*, p. 290.

[17] Llorente, vol. i, pp. 66-97.

[18] Mansi, vol. xxiii, pp. 553-8

[19] See eulogy of Eymeric in Ludovico à Paramo, p. 110.

[20] See Lea, vol. ii, pp. 290-315. For Bohemia, see pp. 427-505.

IV

The Composition and Procedure of the Tribunal

I

The popular fame that the Inquisition has gained is due to the terror which it aroused in the days of its greatness its terror was the result of the thoroughness and efficiency of its methods.

It was efficient, in the first place, because it was the product of experience. Its characteristics were those that had been *proved* to be necessary. The ordinary ecclesiastical courts had been found unsatisfactory for dealing with heresy because their business was too multifarious; the Inquisition was devoted to the trial of one offence and one only. The bishops had failed in part because they were not specially qualified for their task; the inquisitors were trained specialists.

In the second place, the tribunal was strong in having the support of the secular authority as well as of the papacy behind it.

Thirdly, it became widespread in western Christendom, so that flight was a doubtful salvation. It seemed ubiquitous, because the mutual co-operation between inquisitors of different districts, and indeed countries, was highly organized. It seemed all-pervading because of its apparent omniscience, due to the extensiveness of

IV: COMPOSITION AND PROCEDURE OF THE TRIBUNAL

its records and the thoroughness of its spy system. The victim, in short, was made to feel his helplessness before a power which seemed as strong and inexorable as fate.

The Inquisition owed much to the character of its judges. They were, at any rate, enthusiastic and hardworking. The half-hearted inquisitor was of rare occurrence. They were often ardent with the fiery and formidable zeal of fanaticism, believing themselves servants of God and surrounded by that aureole of sanctity, which gave their court the name and reputation of the Holy Office.

Often, beyond question they were cruel but, on the other hand, it is necessary to beware against accepting the traditional idea of the inquisitor as typical.

In the Middle Ages, when he flourished, the inquisitor was not popularly regarded as a man destitute of human sympathy, an ogre; he was regarded, on the contrary, with veneration. Often he was a man of high intellectual attainments; practically always he must have been educated and learned much beyond the ordinary; he had studied in school and university and was a theologian, if not also something of a philosopher and a lawyer. Often too he was the most upright and honourable of men; and it is plain that men like Bernard Gui and Nicholas Eymeric had the highest sense of their responsibilities and the loftiest ideals for their fulfilment.

Bernard Gui gives us a sketch of the ideal inquisitor. He is a man ardent in the faith; never slothful, yet not precipitate; never timid, but always cautious; never credulous, but ever ready to listen; resolute for truth and justice, yet merciful and compassionate; careful in his sentences that no ground shall be given for the charge of cruelty or rapacity. [1]

The inquisitor was a much privileged person, enjoying a plenary indulgence during the whole period of office, and he could only be excommunicated by the direct authority of the Pope. In every way he was under the panoply of special papal favour and protection. He had the right of granting indulgences—this being mainly used to encourage or reward witnesses and informants against heretics. [2]

Privilege was also extended to all assistants of the Holy Office. The assistants were numerous, consisting of delegates, often called vicars, *socii*, familiars, notaries, councillors, prison officials and simple messengers and other servants. To this list should be added the ordinary *curés*, whose services might be utilized to publish citations, make known the sentences of the tribunal, give testimony for or against their own parishioners.

The delegates were assistants of the inquisitors; to them was generally entrusted the task of asking preliminary questions and hearing witnesses, the role of a *juge d'instruction*. They thus relieved the inquisitors of most of the burden of the initial and formal proceedings; but they were strictly subordinates, their powers being carefully stated in their commissions, and they were, as a rule, appointed only for a particular cause and definite period. On the other hand, they might take the inquisitor's place in case of his illness or absence from any other unavoidable cause.

The *socius* was not, as his name seems to imply, a colleague, but only a companion, who merely accompanied the inquisitor on his journeyings in that capacity, and discharged no official functions, save that he might occasionally give informal advice.

The familiar, a most important and distinctive personage of the tribunal, might come from any class of society and usually came from men who lived in the world. A recluse was of no use for the duties the familiar had to perform. But once having adopted the calling (valued on account of its ecclesiastical privileges), the familiar became a member of a quasi-religious brotherhood. His duties were various.

A personal guard for the inquisitor had to be provided. The inquisitors had the right of arming familiars for this purpose, though the Council of Vienne of 1311 recommended that the number of familiars should be kept down to the minimum and that the right of arming them should not be abused. [3]

Familiars also visited prisons, and at *autos-da-fé* had to accompany the condemned and the penitent, exhorting them to unfeigned repentance, and encouraging them to submit to the punishments inflicted upon them. Lastly, and most important, the familiars were secret agents, and were as a rule remarkably efficient spies.

Another important officer was the notary. He was Write indispensable. The number of men qualified to fill the post, in days when writing was not a widely diffused accomplishment, was far from large; and the position grew to be one held in high esteem and much sought after.

The notary's main duty was to take down interrogatories and answers, and to keep the register of them. First of all he would take down rough notes and afterwards he would make a fair copy on a parchment for permanency. As the questions were put in the vernacular and the register kept in Latin, he had to be a translator as well as a clerk.

His task was so heavy that in some cases he was given the help of scriveners but every document had to bear his signature. It would be impossible to exaggerate the significance of this careful recording of evidence in the work of the Inquisition. All the papers were sedulously kept; often they were carefully indexed and annotated. In course of time the registers came to form a wonderful repository of information, which was of immense assistance to the tribunal.

As an illustration of how the careful preservation of exact and minute particulars of cases promoted the success of the Holy Office may be taken the case of an old woman apprehended in 1316. From the records it was ascertained that the same woman had as far back as 1268 confessed heresy and been reconciled. This discovery showed that the prisoner was already a relapsed heretic. [4] The meticulous transcription of some casual and apparently irrelevant remark made by a witness in one case might lead to the arrest of an unsuspecting citizen on the charge of heresy in quite a different part of the world years afterwards.

The councillors or experts—*viri boni* or *periti*—were usually chosen from the ranks of the clergy, priests, abbés, bishops—but they might also be laymen, and were often civil lawyers. Thus, at Pamiers in 1329 we find that out of fifty-one experts twenty are civil lawyers. [5]

The number of experts varied. Fifty is an exceptionally large number; but twenty or twenty-five quite common. [6]

To what extent the councillors had a practical influence in the inquisitorial process must remain doubtful. The idea was that they should act as a check on irresponsible inquisitors, as well as give professional legal opinion when such was needed; and from the frequent references to the system in papal bulls it certainly seems true that the popes showed anxiety to encourage the system of expert assistance as a restraint upon arbitrary action.

On the other hand, it is by no means clear that the system had much practical effect, since inquisitors were not bound to accept the advice tendered, and the number of the periti being so large, the volume of business transacted usually so great, it is doubtful whether any serious deliberation with the councillors took place in the majority of cases. Probably their presence was often purely formal, for the sake of giving additional solemnity to the condemnation of heretics. [7]

Still, it remains true that a place was provided in the inquisitorial organization for the experts; that the means of competent legal advice was forthcoming; that if the inquisitor was a reasonable man he would no doubt pay due heed to such advice on the purely legal aspect at all events of his cases, and also that the experts, being often men of importance, probably did have the power of making their influence tell upon occasion. The system was at all events a potential safeguard.

Finally, there must be mentioned, among the members of the tribunal, one of the most important—the bishop. The relations between bishops and inquisitors, frankly antagonistic in the early days of the Inquisition, probably always tended to be unfriendly. If the bishop, for his part, resented the new jurisdiction, which was a rival to his own, the inquisitor in his own court aspired to be supreme and to arrogate to himself a superiority over the bishop, which the latter was not likely to allow.

The bishop's position was not altogether easy. Required to take cognizance of heresy in his own court, he yet had also to officiate in the special court where the inquisitor, whatever his ecclesiastical status and whatever his pretensions, was bound to be always prime mover in the proceedings.

We know that the inquisitors often acted without the co-operation of the bishop. The relations between them remained none too clear until they were regulated by the Council of Vienne. They were to work together and to concur in the sentence. [8]

As a matter of fact, the concurrence of the bishop was apt to be a mere formality and his position in practice was bound to be

IV: COMPOSITION AND PROCEDURE OF THE TRIBUNAL

subordinate, the inquisitor being a delegate expressly charged by the Pope with the duty of trying heretics.

Such being the composition of the Inquisition, what was the extent of its province? What, technically speaking, was a heretic?

According to Raymond of Peñaforte, he was simply one who denied the faith. St. Thomas Aquinas maintained that no one was a heretic, unless he obstinately maintained an error after its erroneousness had been pointed out to him by an ecclesiastical authority.

One teaching, therefore, was that no one in ignorance could be a heretic. [9] Proof of previous instruction in the truth had to be forthcoming to show that a man was a heretic. But a broader interpretation tended to prevail, and the heretic to be considered as one who, on any grounds whatever, separated himself from the traditional faith of the Church. [10]

The mere fact of separation did not in itself constitute heresy; but every schism must end in heresy, because separation argues an error in belief touching the nature of the Church. Lack of respect for ecclesiastical, and especially papal, authority suggests denial of the faith. [11] To assert anything against the Scriptures, to add to them or subtract from them would be heresy. Certain forms of blasphemy and profanity would make a man at least suspect of heresy. [12]

Obviously the matter of interpretation gave abundant scope for casuistry. Bernard Gui's 'Practica' is an illustration of this. There was an obvious temptation for the inquisitor to discover heresy in all manner of disguises. [13]

Heresy was conceived as a most insidious as well as a most pernicious enemy, to be ferreted out in all sorts of strange lurking-places. The indefiniteness of the term—the inquisitor's definition is always a catalogue—was as a matter of fact unavoidable, seeing that the offence consisted, not in an overt act, but in an intention.

It was a crime of the intellect, a matter of the state of a man's mind and disposition. Sometimes the heresy might be revealed in an act, but very often there would be no formal act at all. The inquisitor must be a searcher of the heart and a prober into the obscure workings of the mind. [14]

It is necessary to add one simpler but important point. No one could be a heretic unless he had been baptized, unless he was a member of the Christian Church. [15] The infidel, the Turk, the Jew, did not come within the Inquisition's purview—unless he had at one time received the Christian religion. By birth or adoption the heretic must have been a Christian: for the heinousness of his crime consists in its being a repudiation, a rebellion.

The Inquisition formulated a number of classifications of heretics. In the first place, they used to distinguish between *affirmative* and *negative* heretics.

The former was one who deliberately avowed some opinion contrary to the faith before the tribunal; the latter was one who either denied being guilty of the incriminating word or act or else, while acknowledging it, protested that he had no culpable intention. [16]

In the second place, a distinction was drawn between the *perfected* heretic and the *imperfect*. The first not only held an error, but also practised the rites appertaining to it, modelled his life on its dogma; the latter merely believed the error without being guilty of the evil practices.

The inquisitors also recognized a class consisting of people who were not really heretics at all, perfect or imperfect, but merely people who gave evidence of heretical disposition or of tendencies which might lead them into heresy. In the fact of its taking cognisance of such a class lies one of the distinguishing features of the Inquisition. [17]

The tribunal deliberately dealt with, and had a specific treatment for, those who were merely suspected of crime. Suspicion was classified as light, vehement or violent. There was no precise definition of what was meant by each of these; it was generally left to the inquisitor to decide in each particular case what degree of suspicion existed.

It was most essential to avoid all contact with heretics. [18] A man proved to have saluted a heretic or listened to his preaching on a single occasion was regarded as *lightly* suspect; if he had done so more than once, he was *vehemently* suspect if he had done so frequently, he was *violently* suspect. [19] But such an offence as this, even if often repeated, was not regarded as in itself sufficient

IV: COMPOSITION AND PROCEDURE OF THE TRIBUNAL

evidence of actual heresy. It only made the offender a marked man. In such cases the Inquisition did not dismiss the accused as not guilty; it would not absolutely dismiss a case, unless satisfied that there was no proof whatever. This was due to the intangible nature of an offence which consisted in an intention.

The consequence was that the Inquisition, in order to be on the safe side, virtually created a minor offence of allowing oneself to be suspected of heresy. For every good catholic must realize that any connection with heresy, however remote, is contamination and therefore take the most elaborate precautions to avoid all contact.

To become an object of suspicion, therefore, meant either that the suspicion was after all well-founded (on the principle that there is no smoke without fire), or that the conduct which led to suspicion was inadvertent. Was it, then, unreasonable to require that the suspect should make a formal abjuration, to prove that in fact he had no sympathy whatever with heresy, that the suspicion was unfounded? Nor, surely, was it unjust to record such cases of suspicion in view of the possibility that the suspect might at some later date come up once more before the tribunal, when naturally his former offence would be legitimate evidence against him?

Such is the line of argument in justification of the penalizing of the suspected, as well as the convicted. The suspect is indeed guilty, not of the major offence of actual heresy, but of a minor offence of misdemeanour, improper or at least imprudent behaviour, unbecoming to a good catholic—an offence legitimately dealt with by the tribunal concerned with heresy.

Another class of offenders were fautors or defenders of heretics. To place any obstruction in the way of the inquisitors was an act of fautorship. A lord who neglected to pursue heretics out of his lands; anyone giving ecclesiastical burial to a heretic; one who in conversation excused a heretic or conferred any sort of favour, however slight, upon one—all these were fautors.

For a doctor to attend a heretic patient, a lawyer to plead a heretic client's case, was exceedingly dangerous, unless they could prove beyond all doubt that they did so in ignorance. The simplest deed of common humanity done to a heretic was in the view of the Church a sin. [20]

Certain crimes were triable by the Inquisition, not for themselves, but because they were indicative of false doctrine. Thus a usurer might be tried and punished by the Inquisition, not because he was a sinner, but because he showed that he did not regard himself as such. Similarly, a bigamist might be tried by the Inquisition, not because bigamy was an immoral thing — if he could prove that he acted under the stress of simple unreflecting passion the Inquisition would dismiss the case as not coming under its purview—but because his act evinced erroneous belief regarding the sacrament of marriage. [21]

It was the same with a number of other moral offences.

Adultery did not in itself come under the cognizance of the tribunal; but if the adulterer maintained that his transgression was not a sin, it did. There is, for instance, the case of a licentious priest living in concubinage being punished by the Inquisition, because he asserted that he was purified of his ill-living by the simple act of putting on his vestments.

In a word, an error in morals is triable only if it is also an error in belief. Otherwise, it is dealt with by the ordinary ecclesiastical courts. As it is arguable that a large number of crimes are indicative of doctrinal error, the Holy Office could put forward a rather sweeping claim to judicature over all manner of wrong-doing; but in practice there was probably not much trouble as a rule, the tribunal being kept sufficiently well occupied with offences *in intellectu*. Only when the implication of heresy was the significant feature of a crime was the Inquisition likely to be interested.

The list of offences coming within the sphere of inquisitorial judicature is completed with the mention of sorcery and witchcraft, practices essentially implying heresy.

II

The ingenious Ludovico à Paramo, ever anxious to discover warranty for all that the Inquisition was and did in the Bible, and particularly in the infancy of the human race, discovered the beginnings of the inquisitorial process in the Book of Genesis. Thus God was the first inquisitor; the call, 'Adam, where art thou?'

IV: COMPOSITION AND PROCEDURE OF THE TRIBUNAL

was a citation to a heretic; the coats of skins made for Adam and Eve were special garb for heretics, the original of the special garb, the *sanbenitos*, with which the Holy Office clad its culprits; and the deprivation of Adam and Eve of paradise was equivalent to the confiscation of the heretic's goods. [22]

We shall find a more practically helpful explanation of the procedure of the Inquisition if we content ourselves by remembering the origins of the tribunal in the Middle Ages.

The fundamental fact, which shaped the whole character of its judicature, giving it its essential distinctiveness apart from other judicatures, was the function of the inquisitor. Originally he had been, not a judge, but a missionary; he never became a judge simply and solely, he never entirely ceased to be a missionary. His primary object was not so much to pronounce a judgment as to guard the faith; his ambition not to condemn a heretic, but to reconcile him to the Church. Every impenitent heretic was in a sense a witness to inquisitorial failure, every penitent was a triumph.

The inquisitor, even when sitting in his tribunal, was not solely a judicial functionary; he was still a confessor, a spiritual guide. This fact is the key note to the procedure of the Inquisition, because it meant that the procedure was not simply and wholly judicial. The Inquisition aimed at being something more than a court. Its ultimate object was not secured by the simple judicial process of deciding the guilt or innocence of the accused; it sought the spiritual end of bringing the accused to a right state of mind and soul. [23]

Consequently, the inquisitor is always actuated by the desire to secure confession. That does not by any means necessarily involve conviction. What is wanted is that everyone arraigned before the tribunal should publicly in the proceedings acknowledge his acceptance of the Catholic faith. If he is not guilty, not a heretic at all, the inquisitor has reason for personal rejoicing—there is one scandal less to the Church and the faith. Or if the accused is guilty, but acknowledges his guilt and is of his own accord, without compulsion, willing to recant, again so much the better.

It was preferable that the lost sheep should voluntarily return, or allow itself quietly to be led back, into the fold than that it should have to be forcibly driven in. What the Church least desired was that the sheep should be lost altogether. Only if all means to secure reconciliation had failed, was it possible to acquiesce in such defeat.

But the Church, in giving the most earnest solicitude to the errant individual, had to think also, and yet more earnestly, of the whole community, and of the sanctity and majesty of the truth which the obdurate heretic had spurned. Consequently, a salutary example must be made, the penalty being duly solemn and impressive. But the mild methods first.

The second distinctive feature of the Inquisition was the methods of originating proceedings before it. Whereas, under Roman law, either the accusation by an individual or the denunciation by an official was necessary before proceedings could be initiated, an *inquisitio* could be instituted as the result of a *diffamatio*, the general report of the inhabitants of any community, a parish, a *seigneurie*, a town. It was indeed laid down that the *diffamatio* must be *apud bonos et graves*, people of standing and gravity of character.

This stipulation was no doubt something of a safeguard: nevertheless it remains true that, as no individual had to take upon himself the onus of showing that he had good cause for preferring a charge, the simple fact of unpopularity with his neighbours might be quite sufficient for the institution of proceedings against a man who was for any reason, just or unjust, taboo among them.

This method of justice belonged to Canon law; there was no trace of it in Roman law; but it has to be remembered that it was not instituted specifically against heretics, but rather against clerical wrong-doers in high places, who passed unchecked because the necessary number of accusers willing to take upon themselves the responsibility, and also possibly danger, of prosecution could not readily be found. [24]

Simple rumour by itself was not of great practical value. It had to be organized. Hence the ruling of Innocent III's decretal, *Licet Heli* (1199), relating to clerical abuses, that superiors are to keep diligent watch over their subordinates, so as to bring their misdoings before judicial authority; hence, as regards heresy,

IV: COMPOSITION AND PROCEDURE OF THE TRIBUNAL

the system of 'synodal witnesses,' whose specific duty it was to vocalize local public opinion or knowledge. The general vague *diffamatio* of the neighbourhood is by them so crystallized as to become of practical value in a court of law.

But while this system of using the depositions of the synodal witnesses and the village clergy, accomplished much, further organization was needed.

The additional device necessary was provided by the institution of the special papal delegates, who were inquisitors in two different senses—judicial officers, examining charges brought before them as members of a tribunal; but also procurators making the preliminary investigations prior to trial.

They had two distinct functions, two distinct inquisitions to make. These are technically *inquisitio generalis* and *inquisitio specialis*.

As the system became elaborated, the inquisitors had at their command a formidable spy system, carried on by their agents, the familiars. At the same time much encouragement was given to wholesale delation. The inquisitor or his vicar would make a sudden dramatic descent upon town or village, and deliver a solemn, perhaps menacing, exhortation to the inhabitants to proffer information against heretics. By thus appealing to the religious zeal or the apprehensions of the populace many accusations would be obtained, often from husbands and wives, parents and children.

But to reinforce such voluntary incriminations it was customary to proclaim a 'time of grace,' which lasted from a fortnight to a month. If within that period the heretic came forward, acknowledged his own guilt and gave any information he possessed against others, he would obtain either complete exemption or considerable alleviation from the penalties merited by heresy. This method, Bernard Gui assures us, was remarkably satisfactory. [25]

The *inquisitio generalis* being concluded, and prisoners obtained either by voluntary self-denunciations or on the information of others, the judge, according to canonical usage, had a choice of expedients. He could either proceed to an *inquisitio specialis* or make use of the method of *purgatio canonica*.

The second method had been solemnly adopted by the Church in 803. [26] It was an appeal to God. The accused solemnly swore by the Gospels that he was innocent, while those of his friends or neighbours willing to support him acted as his *compurgatores* and gave similar solemn testimony to his innocence, their number, from two or three to forty, varying in accordance with the degree of suspicion existing against him.

The device was obviously defective. Its only advantage lay in the impressiveness of its appeal to the devout mind, persuaded of the heinousness of the sin of perjury, while it allowed the innocent man to suffer, if he happened to be unpopular and could not prevail upon the necessary number of compurgators to assist him, and also allowed the guilty to go free, so long as he was not over-scrupulous as regards perjury and had the necessary popularity to persuade, or power to compel, others to act as his compurgators.

Thus, while the system of canonical purgation was never abolished, it had fallen into virtual desuetude before the end of the thirteenth century. [27] In practice the *inquisitio generalis* was followed automatically by the *inquisitio specialis*. The accused was served with a citation to appear before the tribunal and kept in prison pending his trial. [28]

In the case of those who had yielded themselves up of their own accord, the voluntary act constituted the confession, which it was the inquisitor's object to obtain. For those accused who refused to confess there followed the interrogatory. Here the inquisitor acted as prosecutor and cross-examiner, as a sort of *juge d'instruction*. [29]

Only the inquisitor's office, unlike that of the *juge d'instruction*, did not end with the completion of the interrogatory; having conducted the examination, he would also afterwards pronounce the sentence. The interrogatory resolved itself into an unequal contest between inquisitor and accused. It was unequal, in the first place, because there was always a presumption against anyone charged with heresy. As we have seen, it was an offence for anyone to be so criminally negligent in vitally important matters as to allow his conduct to give rise to the slightest rumour of heresy.

IV: COMPOSITION AND PROCEDURE OF THE TRIBUNAL

It was an excellent characteristic of both Roman and Canon law that the accused was held to be innocent until actually proved to be guilty. This characteristic was not shewn, in actual practice, in dealing with one accused of heresy. The mere fact of defamation tainted a man.

It was, therefore, a matter of very great difficulty for the defendant to demonstrate his innocence. He had to demonstrate it; for the mere fact of the *diffamatio*, whether well-grounded or not, was good evidence against him; and to free himself, he must rebut this evidence. The process was indeed so difficult that it was much safer to confess guilt at the outset than to labour to prove innocence.

In the second place, the duel was unequal because the inquisitor considered it perfectly legitimate to disconcert his adversary by means of disingenuous subtleties and subterfuges. It is only fair to add that the inquisitor adopted such devices because he believed that the heretic was apt to indulge in them and might save himself by clever equivocations unless dealt with astutely; and the inquisitor had a lively sense of the extreme undesirability of permitting a heretic to get the better of him in a duel of wits. Such a thing would be ignominious for the inquisitor; a blow to the Church and the truth.

We are told of some of the artifices practised by Waldenses. In answer to the question: 'What is Holy Church?' they will say, 'What you consider to be such,' or assert that they are simple illiterate men standing in need of instruction, and must leave it to the judge to express their beliefs in words. That the inquisitors may have found the rejoinders even of illiterate men at times disconcerting is likely. [30]

But it is certain that they practised their subtleties on many who had not the wits to cope with them: and, in any case, the inquisitor, being both examiner and judge, had an enormous initial advantage.

As a rule, the inquisitor or his vicar was extremely well equipped to conduct the interrogatory skilfully and successfully, even against the most redoubtable antagonists. They possessed, moreover, a rich repository of ready-made devices in the treatises written by the great masters of the inquisitorial art.

The difficulty of escaping from the tentacles of the inquisitorial process inspired Bernard Délicieux to say that even the orthodoxy of St. Peter and St. Paul would not have been sufficient to satisfy the tribunal. [31] It was held to be legitimate to surprise and confuse the defendant by a multiplicity of questions, which would involve him in contradictions. [32]

Altogether the dice were heavily loaded against the accused. Dismayed to begin with very likely by the simple shock of finding himself accused of the terrible crime of heresy [33], confronted by a formidable examiner, who was clearly bent upon securing a confession if at all possible, he had also to face the great obstacle presented by the close secrecy of all the proceedings. There was none of the security that comes from the open trial, none of the encouragement to make a good fight for freedom, for honour, for life that comes from publicity.

Again, the chances of acquittal were very small when the agreement of only two of the witnesses against him was sufficient for the condemnation of the accused, whether he confessed or not: especially as the delicate question of what constituted sufficient agreement was left to the discretion of the judge. It was laid down that agreement in substance was sufficient; and even when there was discord in the evidence of the two witnesses, this was not sufficient to secure acquittal.

Moreover, evidence, not good enough to procure conviction, would be good enough to serve as the basis of a prolonged, searching and perplexing examination, in which the accused was more likely to incriminate than to clear himself. [34]

A further heavy obstacle to the making of a defence was insufficiency of information. While the résumé or *capitula* of the charges preferred against him was communicated to the defendant, on the other hand, the names of the witnesses were withheld from him, and he was not allowed to read their evidence *in extenso*.

This practice of secrecy commenced early in the thirteenth century in Languedoc, and the rule soon came to apply in most other countries. Occasionally the names were given, though in an incomplete or confusing fashion [35]; but the inquisitors themselves were in favour of not disclosing names at all. [36]

IV: COMPOSITION AND PROCEDURE OF THE TRIBUNAL

This was owing to the circumstances in which the Inquisition had originated, amid an unfriendly populace. [37]

There had been cases of the assassination of witnesses by the friends of the acccused; and undoubtedly there was always a certain element of risk in giving evidence against a heretic in a country where heresy flourished and was popular. In those early days the inquisitor was very likely endangering his life in the prosecution of his labours: in such circumstances, if the indispensable evidence was to be collected, some sort of safeguard for voluntary witnesses was reasonable.

But an arrangement, which was justified, and perhaps rendered imperative, by the conditions prevailing when the Inquisition began, was continued indefinitely, and maintained when not the witnesses but the defendant belonged to an unpopular minority and stood in urgent need of some protection. How could anyone put on trial make an effective answer to the charges brought against him when he was never allowed to confront the witnesses, did not even know their identity, and was permitted to see only a *précis* of their testimony?

It is obvious that the system, whatever its origin, became in course of time a positive encouragement to delation and a temptation to perjury. But it is only right to add that the Inquisition, both in the Middle Ages and later on, showed itself at times extremely severe in punishing proved cases of false witness. [38]

Nevertheless, as a rule, the Inquisition was not at all nice in its selection of evidence, and certainly not impartial. It accepted the evidence of persons who were debarred from bearing testimony in the secular courts. It even accepted the evidence of one heretic against another, though it never admitted that the evidence of one heretic in favour of another had the slightest validity. [39]

Similarly the Inquisition permitted, indeed encouraged, husbands to testify against their wives, children against parents, servants against masters; though their favourable testimony was rejected. [40]

The rules as regards age seem to have varied in different countries; but certainly it is, generally speaking, true that persons were permitted to give evidence before the Holy Office at an age when their testimony would not have been received in a lay court. We even hear of a case at Montségur of a child of six incriminating members of his own family and many others.

The ordinary rules regarding the status and character of witnesses were similarly in abeyance. Criminals and men of infamous reputation, homicides, harlots, proved perjurers and excommunicates were none of them debarred from giving evidence against heretics.

Information might be forthcoming from the confessional. What were the duties of a father-confessor in such a case?

There was, on the one hand, the fact of the extraordinary heinousness of this offence which had necessitated the creation of a special court for its suppression; but, on the other hand, the institution of the confessional had to be safeguarded and a feeling of security be assured to the penitent, without which he could not be expected to make a full and free confession of all his sins, whatever their magnitude.

The solution was that the granting of absolution, upon an avowal of heresy, lay outside the powers of an ordinary confessor; he must refer the matter to his superiors.

The question coming up before the Council of Tarragona in 1242, it was indeed decided that, although a confessor granting absolution for heresy without consulting his bishop merited censure, nevertheless his grant of absolution, if duly certified by himself, should entitle the penitent to a limited protection, i.e. immunity from temporal penalties. This, however, was an isolated ruling, and it was generally recognized that heresy was a 'reserved' case.

Absolution by an ordinary confessor was invalid and could be no safeguard from the institution of inquisitorial proceedings against a penitent, should evidence of heresy be preferred against him. But what if, in spite of his knowledge that he could not obtain absolution from his confessor, a penitent incriminated himself; what if he, inadvertently perhaps, incriminated others? Was information derived by a confessor in such a way sacrosanct, because obtained in the confessional? Not apparently in Toulouse and Carcassonne at all events. There priests were positively enjoined to utilize the hearing of confessions to make diligent

IV: COMPOSITION AND PROCEDURE OF THE TRIBUNAL

enquiry concerning heretics, their believers and fautors, and also to confide carefully to writing anything they learnt. They were also to take the penitent before the bishop or his vicar, so that he might there repeat his testimony.

But if the penitent was unwilling to do this, the priest was 'notwithstanding this' to seek advice from expert and God-fearing persons, as to how he should proceed further. What this must involve is not specified; but clearly the only conceivable further proceedings are either to bring more pressure to bear upon the penitent, or else to use his evidence without his consent. Even if the latter never happened, the former course is not in strict accordance with the rules that should regulate the confessional. [41]

Yet another most serious disability, under which the accused laboured, was that he was not allowed the assistance of an advocate, he was thrown entirely on his own resources in making his defence.

Innocent III expressly forbade advocates and notaries to lend any aid to heretics or their abettors. The prohibition at first applied only to the case of open and avowed heretics. Eymeric ruled that counsel were in no wise to be denied to the accused, but he followed this up by the qualification, that advocates espousing the cause of a heretic rendered themselves liable to prosecution before the Inquisition, as suspect of heresy themselves for doing so. [42]

In actual practice what happened probably was that when the evidence against the accused was clear, he need expect no advocate; but when it was weak, then an advocate might be forthcoming. For if the evidence in support of the charge of heresy was strong, then assistance given to the accused was tantamount to fautorship of heresy, which was in itself a very serious offence. In any case the role of advocate was dangerous and there was no inducement to compensate for so grave a risk.

That such assistance was seldom, if ever, actually given seems proved by the absence of any indication of the practice even in the early inquisitorial registers. [43] Very soon, however, it was decided absolutely that the use of advocates was to be prohibited.

Such was the ruling of the Council of Albi in 1254; and the

regulation soon became general. [44] This was the really inevitable consequence of the view which made the suspect a marked, a tainted man even before he had stood his trial. But certainly one consideration which weighed heavily against the use of advocates was the possibility of the practice encouraging the spread of heresy, though the chances of an advocate's allowing himself to be infected by his client's erroneous doctrines were remote.

In its attitude towards this question we are once more reminded of the fundamental fact of the Inquisition's twofold nature. If the inquisitor be considered as a confessor, the accused as a penitent paternally exhorted, lovingly urged to reconciliation, pardon being assured for the truly repentant, what possible need can there be for an advocate? [45] The tribunal gave every facility for the escape of the prisoner from all the possible unhappy consequences of his defamation, down *one* avenue—confession, penance, reinstatement.

If the defendant was obstinately determined on defending himself, instead of throwing himself upon the mercy of the inquisitor, as representative of the infinite compassion of the Church, he was very much limited in his choice of pleadings.

Ignorance was a possible plea—more likely to be accepted in the case of a woman than a man—but inquisitors were on their guard against feigned ignorance. That words complained of were only a *lapsus linguae*, or an idle jest uttered on the spur of the moment, or in drunkenness, might be accepted as a legitimate excuse.

The plea of great perturbation of mind—mortal terror, for instance—might also possibly be accepted; but not the madness of love or the sudden grief of bereavement. [46]

To make out a case on these lines was in any event very difficult, and the only device that promised any really good prospect of success was to challenge a witness on the ground that he was actuated by personal malice. But as the witnesses' names were not disclosed, this was no easy matter. All that the accused could do, was to mention the names of any of his neighbours who might bear him a grudge, on the chance that they might be included among the authors of his defamation. [47]

But it was not sufficient to indicate simple ill-will. The charge of heresy was so terrible that it was assumed that little short of

IV: COMPOSITION AND PROCEDURE OF THE TRIBUNAL

mortal enmity would induce anyone to prefer it maliciously. The accused would, therefore, be carefully examined as to the nature of any quarrel with his neighbours that he might allege in his defence. The only purpose for which he was allowed the use of witnesses was to prove the facts of such a quarrel.

It must be clear that even when the presiding judge was a fair-minded, conscientious man, not too fanatical, the chances of effective defence were small. And the prosecution was exceedingly strong. If preliminary inducements, the subtleties of the interrogatory, the absence of means of defence, all proved insufficient to produce the desired confession, it was possible severely to shake the *moral* of the defendant by subjecting his case to prolonged delay, which was calculated to impose a great strain upon the nerves.

Except in rare instances, time was no consideration to the Inquisition. Its invincible patience was one of the most terrible of its weapons. It was willing relentlessly to wait, not merely weeks and months, but years and many years. It was quite common for an interval of anything up to ten years to elapse between the date of the first interrogatory and that of the final condemnation. The period might be considerably longer. We hear of a man, first brought to trial in 1301, being sentenced to death in 1319. [48]

This slow torture of suspense was generally endured in prison, where the recalcitrant would probably receive frequent visits from the inquisitor or his assistants, who would instruct him and exhort him to make confession. If simple incarceration proved insufficient to overcome the victim's fortitude, great additional hardships could be introduced—insufficiency of food, comfort, rest.

Finally, the most celebrated weapon which the Inquisition possessed for procuring confession was torture itself. Torture had been known to both Roman and barbarian law, being used even for such minor offences as theft. [49]

On the other hand, according to all the best authorities, it was strange to Canon law. It did indeed recognize flogging, but only as a punishment or penance. Gratian laid it down categorically that torture was not to be used as a means of extorting confession. It was not until after the condemnation of the ordeal by the

Lateran Council of 1215 that the Church sanctioned its use for this purpose.

In the bull, *Ad extirpanda*, published in 1252 by Innocent IV, the employment of torture was not merely permitted, but enjoined. [50] The rule was thereby laid down, that any sort of torment short of mutilation was to be utilized in order to obtain confessions and information. But the actual infliction of the torture was to be carried out by the secular arm. The idea of the clergy's personally superintending the infliction of cruelty was very properly repugnant.

The sense of repugnance did not last long, however. [51] The inquisitors of the thirteenth century found Innocent IV's proviso irksome. The employment of a secular official to assist them in carrying through the inquisitorial process was no doubt inconvenient, and in 1256 Alexander IV overcame the difficulty by granting inquisitors and their assistants the privilege of absolving one another, or giving one another dispensations, for any canonical irregularities they might commit in the pursuance of their duties. [52] This was an oblique reference to torture. This rule was reinforced by Urban IV in 1262. [53] The subterfuge satisfied the scruples of the inquisitors.

The extent to which torture was used no doubt varied in accordance with the character of the inquisitor.

In the sentences of Bernard de Caux there is only one passing mention of the practice; there is only one mention of it also in Bernard Gui. Though it is frequently referred to by Geoffrey d'Ablis, this is in a negative way only. [54]

It is stated that so-and-so confessed freely, no torture having to be used. But that torture was being used and with great severity is proved by the intervention of Philip the Fair in 1291 and 1301, and of Clement V in 1306; while in 1311 the Pope endeavoured to moderate the practice by the requirement that torture should not be inflicted save with the concurrence of the bishop of the diocese. [55]

Bernard Gui very much resented the restriction, and though in his sentences there is only the one mention of torture, it is clear from his treatise that he thoroughly approved of it, on account of its great utility. [56]

IV: COMPOSITION AND PROCEDURE OF THE TRIBUNAL

Certainly torture was regarded by inquisitors of the best type, not as a habitual practice, but only as a final measure, to be used solely when other means had failed. Eymeric lays it down that the circumstances justifying its application are that the case against the accused has been half-proved already or that the accused has contradicted himself. [57]

It was a very salutary rule that no prisoner might be tortured more than once; but this humane regulation became a dead-letter. The inquisitors found it galling and surmounted the obstacle with an utterly disgraceful quibble. Torture, they agreed, could not be *repeated* but it might be *continued*. [58] They used this patent sophistry to justify the application of torture an indefinite number of times at indefinite intervals. Thus some of the witches of Arras were tortured forty times, twice in a day. [59]

In such cavalier fashion could rules and regulations be treated. The requirement that confessions must be freely made without restraint was satisfied by another similar subterfuge. A confession, which had actually been wrung from the defendant or witness in the physical anguish of torture, was confirmed some two or three days later in some other place than the torture chamber; and this confirmation of the actual confession was officially regarded as the true confession. [60]

There were no exemptions from the administration of torture on the ground of youth, old age or infirmity, except for pregnant women. Old men and women, young children might all be subjected to the process, only in their case the infliction must be light. [61]

Eymeric laid it down that at all times the application must be moderate and that there must never be any effusion of blood. The term 'moderate' is vague and it is clear that there was no strict general rule, the determining factor here, as so often with the Inquisition, being the discretion of the judge. [62]

The unhappy victim, on being brought into the chamber, was first of all shown the instruments of torment and urged to confess without recourse being had to them. In some cases this alone was sufficient. But if a confession was not immediately forthcoming, the prisoner—male or female, it made no difference—was stripped naked and bound by the executioners.

A second exhortation to confess followed. If still there was no confession, the victim was then actually subjected to the pain of the rack, the pulleys, the strappado and the other devices of calculated cruelty, which were regarded as appropriate for the coercion of recalcitrant suspect or unwilling witness. Continued refusal to speak led to increase in the severity of the application; further obduracy with increase in the severity of the type of torture.

The refinements of cruelty in the machines and devices at the inquisitor's disposal were so exquisite that it is marvellous with what constancy they were often endured. There were many, no doubt, who submitted at the simple threat of torture or at the first turn of the screw; others who with almost superhuman endurance bore frightful extremities of pain.

NOTE:—The important subject of the influence exerted by the procedure of the Inquisition upon the civil courts of Europe has never been thoroughly worked out. There is partial treatment of it in Esmein's *Histoire de la Procédure Criminelle en France*; English version, *A History of Continental Criminal Procedure*; H. Brunner, *Die Entstehung der Schwurgerichte* (1872); C. V. Langlois, *L'Inquisition après des travaux récents*; P. Fournier, *Les Officialités au Moyen Age*; H. C. Lea, *Superstition and Force*, esp. pp. 428-590. Vol. v of the Continental Legal History Series, published by the Association of American Law Schools, while mainly based on Esmein's study of Criminal Procedure in France, is of wider scope and traces the inquisitorial system in Europe generally.

While the system of *inquisitio*, derived from the later Roman Empire, was not passed on to the civil courts of Europe solely through the *inquisitio haereticae pravitatis*, it is the case that 'The Church was able to furnish the secular courts with a lesson and a model... By its example it paved the way for the substitution, consummated in the 1500's, of the inquisitorial procedure for the accusatory procedure in every country of Europe.'

Again: 'This system, originally employed for prosecutions for heresy, afterwards for all crimes, became, under the name of "procédure à l'extraordinaire," the system of common law in force in the royal jurisdictions for the prosecution of serious crimes until 1789.'—*A History of Continental Criminal Procedure*, p. 10 and pp. 10-11, *note*.]

IV: COMPOSITION AND PROCEDURE OF THE TRIBUNAL

[1] *Practica*, pp. 232-3, 'Diligens ac fervens zelo veritatis fidei et salubris animarum ad detestationem et extirpationem heretice pravitatis... Inquisitor sit constans: persistat inter pericula et adversa usque ad mortem, pro justitia fidei agonizans, ut non temerarie praesumat per audaciam que periculose precipiat.' *Cf.* Eymeric, *Directorium*, p. 575, 'Inquisitor debet esse conversatione honestus, prudentia circumspectus, constantia firmus, sacra doctrina fidei eminenter eruditus et virtutibus circumfultus.' See also Frédéricq, *Corpus*, vol. i, Nos. 215, 243.

[2] *Ibid.*, pp. 594, 602; Ludovico à Paramo, p. 106.

[3] Limborch, *Historia Inquisitionis*, p. 124, cap. ix; *Directorium*, pp. 631-2.

[4] See Lea, vol. i, p. 379

[5] See Vacandard, *op. cit.*, p. 139.

[6] Douais, *L'Inquisition*, p. 246; De Cauzons, vol. ii, p. 134.

[7] Vacandard, p. 142; Lea, vol. i, pp. 388-9.

[8] In sentences the name of the bishop preceded that of the inquisitor. Bernard Gui, *Practica*, p. 93.

[9] Arnaldo Albertini, *Tractatus de Agnoscendis Assertionibus Catholicis et haereticis*, in F. Zilettus, *op. cit.*, vol. xi, pt. ii, pp. 52 *et seq.*

[10] See Tanon, p. 218.

[11] Vacandard, p. 162.

[12] Simancas in Zilettus, vol. xi, pt. ii, pp. 96-7, 104, 122.

[13] Moeller, *op. cit.*, p. 740. 'The spirit of the inquisitors is another matter. There is room for distrust of their propensity to discover heresies everywhere. Their *amour propre* was engaged to discover it under the most puzzling appearances.'

[14] See J. à Royas, *De Haereticis*, in Zilettus, vol. xi, pt. ii, pp. 212-24 (*passim*); Albertini, *op. cit.*, p. 53; Ludovico à Paramo, p. 544. See both Royas and Albertini *passim* on the general question of how to recognize a heretic, also Simancas in tit. xxxi.

[15] Simancas, p. 155.

[16] Eymeric, *Directorium*, p. 343. 'Haeretici affirmativi dicti sunt, qui habent eorum quae sunt fidei, errorem in mente, et verbo vel facto ostendunt, se modis praedictis habere pertinaciam in voluntate.'—'Negativi vero haeretici dicti sunt, qui coram judice fidei per testes legitimos de aliqua haeresi, vel errore, quos nolunt vel non possunt repellere, rite sive juste convicti sunt, sed non confessi, immo in negativa constanter perseverant; verbo fidem catholicam profitentur et detestantur etiam verbo haereticam pravitatem. *Cf.* p. 561.

[17] Lea, vol. i, pp. 433-4. 'That a man against whom nothing substantial was proved should be punished merely because he was suspected of guilt may seem to modern eyes a scant measure of justice; but to the inquisitor it

appeared a wrong to God and man that any one should escape against whose orthodoxy there rested a shadow of doubt. Like much else taught by the Inquisition, this found its way into general criminal laws, which it perverted for centuries.'

[18] Simancas in Zilettus, vol. xi, pt. ii, pp. 133-5. See Tanon, p. 334.

[19] See Douais, *L'Inquisition*, Appendix, p. 276, Raymond of Peñaforte's ruling.

[20] See Mansi, vol. xxiii, p. 360. Council of Narbonne, 1235. 'Quinam existimandi fautores haereticorum.' A sin in the eyes of the Church; and, it should be added, highly improper and dangerous conduct probably in the eyes of the average man in those days.

[21] Albertini in Zilettus, vol. xi, pt. ii, p. 82.

[22] Ludovico à Paramo, *op. cit.*, pp. 37, 45.

[23] *Cf.* De Cauzons, *op. cit.*, vol. ii, p. 203.

[24] See Fournier, *op. cit.*, pp. 235-7, 262-73. See also Esmein, *op. cit.*, pp. 66-134 (*passim*). English version, pp. 8-16, 78-94.

[25] *Practica*, p. 182.

[26] Fournier, *op. cit.*, p. 265; Tanon, pp. 272-6.

[27] Fournier, pp. 266-7.

[28] For forms of citation, see Bernard Gui, *Practica,* pp. 3 *et seq.*; Tanon, pp. 339 *et seq.*

[29] Fournier, p. 273. The inquisitor, or his delegate. Supra, p. 180.

[30] Bernard Gui, *Practica*, pp. 235 *et seq.*; Eymeric, pp. 465 *et seq. Cautelae inquisitorum contra haereticorum cavillationes et fraudes.*

[31] B. Hauréau, *Bernard Délicieux et l'inquisition albigeoise* (Paris, 1877), p. 89.

[32] *Cf.* Tanon, p. 357.

[33] On the 'shock' of accusation, see Langlois, *op. cit.*, p. 56. On methods of interrogatories generally, see Molinier, *op. cit.*, pp. 328 *et seq.*

[34] See Tanon, pp. 388-9.

[35] *Ibid.*, pp. 390 *et seq.*; Limborch (Eng. tr.), vol. i, p. 179.

[36] Bernard Gui's *Practica*, pp. 189-90, 243. 'Non... expedit quod omnes interrogationes scribantur, sed tantum ille que magis tangunt substantiam vel naturam facti.' *Cf.* Ludovico à Paramo, p. 523.

[37] See Molinier, pp. 155, 327.

[38] See Simancas in Zilettus, vol. xi, pt. ii, pp. 103-8, 121-2, 202; Lea, vol. i, pp. 441-2.

[39] Eymeric, *Directorium*, p. 662.

[40] *Ibid.*, p. 663, Peña's comment, No. 119. 'Familiares & domesticos non admitti in hoc crimine ad defendendum reum, & ratio non inepta haec potest, nam quemadmodum nemo unquam carnem suam odio habuit, eodem modo

nemo putandus est consanguineos suos odio habere, turn etiam quia cum ex hoc crimine infamia in filios descendat, si filii ad testimonium dicendum pro parentibus admitterentur, facile ut infamiam vitarent, mentirentur.'

[41] On the question of the confessional, see De Cauzons, vol. ii, pp. 214-7; Douais, *L'Inquisition*, p. 279, in treatise ascribed to Raymond of Peñaforte; Lea, vol. i, p. 437 and note. For decree of Council of Tarragona, see Mansi, vol. xxiii, pp. 555-6. See also E. Martène and U. Durand, *Thesaurus novus Anecdotorum* (Paris, 1717), vol. v, p. 1802. *Doctrina de Modo Procedendi contra Haereticos*, the section *Qualiter sacerdos debet inquirere in confessione de facto haeresis*. 'Item, injungitur sacerdotibus quod in poenitentiis diligenter inquirant de haereticis & Insabbatis, credentibus, & fautoribus eorumdem, & si quid invenerint, fideliter conscribant, & mox cum illo vel cum illis qui hoc confessi fuerint, episcopo, vel ejus vicario, quid super hoc invenerint manifestent. Si vero confessus noluerit consentire, ut quod dictum est reveletur episcopo vel ejus vicario, Ipse nihilominus sacerdos requirat consilium non specificando personam a peritis & Deum timentibus, qualiter sit ulterius procedendum.'

[42] *Directorium*, p. 480.

[43] See Tanon, p. 401.

[44] Mansi, vol. xxiii, p. 838.

[45] De Cauzons, vol. ii, p. 188

[46] See Ludovico à Paramo, p. 550; Simancas in Zilettus, vol. xi, pt. ii, pp. 138-40.

[47] See Douais, *Documents*, vol. ii, p. 136. 'Amaldus Pagesii, de Mossoleux, comparuit apud Carcassonam coram domino episcopo Carcassone; et requisites si vult se deffendere de hiis qui in inquisitione inventa sunt contra eum, respondit quod nullus pro vero potest aliquid dicere de ipso. Requisitus si velit ea de scriptis recipere, dixit quod non; et aliter non vult se deffendere. *Item*, requisitus si habet inimicos, dixit quod sic, Ber. Gausbert et Martinum Montanerii, sed nullam legitimam causam inimicitiarum assignavit; et alios inimicos noluit nominare.' *Cf. ibid.*, p. 178. See also Lea, vol. i, pp. 578-9, appendix.

[48] Tanon, p. 402.

[49] *Ibid.*, p. 362.

[50] Mansi, vol. xxiii, p. 573, § 23. 'Teneatur praeterea Potestas, seu rector, omnes haereticos quos captos habuerit, cogere, citra membri diminutionem & mortis periculum, tanquam vere latrones & homicidas animarum, & fures sacramentorum Dei & fidei Christianae, errores suos expresse fateri, & accusare alios haereticos quos sciunt, & bona eorum, & credentes & receptatores, & defensores eorum, sicut coguntur fures & latrones bonorum temporalium accusare suos complices, & fateri maleficia quae fecerunt.' *Cf.* David of Augsburg, quoted by Douais, *L'Inquisition*, pp. 171-2 note.

[51] By the time of the Spanish Inquisition of Ferdinand and Isabella torture had come to be accepted as a most praiseworthy and Christian institution. *Cf.* Simancas in Zilettus, vol. xi, pt. ii, p. 204.

[52] Potthast, *Regesta Pontificum Romanorum* (Berlin, 1874 *et seq.*), No. 18057.

[53] *Ibid.*, No. 18390.

[54] Tanon, p. 379.

[55] See *supra*, p. 161.

[56] Lea, vol. i, pp. 423-4, with reference to the infrequent mention of torture in inquisitorial registers. 'Apparently it was felt that to record its use would in some way invalidate the force of the testimony.' *Cf.* Tanon, p. 377. 'Cette particularité (silence) n'est pas spéciale aux registres de l'Inquisition. La plupart des registres criminels des juridictions laïques, pour les époques auxquelles la "question" était d'une application constante, la présentent pareillement. La question était un incident de procédure qui donnait lieu d'abord à un interlocutoire, puis à un procès-verbal spécial, dont la transcription dans les registres n'était nullement nécessaire. Le greffier qui rédigeait la sentence, lorsqu'il relatait les aveux de l'accusé, était beaucoup moins préoccupé de constater les moyens de contrainte à l'aide desquels ils avaient été obtenus que la réitération de ces mêmes aveux, réputés alors volontiers, hors de la chambre de torture.'

[57] Eymeric, *Directorium*, p. 640; Peña's comment, no, p. 643.

[58] *Ibid.*, comment 39, p. 520. 'Cum reus fuit leviter et molliter tortus, repeti potest in tormentis, ita ut sufficienter torqueatur, …et haec non tarn dicitur repetitio torturae quam continuatio.'

[59] Frédéricq, *Corpus*, vol. i, No. 318.

[60] Eymeric, Peña's comment, p. 521.

[61] *Ibid.*, p. 519.

[62] *Ibid.*, pp. 480, 592, 614.

V

Inquisitorial Penalties

Acquittals being virtually unknown [1], nearly every case brought before the Holy Office involved the sentence of one penalty or another.

The word 'penalty' is not technically exact. Strictly speaking, the Inquisition was concerned not with crimes and punishments, but with spiritual errors and penances. [2] Thus, when the tribunal consigned someone to prison, its formula ran that the man in question shall betake himself to prison and there penance himself on a diet of bread and water.

No confessor will regard the mere expression of contrition as sufficient in itself; nor will the genuine penitent be satisfied. Penance is the outward and visible sign of sincere repentance, and an earnest of future amendment of life.

All the penalties inflicted by the Inquisition had this expiatory character. [3] Some of them were of quite a trivial description. The penitent 'suspect' might simply be enjoined to hear Mass on so many Sundays and festivals, or—if his commercial practice suggested unsoundness of doctrine on the subject of interest—to undertake not to exact usury in the future or to promise to restore ill-gotten gains. [4]

But, as a rule, the penance was a much more serious matter. One of the most frequent was that of pilgrimages. [5] These were of various kinds. In the earlier days of the Inquisition the penitent [6] was often sent to Palestine on crusade against the infidel. But after the failure of St. Louis' expedition and the fall of the Kingdom of Jerusalem, the crusade ceased to find a place among inquisitorial penances.

Ordinary pilgrimages were classified as *greater* or *less*. The former took the penitent out of his own country and involved long travelling; the latter were to shrines in his own country.

Thus for a Frenchman Rome, the shrine of St. Thomas at Canterbury, Cologne, St. James of Compostella, Constantinople would come under the first category; Paris, Boulogne, Bordeaux, Vienne under the latter. The undertaking of the longer journeys might be a most severe imposition. The penitent had to abandon his work and set out upon travels which might well occupy many months and even years. He probably had to endure much real suffering, fatigue, and privation.

In the case of the crusade, and probably in other pilgrimages as well, there was an element of personal danger. In the pilgrim's absence, what happened to his family and dependents? In many instances one supposes that on his return after a long absence he must have found his occupation gone.

Those condemned to make pilgrimages received from the inquisitor letters which explained their itinerary and might give instructions as to certain additional penances they had to undergo, while they at the same time served as safe-conducts, of which there might be much need in localities where popular feeling was strong against heretics. Pilgrims were required to bring back with them written attestations, signed by the chaplains at shrines they were ordered to visit, in proof that they had actually carried out the prescribed programme. [7]

The penance of pilgrimage was often united with two others—scourging and the wearing of crosses, or other mark on the clothing, indicative of the penitent heretic. Flagellation by itself was regarded as one of the lightest of penances. The Councils of Tarragona (1242) and of Narbonne (1243) fixed it as the penance to be undergone by those who voluntarily made confession during the term of grace—that is, by the least culpable of all possible kinds of heretic.

The custom was for the flogging to be inflicted in public and in ceremonious fashion. The penitent was obliged to present himself on the appointed days stripped to the waist, and to bring the rod with him. As a general rule the day appointed was Sunday, and the priest performed the operation of scourging upon the penitent between the reading of the Epistle and of the Gospel during Mass.

Whether the operation was painful or not is disputed. One commentator supposes that it was no light matter and that the penitent was soundly whipped; another argues that, as the whipping was done at the altar by inexperienced hands and the sufferer was in a position to cry out and resist during divine service, the humiliation was the most severe part of the penance. [8]

One may perhaps conclude that the severity of the flagellation depended very much upon the intention of the inquisitors and the strength of arm of the ministering priest. Sometimes the sufferer might have to submit to the scourging in processions through the streets or in every house in which he had been seen in company with heretics; or, in the case of the pilgrim, at the various shrines visited. Such repeated floggings may or may not have been very painful, but even in days when they would not produce such a sense of shame as now, they must have been very humiliating.

In this respect the wearing of crosses was even worse. The origin of this penance was that during his missionary labours St. Dominic had ordered penitents to wear two small crosses, sewn on the breast of their clothing in token of contrition. The Inquisition adopted the practice and it was very frequently inflicted, being prescribed, like flagellation, for those who voluntarily made confession of heresy. Next to imprisonment, this penance figures most often in the sentences of Bernard Gui; it was rather less extensively used latterly.

The small marks which St. Dominic had required became under the Inquisition very large ones—as a rule two-and-a-half palms in height, two in breadth. They were saffron in colour and had to be worn one on the breast, the other on the back. Other symbols besides crosses were sometimes used. Thus false witnesses had to wear the symbol of red tongues, prisoners liberated on bail hammers, sorcerers the representation of demons.

The wearing of distinguishing marks was designed to be, and was felt to be, a less tolerable penalty than flogging. The shameful garb had to be worn continuously indoors and out, exposing the wearer at all times to the jeers, if not the fanatical hostility, of the crowd. The penance was enjoined sometimes for an indefinite period, and so long as he had to wear it, it would be difficult for the penitent to obtain employment.

It is plain that evasion was frequently attempted. The Council of Béziers (1233) prescribed confiscation of goods for those who either refused to wear the crosses or tried to conceal them. [9] The Council of Valence (1248) went further and decreed that evasion should be regarded as a sign of impenitent heresy. But evidently the hardships attendant upon this penance were so great that the Church felt it must do something to mitigate their severity, and the Council of Béziers (1246) commanded that penitents wearing crosses should not be subjected to ridicule or excluded from the transaction of business. [10]

There were penalties of a pecuniary nature—the exaction of fines, the confiscation of property. In earlier days, when it was yet thought of as contrary to the principles of their origin that the Friars should receive money on any pretext, it was felt to be repugnant that inquisitors, being friars, should exact fines.

On the other hand, from of old it had been regarded as a normal and praiseworthy form of showing genuine contrition to give alms; and it would have been surprising had this sort of penance been found absent from Inquisitorial practice.

From the time of the Council of Béziers (1246) onwards, it seems to have been recognized that the exaction of a fine was a perfectly legitimate form of penance, the proceeds to be used for the maintenance of inquisitorial prisons and similar necessary expenses. Eymeric laid it down that this penance should be used 'decently and in such a way as not to give offence to the laity.' [11]

A broader interpretation came to be made of the 'pious' purposes for which the proceeds of fines might properly be utilized; they might even include public work of general utility,

V: INQUISITORIAL PENALTIES

such as the building of bridges. [12] In moderation, the payment of a fine was a form of penance much more easily borne than those already mentioned; and if the money was used for such objects as the erection of a church or chapel or hospital, the maintenance of the poor or other such philanthropic work, it seems an eminently justifiable sort of penalty.

It had, however, one serious drawback—namely, that the profits might be used for ends much less worthy, for the personal enrichment of the judges, and might be a temptation to extortion.

Innocent IV, who in 1245 had directed that fines must be utilized solely for the building and upkeep of prisons, is found in 1249 strongly inveighing against inquisitors for the enormity of their exactions, and in 1251 prohibiting the imposition of fines where any other form of penance would serve. Despite this injunction, the penance was still employed; but the papal pronouncement is evidence, not only of the obvious temptation to extortion, but also of the fact of inquisitors' yielding to it.

A fine was the customary penalty for such a minor offence as the thoughtless utterance of blasphemous words; it was also frequently exacted in commutation of other forms of penance, as for example that of pilgrimage, when the penitent was too old or infirm to perform it, or again in the case of a young girl not fit to undergo the ardours of a journey across Europe. [13] So also when the death of a heretic left his prescribed penance uncompleted, the rule was that his heirs had to make compensation in the form of money, which might be heavy in amount. [14]

The provocation to extortion in both these instances is obvious. The accounts of the Inquisition were unchecked, except by the papal camera, and there was no public opinion able, or as a rule any authority desirous, to prevent abuse. [15]

A more serious matter than the exaction of fines was the confiscation of property. This, strictly speaking, was not a penalty, and technically also the Inquisition was not responsible. The goods of the heretic were simply sequestrated by the State automatically. So it had been in the case of the Manichæans under the Roman empire.

It should, however, be noted that if the children of a heretic were not themselves heretics, they were able to succeed to his estate. It was otherwise in the case of crimes, and in particular of treason, which involved the complete, unconditional confiscation of the delinquent's estate.

As the mediæval Church very plausibly reasoned that heresy was a crime analogous to *majestas*, only more heinous as being treason against the King of Kings, the inference was obvious that heresy involved confiscation. In his Decree of 1184, following the example of Alexander III in 1163, who had enjoined on secular princes the duty of imprisoning heretics and taking their property, Lucius III again declared confiscation of property to be appropriate to heresy, but sought to obtain the benefit for the Church.

The practice as to the sharing of the spoils of confiscation varied in different countries. Invariably, as soon as anyone had been declared a heretic by the Inquisition, the State at once sequestrated his property. [16] In the south of France indeed the confiscation took place even before—as soon as the suspect had been arrested or cited. If the prisoner recanted or, in the latter case, if the suspect were found guiltless, the property was then restored.

Innocent III's fulmination regarding confiscation had been vague in its terminology. What constituted the degree of criminality punishable by confiscation? Did the term 'heretics' mean only the obdurate, those who had to be handed over to the State, or did it include 'fautors'? The interpretation seems to have varied. But the most common interpretation was that all those whose offence was sufficiently heinous as to be 'penanced' by imprisonment, the contumacious who failed to answer to citation and all those in whose houses heretics were found, were liable to the confiscation of their property.

This seizing of estate before the termination of judicial proceedings was obviously a heavy hardship, not only upon the accused, but more especially upon his family. In France the rules regarding confiscation were carried out most remorselessly. Even before the accused had been found guilty his wife and children might find themselves turned adrift, dependent upon a charity which it was dangerous to extend to those even indirectly connected with heresy. [17]

V: INQUISITORIAL PENALTIES

In France, also, the whole of the confiscated property, once the royal power was strong enough to insist upon this, went to the State. Confiscation meant the entire loss of property, movable and immovable, but there were certain exceptions. A wife could claim to retain her dowry, but only on condition that she had not been cognizant of her husband's heresy when she married him.

Elsewhere it was otherwise. In *Ad extirpanda*, Innocent IV laid down the rule that the proceeds were to be divided into three equal portions, a third to go to the local authorities, a third to the officials of the Inquisition, a third to bishop and inquisitor. [18]

Latterly, in Italy, a different tripartite division was made, the third which had originally gone to bishop and inquisitor having to be paid to the pope. The question of distribution was complicated by feudal considerations, the feudal lord being able to put forward a claim to any forfeited possessions of his vassal.

But, however much the allocation of these revenues might vary, it was always understood that they were to be utilized for the prosecution of the war against heresy, and in particular the defraying of the expenses of the Inquisition.

The secular princes no doubt played their part. They had every inducement to do so. It is always good policy, if not to stimulate, at all events to preserve, the goose that lays the golden eggs. [19]

But, neither with regard to the action of the secular princes nor of the Inquisition, is it desirable to over-estimate the significance of the pecuniary penances and penalties suffered by the heretic.

It is no doubt true that their importance used to be underestimated, when the tendency was to rivet attention on the stake and torture-chamber in dealing with the Inquisition. It is also true that the opportunity of reaping mercenary profit from the prosecution of heresy was an encouragement to cupidity. It is only in human nature that it should be so.

It may be true to say that 'persecution, as a steady and continuous policy, rested, after all, upon confiscation.'[20] But that is not necessarily to say more than that the Inquisition had to meet its expenses in some way or other; and it was not unnatural to put to those expenses the proceeds of pecuniary penalties imposed directly by, or indirectly resulting from, the sentences of the tribunal.

Confiscation was a very customary expedient in the Middle Ages, and once granted the Church's reasonable analogy, on its own premises, between heresy and treason, it was an inevitable accompaniment of inquisitorial practice. That extortion and avarice were likely to be excited by the scheme is true; but to suggest avarice as a prime motive in the prosecution of heresy is quite to overshoot the mark. [21]

The Church did not embark upon the destruction of Catharism because it coveted the wealth of Cathari, but because it felt it must preserve itself against a movement, which it regarded as anti-religious, antisocial and immoral. [22]

In the second place, it must be remembered that the majority of mediæval heretical sects consisted of poor men. Only rarely was a rich man a heretic, and Fraticelli, Beguines, Dolcinists and most of the later sects, ardently persecuted by the Inquisition as they were, were certainly not worth pursuing from the point of view of the material profit to be derived thereby.

Eymeric, lamenting the dearth of heretics of substance in Spain in his day to help the tribunal to pay its way, deals cursorily with the subject of confiscation as one scarcely affecting the inquisitor at all. [23]

The most severe of the inquisitorial penances was that of imprisonment: but it is a *penance*. The idea is that, left in solitude, where he is out of reach of heretical contamination and has time to reflect on his offence, where in the simple life sustained on bread and water there are no worldly distractions, the penitent may be enabled by the aid of ghostly counsel to make a sincere return to the bosom of the Church.

Bernard de Caux used this penance frequently; it would appear that he enjoined it upon all who did not voluntarily surrender within the time of grace. [24] This was the ruling laid down by the Council of Narbonne (1244), which ruthlessly declared that no arguments of mercy against the infliction were to be considered, such as the dependence of his family upon the heretic, nor illness, nor old age.

The Council of Béziers, two years later, reiterated this principle, but recommended lenience where the penance might involve death to dependents.

V: INQUISITORIAL PENALTIES

Imprisonment was also frequently the penalty for failure to carry out penances previously imposed. In the sentences of Bernard de Caux a large percentage are for perpetual imprisonment. In Languedoc, to meet the necessities of the battle with Catharism, the Council of Narbonne ruled that imprisonment should always be for life. The tribunal did not at the time possess the resources to render the execution of this order practicable. At a later period it appears to have been carried out.

There were different degrees in the severity of the imprisonment. The most lenient form, known as *murus largus*, allowed of the prisoner's leaving his cell, taking exercise in the corridors and holding conversation with other prisoners, similarly privileged, possibly also with friends from outside the prison.

Much less desirable was the lot of the penitent consigned to *murus strictus*. Placed in a cell of the smallest size and worst description, dark and unsavoury, in some cases chained by both hands and feet, he was not permitted ever to leave his cell. This severer form of imprisonment was reserved for those whose offence had been especially conspicuous and therefore especially scandalous and dangerous to the faith and for those whose confessions had not been wholly satisfactory, complete and open. [25]

Mediæval prisons were all of them apt to be horrible places, and it does not appear that those used by the Inquisition were more noisome than others. That they were terrible enough we know: as for example from the report, as to the conditions in the *Cour de l'Inquisition* in Carcassonne, made by the papal commissioners in 1305. [26]

From other evidence it appears that harsh severity was laid down as a rule for the treatment by gaolers of their charges. [27] And, as a general rule, there was little supervision of the prisons, and their inmates had small chance of redress against ill-treatment. Only the strong ventilation of an alert public opinion can find its way into the dark recesses of prison life: there was no public opinion in the Middle Ages interested in the wrongs of the heretic.

It does not appear that there was separate accommodation provided for those awaiting trial apart from the condemned.

It is only right to add, however, that the Inquisition sanctioned the giving of presents of food and drink, clothing and cash from outside friends to the prisoners, so that they were not wholly dependent upon the diet of bread and water, which was all that the prisons provided.

The Inquisition was apt to find itself in difficulties with regard to the funds necessary for the maintenance of its prisoners. The prisons the tribunal itself built were of the cheapest, and consequently of the most insanitary, description. In France there were few specifically inquisitorial prisons, those belonging to the secular and episcopal authorities being utilized.

Prior to the absorption of Languedoc into the French monarchy at the Peace of Paris, the cost of building and maintaining prisons in that country had been borne partly by the bishops, partly by the holders of confiscated property. [28] Probably after 1230 the lot of heretic prisoners in Languedoc sensibly improved. In Italy the Inquisition seems to have been able to meet such expenses out of the proceeds of confiscation.

A penalty frequently met with in the early days of the Inquisition is that of banishment. Originally used in the Roman empire by the civil authority against Arians, Nestorians, Manichæans, it was ordered by the Council of Rheims in 1157 against heretics, incorporated in the Assize of Clarendon, in the edict of Verona, and in those of Alfonso II and Pedro II of Aragon.

On the surface it appeared an excellent method of ridding a country of the contamination of heresy. But to banish from one country was merely to introduce the virus of the scourge into another. The effect was simply to spread the epidemic.

In the second place, banishment was a confession of failure, as it gave no promise of amendment upon the part of the individual: which was ever the inquisitor's object. Hence he preferred imprisonment of the heretic to his banishment, holding him fast to getting rid of him.

Heresy, being regarded as essentially anti-social, involved exclusion from civil rights. The heretic could hold no office in Church and State, could hold no title or honour of any kind. If a father, his natural authority over his children was rendered invalid; if a husband, he no longer had legal authority over his

V: INQUISITORIAL PENALTIES

wife; if a king, he forfeited the obedience of his subjects; if a baron, the vassalage of his tenants. He could not succeed to property or, having it, leave it by will. His debtors need pay him nothing. The incapacity to hold office in the State affected not only the offender himself, but descendants of the second generation in the paternal, the first generation in the maternal, line. [29]

The idea of the taint of heresy is apparent in another penalty which the inquisitor was competent to inflict—the destruction of houses which had harboured heretical inmates or been the scene of heretical meetings. [30] This penalty is less a punishment than a symbolical act, expressive of the Church's horror of heresy; an attempt to blot out the very memory of the offence.

This practice, sanctioned in Roman law, was enjoined by the Assize of Clarendon, by the Emperor Henry VI in the edict of Prato of 1195, by Frederick II in 1232. It was consecrated by the Church in the days of Innocent III.

Innocent IV actually demanded the demolition, not only of the house in which the heretic had been found, but also of neighbouring houses, if they belonged to the same property; a stringent rule modified by Alexander IV. The houses must never be rebuilt, and more, the places where they had stood must remain unused for other building. There was just one saving clause: the stones of the demolished houses might be used for pious purposes. [31]

Had these regulations been literally carried out, it is obvious that whole towns might have been devastated and remained waste. But it is evident that the rules were not fulfilled to the letter. They were made to apply in Languedoc to houses in which definite heretical acts had taken place, such as the Catharan heretication. Even so, the secular arm was not disposed to approve of a penalty which not only did material damage, but diminished the yield of confiscations.

Both France and Germany protested; and eventually the inquisitors agreed to issue licences to build on the sites of the demolished houses. [32]

So far we have dealt, on the whole, with penalties incurred by those who, in the end, became reconciled to the Church—those who confessed, performed their penance in token of contrition and promised amendment. But there were also those who did not become reconciled. They fall under three headings—the contumacious, the impenitent, the relapsed.

As regards the first, the Inquisition adopted the rule of Roman law. If the accused, being cited three times or given one peremptory summons to appear, failed to do so, he was reckoned as contumacious. The penalty was excommunication and forfeiture of goods. This sentence would be annulled in the event of the accused's surrendering himself to the tribunal within the space of a year from the date of the citation. [33] Otherwise, he was liable, on falling into the hands of the Inquisition, as an excommunicate, to be handed over to the secular arm.

With the stubborn impenitent, resisting up to the last all efforts of the Church to bring him back to her bosom, there was obviously nothing to be done. But the inquisitor, to whom relaxation to the secular arm was an admission of defeat, left no means untried, of persuasion, admonition, force, to avoid such failure.

His reluctance to hand over the heretic as a hopeless recalcitrant, was in most cases perfectly genuine. Even after the sentence of relaxation had been pronounced, indeed after the culprit had actually been handed over, the slightest sign of willingness to repent might suffice to save the victim. [34] Eymeric mentions one case in which a heretic, consigned to the flames at Barcelona, being scorched on one side, cried out in his agony that he would recant, and was at once removed from the fire. [35]

The relapsed were those who, having once erred and been received back into communion, sinned in the same way again. These were incorrigible. Their former repentance had manifestly been a mere sham, and the outrage cried to heaven. Repetition of the sin of heresy could not be suffered. [36] Accordingly the relapsed were the only class of offenders coming before the Holy Office who could not save themselves by penitence.

Relapse came to involve relaxation automatically. But it had not been so at first, perpetual imprisonment being the penalty originally enjoined, for example by the Councils of Tarragona and Béziers. By 1258, however, relaxation had come to be recognized as the sole possible reward for relapse. [37]

V: INQUISITORIAL PENALTIES

Relaxation to the secular arm meant death, and death by burning. The inquisitor himself, who did not and could not pronounce a death sentence, knew, on the other hand, that a sentence of relaxation was tantamount to one of death.

It is true that he made use of a formula [38], expressing a desire that lenience might be shown to the victim and that some apologists have based upon this the contention that the ecclesiastical tribunal was in no way responsible for the death penalty; urging, on the one hand, that the desire that the relaxed heretic might not suffer either death or mutilation was perfectly genuine, on the other that the lay authority was entirely independent in the matter, pronouncing and executing its own sentence, based on a decision of its own, not the Inquisition's relaxation; and that, should it decide to spare the life of the heretic, the Church would make no complaint, but quite the contrary. [39]

The theory cannot be accepted. The attitude of Gregory IX and Innocent IV towards Frederick II's Constitutions, and the bulls, *Cum adversus haereticam* and *Ad extirpanda*, are really decisive in the matter. [40] But there is additional clear proof that the formula of leniency was an empty formula, intended merely to preserve technical conformity with the Canon. [41]

In the first place, what appropriate punishment for the contumacious, the impenitent, the relapsed could there be short of death? Even the contrite heretic, received back into the fold, may have to undergo so severe a penance as perpetual imprisonment. If the Church metes out to the contrite punishment as severe as the impenitent has to face, she is putting a premium upon impenitence.

The simple fact that perpetual imprisonment is numbered among the penances inflicted by the Inquisition is proof positive that the Inquisition desired and anticipated from the secular arm the death penalty for those relaxed to it. For careless as to the ultimate fate of the impenitent the Church cannot possibly be. She cannot be willing that he should go free to rejoice in the triumph of his obduracy among confederates and to spread contagion among the faithful.

Shall he be banished by the secular authority? To what end? Banishment only means the spread of infection. Shall he, then, be imprisoned by the secular authority? Again, to what end?

The Inquisition can imprison as well as the State. It is a strange obtuseness that does not see that the whole attitude of the Inquisition to the heretic points logically, and indeed inevitably, to death as the fate of the obdurate. The tribunal had been created, and it existed, to the end that heresy might be exterminated. To have failed to secure that those who to the last resisted all its most strenuous efforts to obtain confession and reconciliation must expect a worse fate than those who proved compliant would have stultified its very existence.

As a matter of fact, the Church saw to it, that the penalty meted out by the secular arm to the relaxed was death. Hardly ever did the secular ruler show any reluctance to inflict it. But if he forbore, he would probably be excommunicated. [42] Even after the Fourth Council of the Lateran, the Church made it incumbent upon the lay power to carry out the imperial edicts against heresy. The formula of mercy, then, may be called either a 'legal fiction' or bluntly, a 'hypocrisy'; it was never intended to be taken literally. [43]

The scrupulous regard of the Church for regularity in accordance with the Canon showed susceptibility to decorum; as a repudiation of moral responsibility it would have been contemptible.

But the mediæval Church did not repudiate such responsibility, as some of its modern apologists have sought to do. Had it disapproved of the penalty of death for the obdurate heretic, it both could and would have said so. Nay, more. It possessed the authority and practical power to have prevented it. To doubt that is to attribute to the mediæval Church infinitely less influence than it actually possessed.

A papacy, claiming and at times exercising authority in matters temporal as well as spiritual, could have brought pressure to bear upon the secular power in a matter peculiarly the Church's concern. The fact that it never made any attempt to do so is proof that it never desired to.

As a matter of fact, the Church in the Middle Ages felt no such squeamishness, as is natural in these modern days of religious toleration, regarding the drastic punishment of errors

V: INQUISITORIAL PENALTIES

in intellectu. Once granted the point of view that heresy is a more heinous offence than coining—to use St. Thomas' analogy—or than treason, to use a commoner and more forcible comparison, and the penalty of death for heresy appears not shocking and horrible, but something eminently just and proper.

We may take St. Thomas as representative of the best thought of the Church on the subject in the Middle Ages. Later inquisitors were quite unequivocal in their language. 'Pertinax non tantum est relaxandus, sed etiam vivus a saeculari potestate conburendus.' [44] Simancas, likewise, has no qualms. The best human law demands the burning of the heretic; in this according with the divine law. Christ is quoted in proof: 'Igne igitur extirpanda est haeretica pubis: ne nobis Deus irascitur, si haereticos dimittimus impunitos.' [45]

A favourite line of argument was that adopted by Ludovico à Paramo, in comparing the Church to the ark of Noah. As God utterly destroyed the unbelievers outside the Ark by a deluge, so now does he destroy the heretic.[46] It is modern humanitarianism, not Inquisitorial authorities, that seeks to disclaim moral responsibility for the stake.

The outward and visible sign of the Church's approval was its participation in the ceremony of execution. This took place frequently as part of a great and elaborate function known as the *sermo generalis* or 'act of faith'—the *auto-da-fé* of the Spanish Inquisition. There could be a *sermo generalis* without an execution. A burning was not the essential feature of the ceremony.

The auto had humble beginnings. In the early days of the Inquisition in Toulouse there might be one every week or so. In rapid, business-like fashion the sentences against heretics were pronounced in the presence of the civil and ecclesiastical officers. But in course of time the proceedings came to be much more elaborate, the object being to impress the popular mind.

The *sermo generalis* usually took place on a Sunday and inside a church, a platform being erected upon which the culprits were placed. The ceremony, which started in the early morning, began with a sermon appropriate to the occasion, preached by an inquisitor. After this an indulgence was announced for all who had come to take part in the solemnity, the civil magistrates took an oath of fidelity, and excommunication was fulminated against all who had in any way thwarted the Inquisition in the pursuance of its labours.

Next the confessions of the penitents were read, followed by the recital of the form of abjuration, which they repeated word by word. It does not appear that they wore any such distinctive garb as was customary in the Spanish Inquisition of later days. The inquisitor then absolved the penitents from the excommunication which their heresy had incurred, the formal sentences were read out, first in Latin, then in the vulgar tongue; after which the culprits were brought forward in order corresponding with the degree of their guilt, beginning with the least guilty and ending with the impenitent and relapsed.

For the disposal of the latter adjournment was made to another place, where they were handed over to the lay authorities. The victims destined to pay the last penalty were not at once executed. It was not seemly that the execution should take place on a Sunday, and they were given another night to make their peace with God.

The following day they were brought to the stake, accompanied by ghostly comforters, who would earnestly exhort them to penitence, seeing that, except in the case of the relapsed, reconciliation was possible up to the last moment. They were forbidden to exhort the victims to quiet submission for fear that this might suggest that they were doing something to expedite the punishment in store for the heretics. [47]

This would have been an irregularity. Yet so implicitly did the Church believe in death for the obstinate heretic, that she pursued his body even after death. For death did not terminate heresy; and it was evidently felt to be obnoxious that anyone who had been a heretic, even though his heresy had never been detected during life, should pass beyond the reach of ecclesiastical justice.

Notwithstanding the pronouncement of Ivo of Chartres, that the powers of the Church extended only to the present world, by the middle of the thirteenth century it seems to have been generally recognized that the corpses of all persons, whose heresy was discovered only after their demise, were to be dug up and disposed of in accordance with the degree of their guilt. [48]

V: INQUISITORIAL PENALTIES

In 1209 a synod at Paris caused the body of Amaury de Bène to be flung to the dogs, and in 1237 the bodies of certain heretic nobles were carried through the streets of Toulouse and solemnly burnt. [49] The practice seems to have been partly due to a popular feeling that it was a dreadful and scandalous thing that a heretic should be buried in consecrated ground, partly to a desire on the part of the inquisitors to demonstrate their implacable zeal and unlimited power. [50]

All inquisitorial sentences, with the single exception of death—which, strictly speaking, was not an inquisitorial sentence at all—could be, and frequently were, commuted. Thus for imprisonment is substituted the wearing of crosses in view of the penitent's having given information about a plot against the inquisitor's life.

The procuring of the capture of other heretics is similarly rewarded. [51] Commutation to a lighter penance is allowed to a woman, because she has a number of small children; to a man, because he has a wife and family dependent upon him. [52]

Such unconditional remitments were rare; temporary alleviations were more frequent. [53] Penitents might be allowed to leave prison, for periods varying from a few weeks to two years, on account of child-birth or illness. [54] A husband and wife, both in prison for heresy, might be allowed access to one another. [55]

A right of appeal existed, from the bishop to the metropolitan, from the inquisitor to the Pope.

The papacy was at first averse to receiving appeals in cases of heresy, Lucius III in 1185 declaring that he would have none of them. [56] When, however, the Inquisition was established, the right was acknowledged. But it was at best of doubtful and partial utility. It was a condition that the appeal must be lodged before the sentence was pronounced. In other words there could be no appeal against a decision of the tribunal. It was valid only as against an alleged injustice in procedure. [57]

A complaint on the latter ground could easily be rectified by the inquisitors themselves by the simple device of starting the process anew and carefully avoiding the irregularity of which complaint was made. If the inquisitors regarded the appeal as frivolous, they could dismiss it. It is clear that they regarded all appeals as a nuisance, an unwarrantable embarrassment. [58]

The most successful appeals lodged against the tribunal were those brought by powerful nobles and influential towns. [59] For the ordinary person, devoid of influence, the right of appeal offered small hope of deliverance.

We have valuable evidence as to the comparative frequency of the various penances prescribed by the Inquisition. The practice of different inquisitors varied, as was inevitable, when so much was left to the arbitrary decision of the individual judge. But a general computation is possible. Imprisonment, confiscation of property, the wearing of crosses are the sentences that occur most frequently.

No inquisitor in the Middle Ages was more vigorous and efficient than Bernard Gui. In a collection of sentences extending over a period of seventeen years, 1308-23, there are 307 of imprisonment, 143 of wearing crosses, 69 of exhumation, 9 of pilgrimages without the wearing of crosses, 40 of condemnation of fugitives as contumacious, 45 of relaxation to the secular arm; i.e. only 45 sentences of relaxation out of 613. [60]

Another veritable 'hammer of heretics,' Bernard de Caux, has left voluminous records of his cases between the years 1246 and 1248. There are a large number of sentences of life imprisonment; not a single mention of relaxation. [61]

This is very remarkable, as it seems highly unlikely that Bernard de Caux never came across an impenitent in the course of his duties, and the suggestion is at least plausible that the records are incomplete, being only entries of sentences of imprisonment. [62] But the clear indication of the evidence is that the number of cases of relaxation must have been comparatively small in the aggregate and very small in comparison with other sentences.

This may appear strange to those whose sole idea of the Inquisition is that of a court mainly concerned with the burning of heretics. Such a conception rests upon a misunderstanding of the object and function of the tribunal. It did not aim at making great holocausts of victims; it desired only to make a few examples.

Except in Languedoc, where the heretics were in a majority and powerful, a few examples always sufficed. It sought not vengeance, which was a synonym for failure, but reconciliation,

V: INQUISITORIAL PENALTIES

which meant success. More characteristic of the Inquisition than its sentences of relaxation, with their attendant horrible consequence, in reality more effective and perhaps more terrible, was its whole method of procedure, its use of torture, moral as well as physical, the agony of the rack and the nervous strain of prolonged and tortuous examination, its utilization of the humiliation of the cross-wearing, of the dull and hopeless misery of harsh and lengthy imprisonment, by which the spirit of the victim was broken and the purity of the faith preserved.

---

[1] See Tanon, p. 433. Out of 200 cases before the Carcassonne tribunal there was only one acquittal.

[2] Ludovico à Paramo, p. 269.

[3] They were also, of course, a warning. 'The punishment of one is the fear of many,' remarks Simancas sententiously, Zilettus, vol. xi, pt. ii, p. 179. But the main object is repentance and conversion. *Ibid.*, p. 181.

[4] Bernard Gui, *Practica*, p. 38.

[5] *Ibid.*, pp. 94-8.

[6] See Douais, *Documents*, vol. ii, p. 181.

[7] Bernard Gui, *Practica*, p. 95; *Liber Sententiarum* in Limborch, *Historia Inquisitionis*, pp. 218, 347. For an instance of this sort of sentence, see Douais, *Documents*, vol. ii, pp. 116-17. 'Injunctum fuit Ullixi in penitentia per inquisitores pro perjurio, quia non resumpsit cruces sicut juraverat, quod dominica post instantem dominicam in lxxa veniat Carcassonam visitaturus omnes ecclesias Burgi Carcassonensis nudis pedibus in camesis et braceis, cum virgis in manu, eundo de una ecclesia ad aliam; et idem faciet in prima dominica mensium singulorum quousque transeat ultra mare. Et hoc fuit ei injunctum in virtute praestiti juramenti.'

[8] Lea, vol. i, p. 464; De Cauzons, vol. ii, p. 303.

[9] Mansi, vol. xxiii, p. 271, § iv. Bernard Gui's sentences are full of the infliction of this penance. *Cf. Liber Sententiarum*, pp. 40-5, 100-17, 185-91, 218-28.

[10] Mansi, vol. xxiii, p. 693. 'Cum peccatores sint ad poenitentiam invitandi juxta Domiuicam vocem, gaudere oportet si poenitentiam impositam libenter suscipiunt et supportant. Quocirca statuimus, & in virtute sancti Spiritus inhibemus, ne poenitentibus, quibus cruces pro crimine haeresis imponuntur, irrisio ulla fiat, nec a locis propriis seu communibus commerciis excludantur, ne retardetur conversio peccatorum, & ne conversi propter scandalum abjecta poenitentia relabantur. Et si moniti desistere noluerint, per censuram ecclesiasticam compellantur.' *Cf.* Bernard Gui, *Practica*, pp. 101-2.

[11] Eymeric, *Directorium*, pp. 702-4; Molinier, *op. cit.*, pp. 23, 390.

[12] *Practica*, pp. 165, 169.

[13] Douais, *Documents*, vol. ii, pp. 213, 237.

[14] 'Filios haereticorum, etiam natos ante crimen commissum, sub poenis, & prohibitionibus canonicis comprehent.' J. à Royas in Zilettus, vol. xi, pt. ii, p. 231.

[15] See Lea, vol. i, pp. 471-81.

[16] While in France the Inquisition took no official record of confiscation—it was automatically carried out by the State—in Italy the tribunal gave a formal declaratory sentence of confiscation. Zanchino, *Tractatus de Haereticis*, chs. xxiii, xxv, xxvi.

[17] See Lea, vol. i, pp. 520-1.

[18] Mansi, vol. xxiii, pp. 574-5.

[19] See Lea, vol. iii, p. 525. On whole question of confiscation, see also Tanon, *op. cit.*, pp. 523-38.

[20] Lea, vol. i, p. 529. Lea was the first historian to go into the financial aspect of the Inquisition at all thoroughly. He devotes a whole chapter, book i, ch. xiii, to the subject of confiscation. 'It was this,' in his view, 'which supplied the fuel which kept up the fires of zeal, and when it was lacking, the business of defending the faith languished lamentably.'

[21] *Cf.* Langlois, *op. cit.*, p. 74.

[22] See De Cauzons, *op. cit.*, vol. i, pp. 48-53. P. 53. 'Ce n'est pas ambition ni cupidité: c'est instinct de préservation.' But see Vacandard, *op. cit.*, pp. 202-3. 'But would the ecclesiastical and lay princes, who, in varying proportion, shared with the Holy Office in these confiscations, and who in some countries appropriated them all, have accorded to the Inquisition that continual good-will and help, which was the condition of its prosperity without what Lea calls "the stimulant of pillage"? We may well doubt it.'

[23] *Directorium*, pp. 709-22.

[24] See Douais, *Documents*, vol. ii, pp. 6, 7, 15, 18, 20, 23, 26, 29, 30, 34; Tanon, *op. cit.*, p. 482; Vacandard, *op. cit.*, p. 193. Eymeric imposed this penance on the *violently* suspect, *Directorium*, pp. 530-1.

[25] See Lea, vol. i, p. 487.

[26] See *supra*, p. 161; Molinier, *op. cit.*, p. 449.

[27] See Lea, vol. i, p. 492.

[28] See provisions of the decrees of the Council of Toulouse (1229), in Mansi, vol. xxiii, p. 196; and of the Council of Albi (1244), *ibid.*, p. 840.

[29] See Tanon, *op. cit.*, p. 544.

[30] Tanon, p. 519; Simancas, *op. cit.*, p. 133. For form of sentence, *Practica*, p. 59. '…Dirui ac moliri funditus ita quod de cetero in loco seu solo ejus nulla humana habitatio seu reedificatio aut clausio ibi fiat, seu locus inhabitabilis et incultus et inclausus semper existat, et sicut fuit receptaculum perfidorum, sic deinceps ex nunc perpetuo sordium locus fiat.'

[31] *Ibid.*

[32] Lea, vol. i, p. 483.

[33] Tanon, *op. cit.*, pp. 404-7.

[34] Bernard Gui, *Practica*, pp. 129, 144; *Liber Sententiarum*, pp. 93, 208; Douais, *L'Inquisition*, pp. 297, 298, 324.

[35] *Directorium*, pp. 514-16.

[36] *Practica*, pp. 124, 127. 'Cum ecclesia ultra non habet quod faciat pro suis demeritis contra ipsum, idcirco eundem relinquimus brachio et judicio curie secularis.'

[37] Lea, vol. i, pp. 544-6.

[38] The formula ran, 'Eundem N. tanquam haereticum relinquimus brachio et judicio curie saecularis, eandem afiectuose rogantes prout canonice sanctiones, quatenus citra mortem et membrorum ejus mutilationem circa judicium et suam sententiam moderetur.' *Practica*, p. 127. *Cf. Directorium*, pp. 554, 559.

[39] Douais, *L'Inquisition*, pp. 264-8; Maillet, *op. cit.*, ch. iv.

[40] *Supra*, pp. 152-6.

[41] Admitted candidly by Peña. See *Directorium*, p. 131, comm. 20.

[42] See Simancas, p. 147. See Vacandard, *op. cit.*, on the Church's use of secular aid, pp. 27-8. 'Nor were they content with merely accepting it. They declared that the State had not only the right to help the Church in suppressing heresy, but that she was in duty bound to do so.'

[43] 'A legal fiction,' is Vacandard's way of putting it; a 'hypocrisy,' Lea's Langlois calls it 'a miserable equivocation.' See Vacandard, *op. cit.*, pp. 178-9. 'We regret to state, however, that the civil judges were not supposed to take these words literally. If they were at all inclined to do so, they would have been quickly called to a sense of their duty by being excommunicated. The clause inserted by the canonists was a mere legal fiction, which did not change matters a particle.'

[44] J. S. à Royas in Zilettus, vol. xi, pt. ii, p. 231.

[45] Simancas, *ibid.*, p. 181.

[46] Ludovico à Paramo, bk. i, p. 47.

[47] For description of *Sermo generalis*, see *Directorium*, pp. 437-42, 548-59; *Practica*, pp. 83-6.

[48] In 897 Pope Stephen VII had dug up the body of his predecessor, Formosus, solemnly tried and condemned it, had it mutilated and thrown into the Tiber. There is a case in 1022 of the body of a Manichæan of Orleans, who had died three years before, being exhumed.

[49] See Lea, vol. i, pp. 231-2, 553; De Cauzons, vol. ii, pp. 354-61.

[50] For sentences against the dead, see *Practica*, pp. 58, 122-6; *Liber Sententiarum*, pp. 32-4, 162-7, 333.

[51] *Ibid.*, pp. 43, 48.

[52] *Ibid.*, p. 54.

[53] *Liber Sententiarum*, pp. 50, 53.

[54] Douais, *Documents*, vol. ii, pp. 128-36 (*passim*), 151-2.

[55] There is the case also of a man, condemned to life imprisonment, being permitted to stay with his invalid father as long as the latter survived. The father may have been seriously ill and his remaining days likely to be few. The case is, however, interesting. Douais, *L'Inquisition*, p. 232.

[56] In the bull, *Fraternitatem tuam*. See Frédéricq, *Corpus*, vol. i, No. 57.

[57] *Directorium*, p. 491. See De Cauzons, *op. cit.*, vol. ii, p. 397.

[58] Ludovico à Paramo, *op. cit.*, p. 124. See Tanon, *op. cit.*, p. 437.

[59] As for example the Sire de Parthenay, see Lea, vol. i, p. 451; and the towns of Albi and Carcassonne, see Tanon, pp. 439-40. It is worth noticing that the notary, who drew up the appeal of the latter city against Nicholas d'Abbeville, was prosecuted for heresy and imprisoned.

[60] See Douais, *Documents*, vol. i, p. ccv., where the sentences are classified.

[61] *Ibid.*, vol. ii, pp. 1-87.

[62] Tanon, p. 479.

VI

Conclusion

The story of mediæval heresy is but a chapter in a much larger subject, that of the slow and painful development of religious tolerance and freedom of thought.

Heresy—essentially free choice in the sphere of religious belief in contradistinction to implicit obedience to doctrinal authority—was a serious problem to the Church in the early centuries of the Christian era. During the long, distracted and desolate epoch of the barbarian invasions it ceased to be a potent factor in history.

But when Europe recovered from the malady, the lethargy of the Dark Ages, and the human mind was again awake, it became once more a problem. The rationalistic speculations of Eriugena, Roscellinus and Berengar; the disordered ravings of Tanchelm; the aggressive anti-sacerdotalism of the Cathari or Paulicians, and of the vagrant Waldenses, present us with the three outstanding types of mediæval heresy. By far the most influential, those which the Church recognized as the most hurtful and dangerous, were the last.

In the case of the Cathari there was a clear and a very remarkable revival of a heresy that had much afflicted the early

Church, Manichaeism. Their dualist theology was hopelessly pessimistic; their practical teachings a mere gospel of despair. The crude dualism and perverted antinomianism of the sect contained little indeed that either merited respect or promised lasting influence.

Only in the hint of a genuine hatred of the gross and the cruel was there aught to respect; only in its Donatist doctrine and its denunciation of the Catholic clergy was there the likelihood of lasting influence. In their hostility to the claims, and their diatribes against the abuses, of the clergy, Paulicianism and Waldensianism stood united.

These two heresies gave a popular currency in the lands where they secured a foothold to anti-sacerdotalism, which involved not only the condemnation of all backsliding on the part of the clergy from the strictest and most rigid interpretation of the Christ-like life, but also—as the result of this—the rejection of the doctrinal basis of the peculiar privileges of the clergy, namely the conception of the mediatorial character of the priesthood.

The Arnoldist 'Poor Men'; the Petrobrusians, insisting on the sole efficacy of the individual's own faith, unaided by churches and sacraments; the Henricians in their ascetic denunciation of clerical worldliness and rejection of the sacraments; the Poor Men of Lyons, adopting the rule of absolute poverty, preaching in streets and countryside because, although illiterate, they were conscious of an inward vocation, and so being led on to undertake other priestly functions though unordained; the Cathari asserting that the Catholic Church was lost in materialism and worldliness and that *they* were the true church of Christ—all these were inherently the aggressive enemies of the priesthood.

There was a similar note in much of the popular poetry in those southern lands in which these heresies took firmest root. It is a note scornful, defiant, often ribald and profane, that comes into the songs of the goliards and troubadours. With a robust and crude Rabelaisianism they burlesque, not only clerical manners, but the holiest ceremonies and the most sacred doctrines. Even in miracles and mystery plays the note is sometimes heard; in the poems of Rutebeuf, the 'Roman de la Rose' and 'Reynard the Fox,' it is most resonant.

VI: CONCLUSION

In the popular poetry there is undoubtedly something of the unconsecrated paganism of the average man—his innate secularism rebelling against clerical privilege, when it is not fortified by personal worthiness.

Yet between the Provençal troubadour and the Paulician heretic there was something akin; and with the nobleman of Languedoc, only too willing to take the excuse for despoiling the clergy, they were alike popular. We may regret the total extinction of the exotic, semi-Moorish culture of southern France, which the Albigensian crusades involved; we need not regret the virtual extinction, with it, of the heresies. [1] If there was something worthy of esteem in their demand for spiritual reality and personal holiness, this was confused with other elements, which were perverted and absurd, sometimes even repulsive and abominable.

On their constructive side the heresies of Waldenses and Albigenses had nothing of genuine value to offer. In so far as they have significance, it is because of their anti-clerical elements, which are in part a cause, but more a symptom, of a trend of popular sentiment.

The second type of mediæval heresy is that represented by Tanchelm, Eon de l'Etoile, Segarelli, Dolcino, the Flagellants. It belongs to the province, not of the theologian but of the psychologist, specially interested in the study of depraved emotion and diseased imagination. Its foundation is that perverted sexuality which is so strangely connected, as a matter of psychological fact, with intensity of religious enthusiasm. The cases of Tanchelm and Eon are no doubt cases of simple religious mania.

None of the heresies of this type had, or from their character was at all likely to have, any but the most fleeting results. They have, nevertheless, their interest, as symptoms of the powerful emotionalism which seemed equally liable to produce a fierce animalism or an intense religious asceticism.

The same raw material of unregenerate sense and passion gave to the Church saints and heresiarchs. Ever in the Middle Ages there was a tendency to excess, excess of self-abnegation, excess of self-indulgence, a tendency to push ideas both of doctrine and conduct to extremes.

Thus did the Spiritual Franciscans tend to see in their founder a superman, to make the cult of poverty an obsession, to believe themselves a new order destined to inaugurate the era of the Holy Ghost.

The third type of mediæval heresy is of an altogether different nature. It is intellectual, philosophic. In all the other heresies there is a taint of rottenness, disease. Here, on the other hand, there is the health and sanity of honest thinking—and though the thought be crude, obscure or exaggerated, there is at least the possibility of lasting results.

In the re-discovery and re-absorption of the intellectual heritage of classical and patristic times there was always the danger of heresy. The process of adapting knowledge, pagan in source, coming sometimes through infidel channels, was certainly perilous.

It has to be remembered that it was the Church that initiated and carried through this process; that to the Church the world is indebted for the Renaissance of the twelfth and thirteenth centuries.

But the process inevitably presented serious problems.

In the first place, it yielded a copious mass of new comment and interpretation upon the original body of Christian dogma, viewed from a philosophic standpoint. Apply the logical methods of scholasticism and envisage dogma in the light of the metaphysical problem of the relations between the universal and the particular, and you have to decide whether the realist, the nominalist or the conceptualist is the true interpreter of the creeds.

The difficulty was increased with the advent of Aristotelianism in the thirteenth century. One exposition of Aristotle was definitely declared to be heresy—that of the Averrhoïsts. But the Augustinian opponents of St. Thomas Aquinas endeavoured to confound him in the charge of heresy: and it was for a time doubtful whether Aristotelianism in any shape or form could be accepted as orthodox.

Not only Alberto-Thomists in their attack upon the Averrhoïsts, but secular clergy waning with regulars, Franciscans inveighing against Dominicans, all glibly brought the convenient accusation of heresy against their opponents. It was for lawful authority to determine categorically what was orthodox, what heretical.

VI: CONCLUSION

But no authority was, as a matter of fact, impartial or certain to be final. Authority, whether papal, conciliar or academic, was itself wedded to one school of thought or another, swayed by the predominant philosophy of its own passing day.

It was not only a question of new ways of regarding, new interpretations of, existing dogma. There was also the problem presented by new dogmas, such as those of the Beatific Vision and the Immaculate Conception. Such tenets were not in themselves either inherently orthodox or heretical. When a creed is stabilized, completely rigid, it is easy to be exactly faithful to it but when it is fluid, even for the most orthodox of intent, safety can only be found in caution.

But the chief potential source of trouble in the intellectual ferment of scholasticism lay in the fact that it inevitably placed side by side two different authorities, the objective authority of the Church as enshrined in Scripture, tradition, papal and other lawful ecclesiastical *dicta*, and, on the other hand, the subjective authority of the human reason. All discussion, all argument is necessarily an appeal largely to this second authority.

While the great majority of the scholastics only used reason in order to justify revealed truth and never questioned the superiority of the infallible, the divine authority of the Church over the fallible authority of man's intellect, there were others, such as Eriugena and Abelard, who placed reason first.

Finally, there came a scholastic in Wycliffe, whose realism led him into dangerous errors, not only subversive of the cardinal doctrine of transubstantiation, but also threatening the whole status and mediatorial character of the priesthood.

It is most important to remember that the scholastic philosophers were in all cases clerics, representative of, and not antagonistic to, Catholic theology; that even the Averrhoïsts were also clerics, having no desire to break with the Church. On the other hand, the freedom of thought which the universities stood for and dialectic fostered, and which the Church not only did not repress, but even encouraged, had a tendency to produce heresy. Realism evolved pantheism; nominalism unitarianism.

The intellectual influences of university life brought forth Gerson, D'Ailly and the other whole-hearted reformers who made the great effort at revival of the Church from within which failed at Constance and Basel; but it also brought forth Wycliffe and Hus, whom those Councils condemned.

It was never absolutely clear where the dividing line between orthodoxy and heresy would rest. However much they might be reconciled or confused, the ideals and methods of theology and philosophy cannot be the same. The postulates of the one are not those of the other; and the more the scientific spirit is developed, the fewer the postulates of any sort that it is ready to accept. The Averrhoïsts at least saw this, only saving their position by the equivocation of the double truth.

Which was really the more dangerous to Catholic doctrine— the organized heresies, as a rule ignorant, perverted, having the seeds of their own destruction in their very rottenness, which the Church did systematically persecute; or the philosophical speculations of the universities, with their temptations to rationalism which the Church in the main tolerated? [2]

Each produced a force not wholly transient—a force operative in the breaking up of the mediæval system. The first was anti-sacerdotalism; the second a habit of independent thought and criticism.

It is true that the anti-sacerdotalism of Luther and the secular spirit of Renaissance humanism, with its entire indifference to religion, were the decisive factors in breaking up the fabric of mediævalism, and the movements of Lutheranism and humanism were largely new creations.

Yet Luther owed much to Hus, and Hus everything to Wycliffe, the scholastic, and the detached attitude of the Italian humanist was only one step in advance of that of the Latin Averrhoïst. Neither the wandering sectaries, in part suggesting, in part merely articulating, an anti-sacerdotal sentiment, nor the philosophers with their speculations concerning universals and the ultimate cause of being, were without influence in bringing about the collapse of the mediæval structure.

It is of no use studying the question of the attitude of the mediæval Church towards heresy unless one is prepared to use imagination enough to envisage heresy from the mediæval point of view.

VI: CONCLUSION

Men's mental outlook is governed by the intellectual conditions of their own day. A few individuals may be, as the phrase goes, 'in advance of their time'; but at the best they form only a small minority. To consider abstractly the rights and wrongs, the advantages and disadvantages of institutions and systems is the function of the philosopher.

But the historian, while not ignoring the abstract question, has specifically the function of ascertaining what, in point of fact, people's opinions have been and why they formed them. Much that has been written on the subject of religious toleration is of only limited validity because it simply denounces, and does not attempt to explain or to appreciate, the psychology of intolerance. [3]

Thus, for example, Locke's 'Letters on Toleration' have little *argumentative* value, because they are based on a complete *ignoratio elenchi*. Religious toleration is a great principle, but many modern dithyrambs on the inalienable right of liberty of thought and conscience fall rather wide of the mark, can convince only the already converted.

It is not very profitable to bring forward the theory of the indefeasible right of free thought in condemnation of mediæval society—to the whole of which, and by no means to its clerical elements only, the conception of such a right was entirely foreign. After all, even to-day the belief in an absolute toleration is held by only a very few, and even these anarchists will usually be found to hold it with certain reservations. [4]

Organized society cannot tolerate the forces which are subversive of it. It does not tolerate the criminal. 'A universal and absolute toleration of everything and everybody would lead to a general chaos as certainly as a universal and absolute intolerance.' [5] It is undoubtedly true that a certain measure of 'intolerance is essential to all that is, or moves, or lives, for tolerance of destructive elements within the organism amounts to suicide.' [6]

The individual possesses rights in so far as they are not prejudicial to the welfare of his fellows and the interests of the entire community. And the recognition that the maintenance of social order was perfectly compatible with the acknowledgment of the right of individual opinion and the permission of diversity of views, this in the Middle Ages 'was a discovery to be made, not a truth to be proved.'[7]

For the Middle Ages religion was not divorced from the secular life. The *Respublica Christiana* was an unity and a potent reality. The common faith was the panoply of the State. Devotion to it was an integral part of patriotism, and the counterpart of loyalty to the secular prince and of obedience to his laws. The man, therefore, who assailed the faith assailed society; in cutting himself off from the Church he outlawed himself from the State.

Acknowledgment of the sacred truths of Christianity was the foundation of all morality. The mediæval mind could not conceive of morality apart from religion. Hence respect for the divine law, as revealed in the Scripture and the Church, was regarded as the sole guarantee for the security of ordered society. Heresy was considered as essentially anti-social, anarchic; was conceived of as analogous to false coining or treason. Only to falsify truth was more heinous than to falsify the coin and treason against God than treason against man.

The exposition of the nature of heresy in Ludovico à Paramo is most logical. The character of a state depends on its religion; the faith is the foundation of the state. [8] Heretics cannot dwell in harmony with catholics: for if difference of language severs, how much more difference of belief? [9] Heresy is productive of all manner of vice and immorality, which are antagonistic to order and government. [10]

To the Church all this was self-evident. How could she stand neutral as between truth and falsehood, and treat them as if on an equality? She found all the strong walls and bastions, defences of the theocratic city, of which she was the appointed warden, being attacked by an insidious enemy within the gates. She had the power to defend; how could she be justified if she held her hand?

The heretic questioned her credentials, turned her claims to ridicule, threatened to bring down the whole structure of the Christian polity to the ground. Both in self-defence and in common loyalty to her mission she must strike. All the intensity of religious conviction inspired to persecution. Tolerance, argues

VI: CONCLUSION

de Maistre, only indicates religious indifference. [11] Moreover, the mediæval churchman was inevitably much influenced by the injunctions of the Old Testament. The Church succeeded to the heritage of the synagogue. [12]

But it was not the Church only that was persuaded of the essentially dangerous and anti-social character of heresy. Partly, no doubt, as the result of the Church's teaching through many generations, but certainly of their own accord and not as the result of any direct instruction, both secular rulers and the ordinary laity were equally convinced. [13]

They all lived in a thoroughly theocratic atmosphere. The prince sincerely saw in the heretic an enemy of all authority, and therefore of his own. [14] Secular legislation was just as unequivocal in its treatment of heresy as was Canon law. To the ordinary layman the heretic appeared as a thoroughly cross-grained, cantankerous, dangerous person, certainly of some immoral propensities and perhaps sexually perverted. [15]

Such was the mediæval point of view; and, once granted the necessary premises, it is extremely logical and exceedingly hard to combat.

Now-a-days we do not accept those premises; but in the Middle Ages we should probably not have dreamed of questioning them. On the extraordinarily interesting and important question of the causes of this change of attitude authorities do, and are likely to, differ, though many students will agree in combining their conclusions.

To those who, like John Stuart Mill and Lecky for instance, attribute religious persecution almost entirely to the doctrine of exclusive salvation, the causes of the growth of tolerance will appear to be the extension of the sceptical spirit and the process of the secularization of politics. [16]

Others, such as Bishop Creighton (who will not agree that persecution is to be explained by the doctrine of exclusive salvation at all) [17], or as Sir F. Pollock (who classifies different types of intolerance—tribal, political, social), insist strongly upon the simple factor of experience. 'It is not the demonstration of abstract rights, but the experience of inutility, that has made governments leave off persecuting.' [18]

After all, the great justification of liberty of thought lies not in the attempted demonstration of a natural right, but in the records of the painful process whereby toleration has been achieved. [19]

It would have saved an infinity of bloodshed and misery, would have freed the palimpsest of history of some of its most terrible blots, could the principle of toleration have been established without that awful struggle. But none of the great triumphs of mankind have been achieved save after centuries of effort, loss and failure.

To the moral judgment of our own day no instrument of persecution seems more odious than the Inquisition. Protestants have persecuted just as whole-heartedly as catholics, and with far less excuse; but the Inquisition stands by itself, as a regular specialized tribunal for persecution, immensely efficient, with an existence of centuries to its record. [20]

We have seen the way in which the Inquisition came into being. Both the circumstances of its origin and the intentions of its various founders gave the tribunal a character only semi-judicial. Indeed, if we object that the Inquisition was a bad court of justice, its originators could retort with truth that it was not intended to be a simple court of justice.

The Inquisition was created to deal with erring children, not criminals; not merely to pronounce a verdict, but to produce reconciliation and amendment not to punish, but to penance. The Church, through the Inquisition, was dealing in the spirit of a parent with her own children, over whom she had all a parent's rights of discipline and chastisement, but also evincing a parent's deep desire for something more than justice and punishment, for the ending of estrangement and the restoration of loving union in the family.

Such was the pure theory of the Inquisition, a much more benignant conception than that of the ordinary law-court. In the latter, the mere fact of repentance would not avail; in the former, if it were sincere, it availed everything. So de Maistre, defending the Spanish Inquisition, declared it to be the most lenient, the most merciful tribunal in the world.

But we have to consider the point of view, not only of the judge, but of the defendant. Whatever the real nature of the tribunal, the man brought before it was on his trial. The tribunal *did* pronounce a verdict, and upon that verdict his reputation, perhaps his freedom or his life, depended. He wanted justice, not mercy; and the Inquisition might be lenient, but it was not fair.

It was radically unfair. It gave no facilities whatever for the plea of Not Guilty. It cared nought for the reputation of the accused. He had already lost his reputation by being before the court at all. The very fact of defamation, of being 'suspect' inferred guilt. To leave the court of the Inquisition without a stain upon one's character was virtually impossible.

In all manner of ways the accused was at a disadvantage —in the suppression of the names of witnesses and of evidence, in the refusal of legal assistance, in the use of torture, and above all in the fact that the judge was also the prosecutor, who regarded it as perfectly legitimate to browbeat and confuse the defendant, if he was so misguided and unfilial as to endeavour to defend himself.

Inquisitorial procedure was a miserable travesty of justice and its mercifulness was forthcoming only on its own terms. To all save the meekly submissive the Inquisition typified not mercy and love, but remorselessness and cruelty.

While in studying the origins of the Inquisition we are bound to examine, and to seek to understand, the point of view of those who were responsible for its inception, in estimating its character and results we need not, nay we *ought* not, to judge by any other criterion than that dictated by the highest conceptions of right and justice.

The common, the accepted, standard of to-day both as regards justice and humanity is, happily, greatly higher than that of the Middle Ages.

Much that has been written of the Inquisition has been vitiated by an attempt to read into the mind and conduct of men of mediæval times a humanitarianism which is the peculiar product of the modern world, and which they could not even have understood.

Even more vitiated would be any thesis which, not satisfied with justifying the originators of the Inquisition, sought to justify the institution itself. Certainly the motive for such an attempt could not be impartiality. Only moral obliquity can be blind to the transparent abominations of inquisitorial procedure.

If its character as a tribunal was essentially evil, evil also were some of the Inquisition's results. Secular princes discerned its remarkable potential utility to themselves and regarded it with envy and admiration. Its methods had a satisfactory efficiency found in no other court. By such methods conviction could be practically assured. The charge of heresy could therefore be preferred against political enemies with the happiest prospects of advantage.

The destruction for purely political ends was achieved by the use of inquisitorial methods of the Templars, Jeanne d'Arc, Savonarola. [21] Those are the most notorious, but there are other instances of this abuse of the sacred tribunal for purely secular, and sometimes base and immoral, purposes.

Worse still—and possibly this is the worst aspect of the whole story of the Inquisition—its pernicious methods of procedure were borrowed by the admiring secular princes for their courts, which did not pretend to have the double nature which was the explanation, if not the excuse, for the Inquisition's adoption of its system.

Thus civil courts in Europe came to be tarnished by the system of *inquisitio*, the secret enquiry, the heaping up of disabilities for the defence, the application of torture—all these abuses having the august sanction of ecclesiastical use. The lay authority could triumphantly vindicate such innovations, whereby justice became an unequal contest between authority, combining the two characters of prosecutor and judge, and the unhappy prisoner, by pointing to the example of the Church, the repository of the sublime truths of divine justice and Christian charity.

To the fortunate fact that the Inquisition never secured a footing in the British Islands is largely due their maintenance, in contradistinction to Continental states, of the open trial and of the great maxim that no one is presumed to be guilty, that the onus of proof lies with the prosecution.

It was not the fault of the Church that the secular power admired and imitated the methods of the Holy Office; but it is surely a calamity that it should have been able to find in an

VI: CONCLUSION

ecclesiastical tribunal a system which must seem to every fair-minded man to-day so abhorrent to the whole spirit and tenor of the Christian gospel.

No attempt has been made in these pages to present the heresies of the Middle Ages in any heroic light, to slur over the pernicious crudities of many of them. As between the spiritual and intellectual ideals represented by the mediæval Church and those represented by the majority of the sectaries the choice is self-evident. Wycliffites and Husites stand obviously on a far higher plane, but Petrobrusians, Cathari, Dolcinists, Flagellants and many others had no fertile ideas to bequeath to a later day and were, at best perhaps, a nuisance in their own.

Yet it has to be remembered that not only noble-minded men like Hus and Jerome of Prague, whose creed, whether true or not, was in any case sane and pure and exalted, but also innumerable others, whom we know only as names in inquisitorial records, who whatever the faith they professed stood constant through physical and mental anguish, to perish perhaps at the last at the stake in a world barren of pity with no friendly faces to encourage them—these suffered for a great ideal, that of fidelity to the spirit of truthfulness, of intellectual integrity.

All who have died rather than be false to themselves and their vision of truth, thus demonstrating to the world their conviction that belief is worth dying for—whether Catholics or Protestants or the most erring of mediæval heretics—have done service to the cause of human progress.

For, if it be true that only through the tragic experience of centuries of religious persecution could mankind attain to the establishment of the principle of liberty of thought and conscience, then every one of us to-day who enjoys the benefits of such liberty owes a debt of gratitude to the men and women who for conscience' sake braved obloquy, torture-chamber and fire.

---

[1] Taylor, *op. cit.*, pp. 283-4 n. 'The philosophic ideas of such seem gathered from the flotsam and jetsam of the later antique world; their stock was not of the best, and bore little interesting fruit for later times.'

[2] Mandell Creighton, *Persecution and Tolerance* (1895), p. 55. 'Leo X was tolerant of the philosophic doubts of Pomponazzo concerning the immortality of the soul, because such speculations were not likely to affect the position of the Papacy; but could not allow Luther to discuss the dubious and complicated question of indulgences because it might have disastrous effects upon the system of papal finance.'

[3] See Acton, *History of Freedom of Thought*, pp. 569-71.

[4] E. S. P. Haynes, *Religious Persecution* (1904), p. 40. 'A Liberal has recently been defined as one who would never have taken the chance of imposing silence on the deceivers of mankind. If we hold by this definition, very few Liberals have ever existed, or do exist now.'

[5] D. G. Ritchie, *Natural Rights* (1903), p. 160.

[6] *The Catholic Encyclopedia* (1907-14), on Heresy, vol. vii, p. 261.

[7] Creighton, *Persecution and Tolerance*, pp. 9-10.

[8] Ludovico à Paramo, *op. cit.*, pp. 281-2.

[9] *Ibid.*, pp. 288-9.

[10] *Ibid.*, pp. 333-4.

[11] Joseph de Maistre, *Considérations sur la France suivies… des lettres é un gentilhomme russe sur l'inquisition espagnole* (Brussels, 1844), pp. 281 *et seq*. Cf. *Catholic Encyclopedia*, vol. vii, p. 261. 'Toleration came in when faith went out.'

[12] De Cauzons, *op. cit.*, vol. i, p. 9.

[13] Pollock, *Essays in Jurisprudence and Ethics* (1882), on *The Theory of Persecution*, pp. 144-5. 'However eager the clergy might be to stimulate and direct the anger of the faithful against heretics, their efforts would have been in vain if the bulk of the laity had not been predisposed to persecute heretics when duly pointed out. So far from persecution being merely the creature of priestcraft, it would be as near the truth to say that priestcraft was invented in order to organize persecution.'

[14] Haynes, *op. cit.*, pp. 52-9.

[15] *Ibid.*, p. 3. 'And the heretic—often lacking in tact and a sense of proportion—is as offensive to the believer as one who should rudely tell him that his doctor was a quack and his solicitor a swindler.' Cf. p. 55.

[16] Mill, *On Liberty*; Lecky's Rationalism, esp., chs. iv and v.

[17] *Op. cit.*, pp. 5, 113-15.

[18] Pollock, *op. cit.*, p. 175.

[19] J. B. Bury, *A History of Freedom of Thought* (Home Univ. Lib.), p. 14. 'A long time was needed to arrive at the conclusion that coercion of opinion is a mistake, and only a part of the world is yet convinced. That conclusion, so far as I can judge, is the most important ever reached by man. It was the issue of a continuous struggle between reason and authority…'

VI: CONCLUSION

[20] *Cf.* Langlois, *op. cit.*, pp. 21-47.

[21] For the trial of the Templars, see H. Finke, *Papsium und Untergang des Templerordens* (Münster, 1907); M. Lavocat, *Procès des Frères et de l'ordre du Temple* (Paris, 1888); *Collection de Documents inédits sur l'histoire de France—Procès des Templiers*, J. Michelet (Paris, 1841); Lea, vol. iii, pp. 238-334. Lea's treatment of this complicated subject is masterly, and is conclusive against Philip IV and Clement V. For the trial of Jeanne d'Arc, see J. Quicherat, *Procès de Condamnation et de Réhabilitation de Jeanne d'Arc* (Paris, 1841-9); H. S. Denifle and E. Chatelain, *Le procès de J. d'Arc et l'Université de Paris* (Paris, 1897); A. France, *Vie de Jeanne d'Arc* (Paris, 1908); A. Lang, *The Maid of France* (1908); Lea, vol. iii, pp. 338-78, etc. For trial of Savonarola, see P. Villart, *Life and Times of Savonarola* (Eng. trans.), 1899; Lea, vol. iii, pp. 209-37. For papal use of the Inquisition for political purposes, see Lea, vol. iii, ch. iv, generally.

Note On Authorities

A full bibliography of the subject of Heresy and its Repression in the Middle Ages would be exceedingly lengthy. All that is attempted here is to give a select list of a few of the most useful, important and most easily accessible works. The most thorough bibliography for the subject available is that in T. de Cauzons, *Histoire de l'Inquisition en France* (*q.v.*), the list of books covering forty pages and including 850 works. This is for the history of the tribunal in France alone.

It has to be borne in mind that by far the greater part of our contemporary evidence for the history of mediæval heresies is hostile evidence, consisting of denunciations of them by orthodox theologians, the treatises of inquisitors who condemned their adherents, notes made of evidence given by defendants.

Only those heretics who were themselves philosophers or theologians—and these, such as Siger of Brabant, Wycliffe and Hus, are relatively very few—have left their own records behind them. Due allowance, therefore, has to be made in using most contemporary authorities for considerable bias.

I

INQUISITORIAL TREATISES

These are, on the whole, the most generally valuable of contemporary sources. The two most important for the period dealt with in this book are:

NOTE ON AUTHORITIES

Nicholas Eymeric, *Directorium Inquisitorum cum commentariis F. Pegnae* (Rome, 1585; also Venice, 1607).

Bernard Gui, *Practica Inquisitionis haereticae pravitatis* (ed. C. Douais, Paris, 1886).

Eymeric was inquisitor in Aragon in the latter half of the fourteenth century. His compendious work is probably the most authoritative of all inquisitorial treatises, being a complete exposition of the principles of the tribunal and the doctrines of the different sects with which it had to deal, and giving the minutest details of its procedure.

Bernard Gui, appointed inquisitor at Toulouse in 1306, was the most vigorous and remarkable of those who helped to stamp out Catharism in Languedoc after the Albigensian crusades. The following treatises are not contemporary, but they are valuable as expositions of the permanent principles and methods of the tribunal. They are also useful for the occasional comments made by these later experts on the work of their predecessors:

J. Simancas, *De Catholicis Institutionibus*.
A. Bzovius, *Historiae Ecclesiasticae*.
J. à Royas, *De Haereticis*.
Bernard of Como, *Lucema Inquisitorum haereticae pravitatis*.
Arnaldo Albertini, *Tractatus de agnoscendis assertionibus Catholicis et haereticis*.
Zanchino Ugolini, *De Haereticis*.

All these, among other similar tracts, are included in Zilettus, *Tractatus Universi Juris* (Venice, 1633), vol- xi, pt. ii.

See also Ludovico à Paramo, *De origine et progressu officii Sanctae Inquisitionis* (Madrid, 1598).
Umberto Locati, *Opus iudiciale inquisitorum* (Rome, 1572).
F. Peña, *Inquirendorum haereticorum lucerna* (Madrid, 1598).
Carena, *Tractatus de officio Sanctae Inquisitionis* (Lyons, 1669).

II

COLLECTIONS OF ORIGINAL DOCUMENTS

There are records of the proceedings and sentences pronounced in the inquisitions in the South of France in *Liber sententiarum*

Inquisitionis Tholosanae, 1307-13, printed as an appendix to Philippe à Limborch, *Historia Inquisitionis* (Amsterdam, 1692). Note that this *Liber sententiarum* is not included in Chandler's English translation of Limborch. These are the sentences pronounced by Bernard Gui. The proceedings of the inquisition of Carcassonne, notably the sentences of Bernard de Caux, are contained in *Documents pour servir à l'histoire de l'Inquisition dans le Languedoc* (ed. C. Douais, Paris, 1900).

There are exceedingly useful extracts from original documents of various sorts relating to mediæval heresies in the following:

J. J. Döllinger, *Beiträge zur Sektensgeschichte* (Munich, 1890), vol. ii.
P. Frédéricq, *Corpus documentorum Inquisitionis haereticae praviiatis Neerlandicae* (Ghent, 1889-1906), vols, i-iii.

For the edicts of ecclesiastical Councils the best collection is:

P. Labbe, G. D. Mansi, etc., *Sacrorum conciliorum nova et amplissima collectio* (Paris, 1901-13), esp. vol. xxii, 1 166-1225; vol. xxiii, 1225-1268; vol. xxiv, 1269-1299; vol. xxv, 1300-1344; vol. xxvi, 1344-1409.

For papal bulls between 1198 and 1304 see A. Potthast, *Regesta Pontificum Romanorum* (Berlin, 1874 et seq.).

Important documents relating to the Dominican order are in Ripoll et Brémond, *Bullarium ordinis S. Dominici* (8 vols., Rome, 1737 et seq.).

The Constitutions of the Emperor Frederick II are in J. L. A. Huillard-Bréholles, *Historia diplomatica Friderici Secundi* (Paris, 1852-61).

III

HISTORIES OF THE INQUISITION

There are two useful histories of comparatively early date:

J. Marsollier, *Histoire de l'Inquisition* (Cologne, 1693).
P. à Limborch, *Historia Inquisitionis* (Amsterdam, 1692). The English version is *History of the Inquisition* (tr. S. Chandler, London, 1731). The latter is used in this book except when the *Liber*

NOTE ON AUTHORITIES

sententiarum, only printed in the original, is referred to. Limborch's, although avowedly a propaganda work, is still of value, because it was based on the treatises of inquisitors, making particularly full use of Eymeric, and it is easy to make proper allowance for the avowed bias.

In 1817 appeared the first version (a French translation) of the great work on the Spanish Inquisition by J. A. Llorente under the title, *Histoire critique de l'Inquisition d'Espagne*. The original Spanish text was not published till 1822. Only the introduction and first four chapters are relevant to the mediæval Inquisition.

English writers have been mainly interested in the Spanish Inquisition, as founded by Ferdinand and Isabella, and in the Inquisition in Portgual. English seamen and traders suffered at their hands, either in the Peninsula or its dependencies, in the sixteenth and seventeenth centuries.

See, for example, *English Merchants and the Spanish Inquisition in the Canaries* (Royal Historical Society, ed. L. de Alberti, A. B. Wallis Chapman, 1912); R. Dugdale's *A Narrative of popish cruelties; or a new account of the Spanish Inquisition* (1680) in *Harleian Miscellany*, vol. vii, p. 105; J. Stevens, *The Ancient and Present State of Portugal... containing... A curious Account of the Inquisition* (London, 1705).

Later English writers show a similar strongly Protestant bias, e.g. F. B. Wright, *A History of Religious Persecution from the Apostolic to the Present Time; and of the Inquisitions of Spain, Portugal and Goa* (1816); W. H. Rule, *History of the Inquisition* (London, 1868). Only the first nine chapters of the last-named book are concerned with the Middle Ages.

All previous works were superseded by the monumental labours of the American historian, H. C. Lea, in his

Superstition and Force (Philadelphia, 1866; 4th ed., 1892).
A History of the Inquisition of the Middle Ages (New York, 1887).
A History of the Inquisition of Spain (New York, 1906-7).
The Inquisition in the Spanish Dependencies (New York, 1908).
Chapters in the Religious History of Spain connected with the Inquisition (Philadelphia, 1893).

Together, these volumes represent an immense fund of learning and the most painstaking research. For this reason it will be long indeed before they are superseded. They have been adversely criticized, as being marred by strong anti-Catholic prejudice.

Colour is undoubtedly lent to the charge by the rather unfortunate fact that the *History of the Inquisition of the Middle Ages* opens with an account of the abuses of the mediæval Church and that the whole argument of the book appears as though largely based upon these initial contentions.

Lea is also inclined to be biased in favour of all heretics as against their persecutors. But while in detail he may be open to criticism and his attitude is quite clearly Protestant, the great bulk of his work remains unshaken.

The Romanist point of view with regard to it should, however, be studied. It is summarized, for example, in P. M. Baumgarten, *H. C. Lea's Historical Writings: a critical inquiry* (New York, 1909), and will be found incidentally in the works of recent Catholic historians of the Inquisition (*q.v. infra*). There are admirable *critiques* of Lea's work in:

> Lord Acton's *The History of Freedom of Thought and other Essays* (London, 1909)
>
> P. Frédéricq's Introduction to the French translation of Lea's *History of the Inquisition of the Middle Ages* (tr. S. Reinach, Paris, 1900, pp. i-xxviii);
>
> and in articles by S. Reinach on his *Spanish Inquisition* in *Revue Critique*, No. 18, May 1906, p. 300; No. 42, Oct. 1907, p. 301; No. 5, Feb. 1908, p. 86.

Recent works from the Romanist standpoint have been:

> C. Douais, *L'Inquisition; ses Origines, sa Procédure* (Paris, 1906).
>
> H. Maillet, *L'Église et la répression sanglante de l'hérésie* (Liége, 1909).
>
> E. Vacandard, *The Inquisition, a Critical and Historical Study of the Coercive Powers of the Church* (tr. B. L. Conway, 1908).
>
> C. Moeller, *Les Bûchers et les Autos-da-fé de l'Inquisition depuis le Moyen Age in Revue d'histoire ecclésiastique* (Louvain, 1913, vol. xiv, pp. 720-51).

NOTE ON AUTHORITIES

Mgr. Douais has done much able and learned work on the history of the mediæval Inquisition, and the Abbé Vacandard's book is most moderate and fair-minded. The most considerable work of scholarship written on the subject of recent years has, however, been T. de Cauzons, *Histoire de l'Inquisition en France* (2 vols., Paris, 1909, 1913, unfinished).

There is a critical survey of some of the most recent work done on the Inquisition by P. Frédéricq, *Les récents historiens catholiques de l'Inquisition en France* in *Revue historique*, (vol. cix, 1912, pp. 307-34). Mainly critical is C. V. Langlois, *L'Inquisition après des travaux récents* (Paris, 1902).

IV

LEGAL ASPECT OF THE INQUISITION

On this important subject there is not a great deal, but the following are excellent and most valuable:

> L. Tanon, *Histoire des Tribunaux de l'Inquisition en France* (Paris, 1893).
> P. Fournier, *Les Officialités au Moyen Age* (Paris, 1889).
> A. Esmein, *Histoire de la Procédure Criminelle en France, et spécialement de la procédure inquisitoire* (Paris, 1882).

Esmein's book forms the substantial foundation of a more comprehensive work in the American *Continental Legal History series*, viz. *A History of Continental Criminal Procedure* (Boston, 1913).

See on this subject note on p. 205 *supra*.

V

WORKS DEALING SPECIALLY WITH THE ALBIGENSES AND THE ORIGINS OF THE INQUISITION

J. J. Vaissete and C. Devic, *Histoire Générale de Languedoc* (Toulouse, 1872-1904).
Moneta, *Adversus Catharos et Waldenses* (Rome, 1743).
P. Melia, *The Origin, Persecutions and Doctrines of the Waldenses, from Documents* (London, 1870).

243

C. Schmidt, *Histoire et Doctrine de la Secte des Cathares ou Albigeois* (Paris, 1848).

A. Monastier, *Histoire de l'Église Vaudoise depuis son origine* (Paris, 1847).

B. Haureau, *Bernard Délicieux et l'Inquisition Albigeoise* (Paris, 1877).

C. Douais, *Les Hérétiques du midi au XIIIe siècle* (Paris, 1891); *L'Albigéisme et les Frères prêcheurs à Narbonne au XIIIe siècle* (Paris, 1894); *Les Albigeois, leur origine* (Paris, 1879).

J. Ficker, *Die Gesetzliche Einführung der Todesstrafe für Ketzerei* in *Mittheilungen des Instituts für oesterreichische Geschichtsforschung* (1880), pp. 177-226.

J. Havet, *L'Hérésie et le Bras séculier au Moyen Age jusqu'au treizième siècle* in *Œuvres* (Paris, 1896), vol. ii, pp. 117-81.

C. Henner, *Beiträge zur Organisation und Competenz der päpstlichen Ketzesgerichte* (Leipzig, 1890).

A. Luchaire, *Innocent III*, vol. ii, *La Croisade des Albigeois* (Paris, 1905).

VI

WORKS DEALING WITH JOACHIM OF FLORA AND THE 'EVERLASTING GOSPEL'

Joachim of Flora, *Concordia novi et veteris Testamenti* (Venice, 1579); *Expositio in Apocalypsin* (Venice, 1527); *Psalterium decem Cordarum* (Venice, 1527).

Chronica Fr. Salimbene Parmensis (Parma, 1857); also in *Monumenta Germ. Hist.*, vol. xxxii (1905-13), ed. O. Holder-Egger.

E. Renan, *Joachim de Flore et l'Evangile éternel in Nouvelles Études d'Histoire Religieuse* (Paris, 1884).

E. Gebhart, *L'Italie Mystique; la Renaissance religieuse au Moyen Age* (6th ed., 1908); *Recherches nouvelles sur l'histoire du Joachitism* in *Revue historique*, vol. xxxi (1886).

S. Reinach, *Cultes, Mythes et Religions* (Paris, 1905), vol. i, pp. 173-83

J. J. Döllinger, *Prophecies and the Prophetic Spirit in the Christian Era* (ed. A. Plummer, 1873).

E. G. Gardner, *Joachim of Flora and the Everlasting Gospel* in *Franciscan Essays* (1912).

NOTE ON AUTHORITIES

VII

ON SORCERY AND WITCHCRAFT

The principal authorities are:

Sprenger's *Malleus Maleficarum* and F. Bartholomew de Spina's *De Strigibus*.

Both are included in *Malleorum quorundam Maleficarum tam veterum quam recentiorum authorum tomi duo* (Frankfort, 1582). In Zilettus (*q.v. supra*) there is Bernard of Como's *De Strigibus*.

See also W. E. H. Lecky's *History of Rationalism in Europe* and authorities there cited.

VIII

FOR WYCLIFFE, HUS AND THE COUNCIL OF CONSTANCE

The principal works of Wycliffe are published by the Wyclif Society. See especially *De Dominio Divino* (ed. R. L. Poole, 1890); *Tract, de Civili dominio liber primus* (ed. R. L. Poole, 1885); *De Eucharistia* (1892); *De Potestate Pape* (ed. J. Loserth, 1907. See also *Fasciculi Zizaniorum Magistri Johannis Wyclif* (Rolls series, ed. W. W. Shirley, 1858).

See also the *Chronicon Angliae* (ed. Maunde Thompson, 1874); *Chronicon* of Henry Knighton (ed. Lumby, 1895), vol. ii; D. Wilkins, *Concilia M. Britanniae et Hiberniae* (1737), vol. iii.

The Letters of Hus are edited by H. B. Workman and R. M. Pope (1904). Invaluable is F. Palacky's *Documenta Mag. Joannis Hus* (Prague, 1869).

For the works of Gerson and D'Ailly see J. Gerson, *Opera* (Antwerp, 1706). Works of D'Ailly are included in this volume.

See also Theodoric de Niem, *De Schismate* (Leipzig, 1890).

The works of Marsiglio of Padua and of William of Ockham are in Melchior Goldast, *Monarchia S. Romani Imperii* (Hanover, Frankfort, 1611-14), vol. ii. They are summarized in S. Riezler, *Die literarischen Widersacher der Päpste zur Zeit Ludwig des Baiers* (1874).

See also the following relating to Bohemia or the Council of Constance:

Aeneas Sylvius, *Historia Bohemica* (1453)
Etienne Baluze, *Vitae Paparum Avenionensium* (Paris, 1693)
H v. der Hardt, *Magnum oecumemcum Constantiense Concilium* (Frankfort, 1697-1742).
E Martène and V. Durand, *Veterum Scriptorum et monumentorum amplissima collectio* (Paris, 1724-33), vol. vii, pp. 425-1078).

The following also are useful:

N. Valois, *La France et le Grand Schisme d'occident* (Paris, 1896-1902).
J. B. Schwab, *J. Gerson* (Würzburg, 1858).
B. Labanca, *Marsiglio da Padova* (Padua, 1882).
H. B. Workman, *The Dawn of the Reformation: the Age of Wyclif* (1901); *The Dawn of the Reformation: the Age of Hus* (1902).
J. Lewis, *History of the Life and Sufferings of John Wicliffe* (1720).
J. Loserth, *Wyclif and Hus* (tr. W. J. Evans, 1884).
G. M. Trevelyan, *England in the Age of Wycliffe* (1904).
G. V. Lechler, *Wyclif and his English Precursors* (tr. P. Lorimer, 1878).
R. L. Poole, *Wyclif and Movements for Reform* (1889); *Illustrations of the History of Mediæval Thought* (1884).
H. Rashdall, Article on Wycliffe in *Dictionary of National Biography* (1900), vol. lxiii.
A. H. Wratislaw, *Native Literature of Bohemia in the Fourteenth Century* (1878).
Count Lützow, *The Life and Times of Master John Hus* (1909).
H. Rashdall, *Universities of Europe in the Middle Ages* (1895), vol. ii.
Also of course M. Creighton, *History of the Papacy* (1903-9), Introd. and Books I and II.

IX

GENERAL ECCLESIASTICAL HISTORIES AND WORKS ON HERESIES

C. H. Hahn, *Geschichte der Ketzer* (Stuttgart, 1845-50).
J. J. v. Mosheim, *Institutes of Ecclesiastical History* (Eng. tr., 2nd ed., 1850).

NOTE ON AUTHORITIES

J. C. L. Gieseler, *Ecclesiastical History* (Eng. tr. 1853), esp. vol. iii, which contains extracts from documents.

F. Milman, *History of Latin Christianity* (4th ed. 1883), esp. vols. v and vi.

J. J. Döllinger, *Beiträge zur Sektensgeschichte* (Munich, 1890).

A. Harnack, *History of Dogma* (tr. W. Gilchrist, 1894-9).

See also on special subjects the following:

F. Gregorovius, *History of the City of Rome in the Middle Ages* (tr. A. Hamilton, 1894-1902), vols. v and vi.

J. H. Reusch, *Der Index der verbotenen Bücher* (Bonn, 1883).

J. Guiraud, *Saint Dominic* (Eng. tr., 1901).

P. Sabatier, *Life of Saint Francis of Assisi* (tr. L. S. Houghton, 1904).

H. O. Taylor, *The Mediæval Mind* (1911).

E. Renan, *Averroës et l'Averroïsme* (Paris, 1861).

P. F. Mandonnet, *Siger de Brabant et l'Averroïsme latin au XIIe siècle* (Fribourg, 1899), with invaluable appendix containing Siger's Works.

M. de Wulf, *History of Mediæval Philosophy* (Eng. tr., 1909).

B. Haureau, *Histoire de la Philosophie Scolastique* (Paris, 1880).

C. Douais, *Essai sur l'organisation des études dans l'ordre des Frères-Prêcheurs* (Paris, 1884).

Registrum epistolarum fratris Joannis Peckham (Rolls Series, ed. C. T. Martin, 1884).

Rutebeuf, *Œuvres Complètes* (1874-5), vol. i, passim.

De Tribus Impostoribus (ed. Philomneste Junior, i.e. P. Gustave Brunet, Paris, 1861).

J. Owen, *Skeptics of the Italian Renaissance* (1893).

X

ON THE GENERAL QUESTION OF FREEDOM OF THOUGHT AND THE THEORY OF RELIGIOUS PERSECUTION

Representative works, among many:

J. Locke, *Letters concerning Toleration*.
J. S. Mill, *On Liberty*.
W. E. H. Lecky, *History of Rationalism in Europe*, ch. iv.

Sir F. Pollock, *The Theory of Persecution in Essays in Jurisprudence and Ethics* (1882).

M. Creighton, *Persecution and Tolerance* (1895).

D. G. Ritchie, *Natural Rights* (1903); *The Principles of State Interference* (1902).

E. S. P. Haines, *Religious Persecution* (1904).

Joseph de Maistre, *Lettres à un gentilhomme russe sur l'Inquisition espagnole* (Brussels, 1844).

Lessing's *Nathan der Weise*.

Sir J. Stephen, *Liberty, Equality, Fraternity* (2nd ed., 1874).

J. M. Robertson, *A Short History of Free Thought, Ancient and Modern* (1906).

The Catholic Encyclopedia (1907-14), articles on Heresy and Inquisition.

J. B. Bury, *A History of Freedom of Thought* (Home University Library).

www.ingramcontent.com/pod-product-compliance
Lightning Source LLC
Chambersburg PA
CBHW021431080526
44588CB00009B/490